LAW IN THE LIBERAL ARTS

LAW IN THE LIBERAL ARTS

Edited by Austin Sarat

CORNELL UNIVERSITY PRESS
Ithaca and London

First published 2004 by Cornell University Press
First printing, Cornell Paperbacks, 2005
Printed in the United States of America

Design by Victoria Kuskowski

Library of Congress Cataloging-in-Publication Data

Law in the liberal arts / edited by Austin Sarat.
    p. cm.
  ISBN 0-8014-4269-9 (cloth : alk. paper)
  ISBN 0-8014-8905-9 (pbk. : alk. paper)
  1. Law—Study and teaching (Higher)—United States. 2. Education,
Humanistic—United States. I. Sarat, Austin.
  KF4245.5.L3L39   2004
  340'.071'173—dc22

                                                    2004007160

Cornell University Press strives to use environmentally responsible suppliers and materials to the fullest extent possible in the publishing of its books.
Such materials include vegetable-based, low-VOC inks and acid-free papers
that are recycled, totally chlorine-free, or partly composed of nonwood fibers.
For further information, visit our website at www.cornellpress.cornell.edu.

Cloth printing   10 9 8 7 6 5 4 3 2 1
Paperback printing   10 9 8 7 6 5 4 3 2 1

TO BENJAMIN, WHO HELPS ME CROSS BOUNDARIES—A.S.

Contents

LAW IN THE LIBERAL ARTS

SITUATING LEGAL SCHOLARSHIP IN THE LIBERAL ARTS

An Introduction

AUSTIN SARAT

P erusing the catalog of almost any college or university in the United States, the casual reader finds countless courses in which law figures prominently, for example, constitutional law, judicial process, anthropology of law, philosophy of law, law and economics, law and literature, sprinkled throughout the curriculum of the arts and sciences. Historically disciplines such as political science, sociology, and philosophy, to name just a few, have provided space for the examination of law. And some of the most important scholarship on law traditionally has been done by scholars with academic appointments in the liberal arts.[1] From this vantage point, legal scholarship looks like it has a firm foothold in the education of undergraduates, and legal scholars look like they are completely at home in traditional academic disciplines.

Yet from other vantage points the situation looks quite different. Unlike Europe and elsewhere in the world where law is readily available as a subject of study for undergraduates, and where law departments and faculties are as common as departments of history or literature, legal education in the United States is generally thought of as postgraduate education, located primarily in law schools dedicated to professional training. So complete is the equation of legal scholarship with the work of law schools that fifty years ago at a Harvard conference on the teaching of law in the liberal arts, the orienting question was "Is law a proper subject of study in the liberal arts curriculum?"[2] Turning the clock forward to 2002, we find *Harvard Law Review* devoting a symposium issue to the subject of the future of legal scholarship yet including nothing about the work of legal scholars in the liberal arts.[3] Today respected scholars can argue about the need to develop law as an academic discipline without making reference to anything done in the liberal arts.[4]

This book inquires about the situation of legal scholarship in the liberal arts, attending to work now being done by teachers and scholars outside professional schools, pointing to its promises and possibilities. It aims to assess the place of legal scholarship in the liberal arts by asking whether and how law teaching and research are different in liberal arts settings than they are in law schools. Another way of putting this concern would be to ask what does the study of law contribute to the liberal arts and what does the former contribute to the latter. Still another way of stating the topic of this book is to say that it aims to answer the question Can the study of law in the liberal arts save law from the lawyers?

LAW IN THE LIBERAL ARTS: HISTORY AND POSSIBILITY

This volume joins a long history of efforts to claim a place for legal scholarship in the liberal arts. As early as 1887, Yale University established a course of study "for those not intending to enter any active business or professional career, but who wish to acquire an enlarged acquaintance with our political and legal systems, and the rules by which they are governed." In 1894 Woodrow Wilson said that "we need laymen who understand the necessity for law and the right uses of it too well to be unduly impatient with its restraints." The function of a college course in law, he went on, is to teach students "what law is, how it came into existence, what relations its form bears to its substance, and how it gives to society its fibre and strength."[5] During the 1920s, Johns Hopkins University created the Institute for the Study of Law, devoted "to the nonprofessional study of law, in order that the function of law may be comprehended, its results evaluated, and its development kept more nearly in step with the complex developments of modern life." Moreover, the 1954 Harvard conference answered its opening question about law in the liberal arts by suggesting that "the study of law—not as a matter of professional training but as a matter of humane, or liberal, education, can enrich the minds of students."[6] And in 1975, the report of the Law Center Consultative Committee at the University of Massachusetts contended that there is a

> coherent body of knowledge about the social functions and consequences of legal institutions and processes . . . [that amounts] to more than the extraprofessional study of law; it is itself a new scholarly enterprise. . . . The perspectives of law, on the one hand, and of social science or humanities on the other, cannot merely be placed side by side. Only an uneasy accommodation, perhaps spliced by occasional moments of communication, can result from that approach. What is needed is an effort toward a real synthesis

of the intellectual heritage and analytic capabilities of law, social science, and the humanities—one that aims at the creation of a distinctively new and broader scholarly discipline with law and legal systems at its core.[7]

Despite these efforts, only sixty colleges and universities in the United States today allow their students to concentrate in something variously called legal studies or law and society.[8] A handful of those programs are full-fledged majors; the rest are minors or certificate programs. Noticeably absent from this list are the Ivy League universities and most of the best liberal arts colleges. In addition, no more than a handful of universities offer interdisciplinary Ph.D.'s in law, with the result that law teaching, at the undergraduate level, is usually done by people trained within social science or humanities disciplines, in which law is rarely at the center of concern.

This is unfortunate both for legal scholarship and for the liberal arts. For the former, it means that the work of understanding law is generally coupled with the lawyer's need to understand how to use law or with the policymaker's desire to reform it, impoverishing our ability to see the complex connections of law, culture, and society in all their variety and to connect theorizing about law with the humanities and social sciences. The failure more fully to articulate and institutionalize legal scholarship in the liberal arts deprives its fields of a subject of enormous richness and interest. Systematic study of law advances the goals of a liberal education. This conclusion is based on two general observations: one concerns the importance of law in culture and society, the other the capacity of legal study to engage and enhance the intellectual, analytic, and imaginative capacities of undergraduates.

First, law is ubiquitous. It pervades much of our lives and provides a forum in which the distinctive temper of a culture may find expression. In this country and abroad it plays a major, though variable, role in articulating values and dealing with conflict.[9] Although the role of law has never been more substantial or controversial in the United States, in countries from Argentina and Brazil to South Africa and those of Eastern Europe, people are now seeking to develop their own versions of the rule of law as a means of ordering their societies.

The pervasiveness of law reflects human tendencies to engage in normative argument as a regular part of social interaction and to interpret social action in the language of right and wrong.[10] Law, however, is more than a branch of applied ethics; in many cultures, the concept of legal legitimacy is associated not only with the adequacy or normative appeal of legal commands but also with elaborate rhetorical practices and traditions of reading and interpreting that have parallels in the rich history of biblical hermeneutics.[11] Finally, law finds its most vivid expression when moral argument and interpretation issue in force. Although law depends on persuasion, inducements, and voluntary compliance, force (or its possible application) remains the critical tool for legal enforcement.

The study of law invites examination of a wide range of critical questions about persons and the ways they live together, raising issues traditionally linked to liberal inquiry. For example,

- Why are some societies highly dependent on law while others resist legal regulation and favor different modes of organizing, regulating, and changing behavior?

- How does law change, and how do social forces precipitate legal change? What role does legal continuity play in historical change and the structuring of historical time?

- Can immoral law nonetheless be valid and binding?

- How is the power of law exercised, and what role does law play in the calculus of sociopolitical legitimacy?

- What is the relationship between the official law and the lives of persons law is supposed to regulate? Is legal regulation efficient? Does law facilitate or impede the growth of scientific knowledge and technological innovation?

- In what ways are the narrative styles used by legal officials distinctive, and in what ways do they resemble rhetorical modes in other domains of social life? How do the canons of argument and proof used in law compare with those used elsewhere, for example, in philosophy, science, or mathematics?

- How is the legal concept of authority grounded in a tradition of reading and re-reading canonical texts? How does this tradition of reading conserve and alter the meaning of written law?

- How ought law to be understood as a cultural system? How does it reflect or embody the debates and divisions of the cultures in which it is found? How have legal institutions embraced and constructed, as well as silenced and stigmatized, various national, social, cultural, and personal identities?

Legal study provides a useful and engaging way to sharpen students' skills as readers, as interpreters of culture, and as citizens schooled in what Aristotle would have regarded as a kind of practical wisdom, a knowledge that extends beyond theoretical understanding to civic and moral action. To understand legal materials, students are required to develop habits of close reading and hone their interpretive, imaginative, and analytic abilities. Understanding those materials requires great attentiveness, the ability to see how arguments are constructed, and the willingness to imagine alternative possibilities. Because law is concerned with resolving disputes, the student of law is invited to test his or her ethical arguments and textual understandings in a context in which decisions must be made and force often must be deployed. In each of these respects, legal study complements general education objectives of a liberal arts education.[12]

New interest and energy are now being focused on the situation of legal scholarship in the liberal arts. Evidence of this fact is found in the proliferation of organizations now promoting legal study within social science and humanities disciplines, for example, the Organized Section on Courts, Law, and the Judicial Process of the American Political Science Association and American Psychology-Law Society/Division 41 of the American Psychological Association. Other scholarly associations, such as the Research Committee on the Sociology of Law of the International Sociological Association, the Society for the Study of Political and Legal Philosophy, the American Society for Legal History, the Law and Society Association, the American Legal Studies Association, and the Association for the Study of Law, Culture, and the Humanities, cross disciplinary lines. Moreover, 2003 saw the incorporation of the Consortium of Undergraduate Law and Justice Programs, whose stated purpose is

> to support and promote undergraduate programs in law and justice studies broadly conceived . . . through such activities as the collection and distribution of information concerning the content, structure and curricular design of existing undergraduate law and justice programs; the formulation of guidelines and procedures designed to improve the operation and assessment of such undergraduate programs; the advising of faculty engaged in the creation and/or development of undergraduate law and justice programs; the mentoring of younger scholars teaching in such programs; and the provision of services (such as a newsletter and website) to facilitate communication and discussion among the Consortium's constituent programs and other interested persons.[13]

In addition, in a growing number of widely read journals, interdisciplinary legal scholarship is well represented.[14]

Nonetheless, one might ask why study law in the liberal arts when there is a well-developed tradition of legal study in professional schools? Or more simply put, why should a liberal arts college do what some believe is now done in law schools? The short answer is that if law schools did anything like what I am describing, then it might be less necessary to study law in the liberal arts.[15] But they do not.

It is true, however, that the law school of the twenty-first century is a far more open and accommodating place than it has ever been. The boundaries between the law school and the rest of the university have been blurred to the extent that many faculty at the best law schools now have Ph.D.'s in addition to law degrees and interdisciplinarity is a watchword. Yet this blurring has occurred at the margins of even the most interdisciplinary law schools.[16] At the center, law schools are still "lawyering schools."

The education of lawyers is important in its own right, and legal education emphasizes doctrine and teaching students to "think like lawyers." Law school has the same relationship to legal study in the liberal arts as medical school does to the study of biology or business school does to the study of economics. In law schools, legal study is treated as a subject for professionals and practitioners who must understand what the law says and how it can be used to serve the interests of clients. It focuses on law as a tool rather than its place in society or its ethical and rhetorical dimensions. Consequently, law schools largely ignore broad regions of legal knowledge. This volume is premised on the belief that neither our students nor our society is well served when legal education is surrendered to professional schools.[17]

OVERVIEW OF THE BOOK

The chapters that follow seek to chart or exemplify the work of legal scholarship in the liberal arts. Each gives evidence of the work that legal scholars do to connect their subject to the disciplinary concerns and interdisciplinary aspirations of the liberal arts. Although each speaks in its own distinctive voice, together they explore the practices, possibilities, and pitfalls of legal scholarship in the liberal arts.

The book begins with Douglas Goodman and Susan Silbey's "Defending Liberal Education from the Law." Goodman and Silbey articulate a vision of legal scholarship in the liberal arts that differentiates it from the professional school vision discussed earlier. Liberal arts education, they argue, "is meant to prepare students to grasp the nature and range of human problems and to provide a variety of tools to manage them." Professional education in law is mere "training." Training, unlike education, involves " 'the acquisition of techniques for which norms or standards have been commonly agreed upon.'" Education subjects the norms and standards that guide training to critical examination and opens up the discussion of what we should, not just what we can, do.

Colleges and universities have historically avoided systematic study of law because of the fear that it would slide too easily from education to training. Goodman and Silbey argue that this exclusion has been, and is today, a mistake with serious consequences for the educational enterprise itself. The exclusion of legal scholarship from the liberal arts has encouraged a "complicity with law" such that students graduating from college take law to be something to be manipulated rather than questioned and treat it as "fact rather than as a social and moral accomplishment."

In addition, Goodman and Silbey suggest that the lack of explicit engagement with legal scholarship and the lack of informed critique of law have allowed "law as social fact to invade the educational relationship itself." The result is the "juridification" of many of the activities of colleges and universities. Goodman and Silbey praise legal scholarship in the liberal arts for treating law as a "moral accomplishment" produced by *discussion* about what we should do. They praise it for its critical and discursive engagements and its redemptive possibilities. "The moral force of law," they contend, "depends on lifeworld discussions," which legal scholarship in the liberal arts advances. Without that, "law loses its moral dimension and becomes a juridified system."

The remaining chapters in this book respond to and engage in various ways with Goodman and Silbey's argument that legal scholarship in the liberal arts highlights the moral and political dimensions of law rather than its technical force. The next three chapters develop particular conceptions of the moral and political work of legal scholarship in the liberal arts, whereas those that follow provide several examples of the pedagogical practices of those who teach law in the liberal arts. This book concludes with a chapter that raises questions about Goodman and Silbey's redemptive view of legal scholarship.

Like Goodman and Silbey, Keith Bybee, in his chapter titled "The Liberal Arts, Legal Scholarship, and the Democratic Critique of Judicial Power," also emphasizes the antivocationalism of the liberal arts. Bybee suggests that differences between professional education in law and legal scholarship in the liberal arts do not result primarily from disciplinary divides between them. They result, he suggests, from something much more profound, namely, the historical connection between the liberal arts and political life. Like Goodman and Silbey, he sees legal scholarship in the liberal arts in moral and political terms and evaluates it in terms of its ability to contribute to a democratic political project.

Legal scholarship contributes to democracy by equipping students to comprehend, critique, and ultimately to control the countermajoritarian exercise of power by courts and judges. Legal scholarship does this by decoding and demystifying the frequently muddied and incoherent decisions that courts produce as they negotiate diverse disputes in a fractious political system. Bybee thus emphasizes attention to language and argument as central to legal scholarship in the liberal arts.

He does not criticize judicial decisions for being muddied and incoherent, however, nor does he wish them to be otherwise. Instead Bybee reads them symptomatically, as signs that courts respond to the healthy pluralism of our society with efforts to accommodate and give voice to diverse views rather than imposing doctrinal purity. Legal scholarship should, he suggests, help students first to understand and then to appreciate such responses. It should help them cultivate an appreciation of diversity and provide practice in handling disagreement and uncertainty. In this way, legal scholarship in the liberal arts instills in students skills necessary for successful democratic self-government.

Marianne Constable, in her chapter titled "On Not Leaving Law to the Lawyers," focuses, like Goodman and Silbey, on the dangers of particular conceptions of law, conceptions that sometimes appear in the liberal arts. For Constable, that scholarship is, like the work done in professional schools, too much concerned with technique. As a result, it cannot provide a satisfactory explanation of why "law is too important to be left to the lawyers."

What does/might this phrase mean, Constable asks? And why/how can/should law not be left to the lawyers? She notes several possibilities, one that seems remarkably like the conception of the role of law in the liberal arts advanced by Goodman and Silbey and Bybee. Following Harold Berman, Constable notes that some legal scholars worry that lawyers divorce the technical means by which law achieves its ends from the " 'larger dimensions of law which relate it to justice, equity, to social welfare.'" Following Frank Munger, she suggests that some scholars think that "law is too unequal or unjust for . . . [those] committed to the fight for equality and justice to leave law alone." Following Robert Nelson, she notes efforts of scholars to " 'develop theories that connect context with broader structures'" in the explanation of legal phenomena. Following Lawrence Friedman, she observes that some scholars think that "the meaning . . . of law is too big and alive to be left to the narrow theorizing, model building, and deadening . . . thought of lawyers."

All of these statements focus of law's practices, not on the discursive, rhetorical, linguistic dimensions. But law, Constable contends, is "a discourse that matters and a practice . . . involving speech." Legal scholarship in the liberal arts needs to attend to the discursive work of law, the way it "tells" people what to do. Law is, in this sense, too discursive to be left to lawyers or to social scientists eager to rescue it from them. If we are to engage, as Goodman and Silbey urge, with law as a moral accomplishment rather than as a social fact, legal scholarship in the liberal arts must, Constable argues, attend closely to the way law speaks.

Austin Sarat, in his chapter titled "Crossing Boundaries: Toward an Integrated Conception of Legal Scholarship," acknowledges the importance of Constable's insight, but he argues that attending to the way law speaks should be part of a broader, integrative conception of legal study in the liberal arts. He begins his argument by reflecting on the challenges that those who teach law undergraduates face every day. These challenges arise, in part, from a message that the culture transmits to those students, namely, that the "real" law teachers are to be found in law schools, not in liberal arts colleges.

Sarat argues, in the spirit of Goodman and Silbey, that this way of thinking arises from the equation of legal knowledge with technical knowledge. Despite signs of what he calls "liberal arts envy" among some law professors, he contends that at the heart of the study of law as technique is the separation of law from morality and politics, which is the key to law schools' efforts to get their students to think like lawyers. The work of legal scholarship in the liberal arts is to reconnect what professional legal education seeks to keep separate.

Legal scholarship in the liberal arts invites students to explore law's complex relations to morality and politics as well as the ways these relations get worked out in distinctive interpretive practices. Morality and politics then get connected to the study of law, rhetoric, and discourse. But, Sarat contends, what gives law its distinctive temper is that it seeks to work in the world through the deployment of legitimate violence. Appreciating this, students are challenged to cultivate their capacity to judge, to find their way to understand when law does, and should, deploy its lethal will in the world. Sarat advocates an "integrative" conception as an alternative to the idea of law as technique—a conception that examines what happens when moral argument, distinctive interpretive practices, and violence come together.

The remaining chapters exemplify what legal scholarship in the liberal arts looks like when it treats law as a moral accomplishment rather than as a social fact. The first, by James Boyd White, explicitly engages with Constable's argument about the importance of law's discursive and linguistic qualities for legal scholarship. For White, however, the focus is not on how we interpret language; it is instead on the attitude we take toward writing. The title of White's chapter, "Meaning What You Say," captures the essence of his argument. Legal scholars, like others in the liberal arts, should be attentive to the quality of writing in the texts they produce as well as in those they read and interpret.

White argues that one of the central vocations of legal scholars in the liberal arts is to help students master "forms of expression so fully that they can turn them to their own purposes" and, echoing Bybee, develop "a new sense of the possibility of expressive and active life, indeed a new sense of the self." Meaning what one says is by no means an easy task; it is itself a moral accomplishment. Legal scholars in the liberal arts should, White suggests, turn their critical gaze on legal writing, exposing and criticizing those who treat law as "a set of rules to be applied more or less routinely to the facts of cases as they arise." For White, like Constable and Bybee, language matters. Good legal writing honors language by making present through it "the life of the mind, of thought and argument, that is generated by the recognition that we live in a world in which there are many valid things to say, from many points of view, with which it is the task of the legal mind . . . to come to terms."

Good writing is writing in which an author means what she says. It is writing with qualities of "immediacy, authenticity, care . . . of real significance" to its author. The opposite of such writing is alienated, formulaic, dutiful writing, the kind produced by many undergraduates and, on White's account, by many judges as well. The practices of good writing are no more aesthetic fixation; instead they touch on the central themes of the liberal arts and legal scholarship's contribution to it—they go to "the very value of the human being," "our practices of self-government," "the idea of justice at work . . . in our legal system." One can, White contends, "deny humanity in the way one speaks just as effectively as in the way one acts."

Jeffrey Abramson's chapter, titled "Teaching Civil Liberties as a Branch of Political Theory," provides a second example of how legal scholarship in the liberal arts advances the understanding of law as a moral accomplishment. Like Bybee and White, he is interested in the writings of appellate judges and in a limited slice of legal cases, namely, those involving civil liberties issues, and, like them, he sees the indeterminacy of law as providing a rich opening for liberal arts inquiry. One of the special opportunities of legal scholars in the liberal arts, Abramson contends, is to use legal materials to illuminate significant issues in political theory and to read legal decisions with a view toward identifying the theoretical choices that drive them.

His chapter illuminates that claim in the context of legal decisions in the areas of freedom of speech and religion. Those cases, Abramson argues, often are animated by a philosophical choice between tolerance (an agreement to disagree) and respect (genuine appreciation of what is different). Tolerance, he claims, forms weak social bonds even as it commits its advocates to tolerating those who would not tolerate them. Respect is deeper, more engaged and engaging. Whereas tolerance is neutral and impartial as to the moral worth of that which is tolerated, respect requires affirmation and embrace at the level of substance.

By teasing out the philosophical bases of legal decision, Abramson believes that the legal scholar in the liberal arts alerts students to the richness and complexity of the choices that judges make. He also illuminates the apparatus through which judges deny that they are making choices and thereby exposes one of the ways in which legal decisions are made to appear legitimate. Abramson concludes his chapter by highlighting the urgency of this work in post–September 11 America, where both law's choices and the maintenance of its legitimacy are as, if not more, consequential than they have ever been.

Hendrik Hartog, in a chapter titled "Romancing the Quotation," speaks in a quasi-autobiographical voice about the vocation of legal history, about what moves him in his scholarship, about the purposes of legal history as he does it. He self-consciously resists abstract generalizations in favor of what he calls "the particular story (which sometimes might be a case)." Romancing the quotation is, Hartog says, one "peculiar 'liberal arts' way to gain understanding about law." Allied forms of legal scholarship in the liberal arts often analyze "the trouble case."

Hartog's view of legal scholarship in the liberal arts is, like Constable's, self-consciously antipositivist and antistructuralist. He develops this view through a reading of a story, an account of the work of the anthropologist David Schneider and of his quarrel with his wife, Addie Schneider, over the status of evidence, data, and quotations in ethnographies of family and kinship. Hartog uses this story to consider "dilemmas of how particulars join to become generalizations, singulars become plurals and explanations . . . how cultural history and legal history and cultural anthropology and legal anthropology and literary theory all converged at a particular historical moment."

As legal scholarship, Hartog's work speaks to "the significance of nonstate legal actors in narratives about the evolution of law and the uses of the trouble case . . . as offering access to counterhegemonic . . . conceptions of legality." His brand of the "cultural history of law" is driven, or so it seems, by the same impulses that animate Goodman and Silbey, Bybee, Constable, and White, although he is suspicious of the large theories that some of these authors mobilize to justify their work. Understanding law as a moral accomplishment requires Hartog to study the law as it was lived in the quotidian lives of " 'actual people' " and to uncover the " 'informal logic of actual life.' " As he puts it, "I . . . insist that one humanistic task for those of us who are not of . . . the law school world is to reconstruct and play out the meanings and tonalities located in the stories, quotations, and anecdotes that offer our primary access to the ways women and men work through and think about their relationships to law."

Susan Heinzelman concludes this volume with a caution about the search for a single political meaning or epistemological project for interdisciplinary work in law. Advocacy of an antitechnical view of law, a view of law as a moral accomplishment, pointing to the democracy-enriching qualities of legal scholarship in the liberal arts, celebrating language and good writing, romancing the quotation—these ideas all replicate the "previous claims of men of learning, like Blackstone and Burke, that a complete education implied knowledge of the law." This replication runs the danger, she warns, of being deeply "regressive." Although legal scholarship in the liberal arts may seek to liberate law from the technocrats, it should not fall into an easy alliance with aristocracy and patriarchy.

The danger that informs Goodman and Silbey's critique of "juridification" as well as the search for a humanistic version of legal scholarship is the danger of nostalgia, "a nostalgia for an Edenic moment, that original time when law and humanities were not separated but rather were inextricably united, one discipline, one body of knowledge such that people instinctively knew how to live in a state of harmony with one another and with the world around them." Such harmony, she argues, is only and always gained through exclusion and silencing. Through a close reading of two episodes in Chaucer's *Canterbury Tales*, Heinzelman warns that the turn to the humanities, to the liberal arts, to poetic representation may replicate, rather than challenge, this process. As she puts it, "although the relationship of poetics to law may be represented between disciplines as the relationship of the feminine to the masculine, poetics nevertheless performs as masculine within its own representational protocols."

Heinzelman insists that we look hard at the gendered dynamics of the relationship between law and the humanities. These dynamics are "uncanny" in that they will not "remain silenced, hidden, or suppressed." Examining law as a moral accomplishment and praising legal scholarship in the liberal arts should not/will not forestall interruptions of the emergent narrative. These interruptions may disrupt the nostalgic wishing for the harmony of another time even as they remind us that "no law comes unattended by fantasy," whether the fantasy of escape from the professional project of legal education or of using legal scholarship in the liberal arts to save law from the lawyers.

From the appreciation of law as a moral achievement rather than a social fact to a warning about the dangers of nostalgia, exclusion, and silencing in that appreciation, the essays in this book suggest that legal scholarship in the liberal arts is neither a panacea for disenchantment with law schools and lawyers nor a hollow hope devoid of moral, political, or pedagogical significance. They alert us to the possibilities as well as the pitfalls of turning to the liberal arts to redeem legal scholarship or of turning to the latter to enrich the former. Although the full significance of legal scholarship in the liberal arts cannot be determined, such scholarship opens up a space in which the issue of what law is, how it should be studied, and toward what ends it might be put can be contested and the weight of these questions can be assessed.

NOTES

1. Examples include Edwin Corwin, Henry Steele Commager, Robert McCloskey, and Laura Nader.

2. See Harold Berman, *On the Teaching of Law in the Liberal Arts Curriculum* (Brooklyn: Foundation Press, 1956), 9.

3. "Symposium: Law, Knowledge, and the Academy," *Harvard Law Review* 115 (2002): 1101.

4. See Paul W. Kahn, *The Cultural Study of Law: Reconstructing Legal Scholarship* (Chicago: University of Chicago Press, 1999).

5. Woodrow Wilson, "Legal Education of Undergraduates," *Reports of the American Bar Association* 17 (1984): 439.

6. Berman, *On the Teaching of Law*, 17.

7. These early efforts are discussed in *LJST and Interdisciplinary Legal Scholarship*, http://www.amherst.edu/~ljst/aboutus.htm#program.

8. See American Bar Association, Section on Public Education, http://www.abanet.org/publiced/undergrad/home.html.

9. The variety of legal forms and the different ways law is used and understood in different times and places are as notable and instructive, as is the ubiquity of law itself.

10. Legality, of course, does not exhaust morality and at times contravenes it. Thus legal justice is not coextensive with justice itself.

11. Hermeneutics is, strictly speaking, the study of the principles of interpretation. However, when we refer to hermeneutics we are referring to the way those principles are organized and reproduced within any cultural system.

12. Lawrence A. Babb et al., *Education at Amherst Reconsidered: The Liberal Studies Program* (Amherst: Amherst College Press, 1978), describes the objectives of general education to include the fostering of "a critical engagement with life, a willingness to examine the given and to question dogma, an ability to entertain novel ways of thinking. . . . In truth, the critical faculty is most directly exercised in reasoning that accompanies choosing: the choice of a course of action, a moral position, a problem for investigation, a method of approach" (36–37). See also "Report of the Select Committee on the Curriculum," October 1990.

13. Bylaws of the Consortium of Undergraduate Law and Justice Programs, on file with author.

14. For example, *Law and Society Review, Law and Policy, Law and Social Inquiry, Yale Journal of Law and the Humanities, Law and History Review, American Journal of Legal History, Law and Philosophy, Philosophy and Public Affairs, Cardozo Studies in Law and Literature, Journal of Legal Studies, International Journal of the Sociology of Law, Studies in Law, Politics and Society, Social and Legal Studies: An International Journal*.

15. See Austin Sarat, "Law's Two Lives: Humanist Visions and Professional Education," *Yale Journal of Law and the Humanities* 5 (1993): 201.

16. Some think that interdisciplinarity has gone too far in law schools. See, e.g., Harry T. Edwards, "The Growing Disjunction between Legal Education and the Legal Profession," *Michigan Law Review* 91 (1992): 34.

17. One analogy to our project is provided by the development of religious studies in America. Just as the study of religion in America no longer is directed exclusively toward those studying for the ministry, priesthood, or rabbinate, so law, as an academic subject, is not the exclusive domain of the legal practitioner. Just as religion established its independent identity as a field of study in colleges and universities, so too should law. For an elaboration of this analogy, see Kahn, *Cultural Study of Law*.

ONE

Perspectives on Legal Scholarship

in the Liberal Arts

DEFENDING LIBERAL EDUCATION
FROM THE LAW

DOUGLAS J. GOODMAN AND SUSAN S. SILBEY

There are, of course, many positive reasons for including a study of law in a liberal arts education.[1] A liberal arts education is, by definition, expansive, since it is meant to prepare students to grasp the nature and range of human problems and to provide a variety of tools to manage them. It is easy enough to argue that the study of law—as a set of tools designed to handle social problems—is a valuable addition and thus that legal scholarship should have a central place. Furthermore, a liberal arts education is meant to provide students with the essential knowledge that is relevant to their particular era, and it certainly takes little argument to convince us that our era is particularly legalistic. Even more to the point, a liberal arts education is meant to equip students to meet the demands of intelligent citizenship. That the liberal arts create well-informed citizens has long been cited as the primary practical justification for this seemingly impractical endeavor. This ambition alone seems so compelling for the explicit inclusion of legal scholarship in a liberal arts education that it makes us wonder why there has ever been any resistance.

We can suggest a practical explanation although we do not defend it. Liberal arts colleges have always defined their vision of education in opposition to an idea of training. Training, as used in this opposition, involves "the acquisition of techniques for which norms or standards have been commonly agreed upon, as in the trades and professions."[2] Education, however, is more than simply the acquisition of techniques. In education, norms and standards are explored, critically examined, discussed, and submitted to continuous challenge. Training is to teach us what we can do, whereas education opens up the discussion of what we should do.

In the area of law, a liberal arts education would be focused on law's critique rather than training students in its use. In education as opposed to training, the law must be empirically explored, discussed, critiqued, and perhaps challenged instead of memorized, manipulated, and applied. But in traditional conceptions of law, the line between education and training may appear to be too difficult to maintain. Certainly law has been allowed to appear as a subject of a liberal arts education, but only as minor topics in sociology (of law), history (of law), or political science (of law). The fear of sliding over into training, which characterizes the professional definition of legal education, has kept the *explicit* study of law off of the liberal arts agenda.

Liberal arts colleges have, consequently, avoided training their students in the law as a set of terms and techniques to be memorized, manipulated, and applied. The colleges' vision of the good citizen has meant the citizen capable of interrogating the law, not the citizen who blindly accepts or the technician who uses the law.[3] This is the reason colleges have avoided the explicit study of the law—because it will slide too easily into the production of good lawyers rather than the liberal arts' idea of a good citizen.

However, it is not at all clear that they have accomplished this goal. On the contrary, the exclusion of the law as an explicit area of study seems to have encouraged a complicity with the law even more effective because it is too often unquestioned and perhaps soon unquestionable. Could it be an accident that most of the student unrest during the 1960s and early 1970s over race relations, the Vietnam War, and the environment did not have its genesis at liberal arts colleges? Could it be that precisely because it has not been explicitly discussed, the liberal arts colleges are producing students who take the law as fact rather than as a social and moral accomplishment?[4] Are we not producing students who feel perfectly at home in either the most professional or the most reprehensible law office, who have been trained in that most important of attributes for getting ahead in the legal profession—the unquestioning acceptance of the law as something to be manipulated and used rather than questioned? Has not the lack of education in legal scholarship been the best training possible for showing us what the law can do without ever discussing what the law should be?

In this essay, we develop this more negative tack. Rather than ask why it would be good for a liberal arts education, and by extension, research at liberal arts colleges, to include legal scholarship as an explicit field of study, we ask what harm is being done because we do not include legal scholarship. We do not in any sense intend this as a repudiation of what is good in the study of the law and what is instructive in legal scholarship, but we leave that ground for others to till.

Indeed, the main point of this chapter is to suggest that the case is even worse than we have indicated thus far. The lack of explicit engagement with legal scholarship and lack of informed critique of the law do more than prepare students to accept law as a necessary and self-determining social fact rather than as a social and normative accomplishment. It also allows the law as a social fact to invade the educational relation itself. We are going to argue that the acceptance of the facticity of law has affected the way in which students and professors view their relations with each other and that this is eating away at the basis of liberal arts education. The relation between students and professors is increasingly seen as a legal relationship defined by an assumed legal contract rather than as a moral accomplishment. In such a juridified relation, the traditional mission of the liberal arts college becomes progressively more difficult. As students become consumers with implied contractual rights and professors become employees of an institution that markets socially valued qualifications, the question of moral and political education becomes irrelevant or even discouraged.

This increasingly legalized relation underlies some of the critiques from those on the left, such as Jerome Karabel and John Marciano,[5] who decry the lack of moral criticism in education, and those on the right, such as William Bennett, Allan Bloom, and Lynne Cheney, who bemoan the lack of moral principles. Some of these critics see a solution in a return to "eternal verities," instead of coping with the underlying change in the social structures. We see this even in the leftist critics who should certainly know better. Marciano, for example, urges the adoption of different texts and more critical lesson plans, but he never looks at the social relations that have led to the regressive changes in the first place.

Of course, it is true that the history of the liberal arts has been one of continuing, or at least successive, crises. David Breneman notes the irony of this: "Indeed, the private liberal arts college stands out as one of American society's greatest success stories. Ironically, however, the literature on the private (or independent) college portrays a nearly unbroken history of concern for its survival. Are we looking at one of the hardiest of institutions, or one of the most fragile?"[6] Here though, we are not asking whether or not it will survive; instead we wish to look at its transformation into something that formally resembles its founding mission but that in practice subverts it.

We point out here at the beginning that we do not believe that this transformation can be halted by simply carving out an area, such as that of liberal arts education, that is free of legal relations. The intrusions of the law into education have not been the result merely of legal overreaching, nor are they wholly due to a contagion from the increasing legalization of almost every sphere of contemporary society. As we discuss more fully later in the chapter, much of the intrusion of legal relations into liberal arts education has been in response to racist, sexist, classist, or other pernicious customs and traditions that are embedded in the institutional structures, personal relations, and ideological goals of the liberal arts education. The recourse to legal techniques, contracts, duties, and liabilities has been the most successful avenue of challenge by those who were disadvantaged by the liberal arts tradition as it existed throughout much of its history. Even if all discriminatory practices were erased, we still would not call for the reversal of this legalization. We are persuaded that the interdependent relations of modern society, of plural values and normativities, require a self-conscious system of mediation and regulation of those plural normative orders, that is, we require a legal system. It is unlikely that we will ever return to the types of regulation available in more homogeneous social worlds.

We are caught between the discriminatory but living traditions of the liberal arts education that we have known and the more just but lifeless and impersonal form that it is becoming. We argue that the solution to this problem cannot be a rearguard action or a fencing off of a liberal arts preserve. The solution can only be to involve the students in a project that transforms the legal form that the college is assuming from a legalistic social fact into a critical engagement and thus a moral accomplishment. Liberal education must involve an explicit embrace of legal scholarship, a discussion of the development and extent of this legal encroachment, the reasons it came about, its moral and educational effects, and the reasons it must be transformed through cooperative effort, understanding, and critique.

Before proceeding, we think it is useful to clarify two points. First, when we say that the law is a moral accomplishment, we do not mean that the law is morally right but rather that it comes out of discussions related to what is right. In other words, the law is a moral accomplishment when it is produced by discussions about what we should do, what it is good to do, what it is right to do, rather than discussions about what we can do, what is technically feasible. We use the term *moral accomplishment* to mean that law is constituted through the transactions of persons deploying diverse motives and meanings, instrumental, normative, affective, and habitual.[7] Even a law that emerged from discussions that conclude that there ultimately is no universal morality would be a moral accomplishment, since the discussions out of which it originated were focused on what should be done and not on what can be done. Therefore, to say that the law is a moral accomplishment is not to say that the law conforms to any moral system. To identify the law with a particular moral system would be to present the law as a self-determining fact. The law is a moral accomplishment only when the discussion includes the confrontation of moral systems.

Second, we should clarify how we see the relation between teaching and research in the liberal arts. When we speak about law in the liberal arts curriculum, we mean to include both the production of legal scholarship and the teaching of it. We do not believe that it is only a historical accident that teaching and research are often linked by their common institutional base. As for our particular focus—the role of law in the liberal arts—it is not important to distinguish between institutions that demand that undergraduate faculty be active scholars and institutions that do not make such stringent research demands. Similarly, it is not important to distinguish between liberal arts colleges and universities. At the heart of this inquiry is not the liberal arts college per se or the relationship between teaching and research specifically. Rather, we are talking about the goal that historically has been identified with the liberal arts college but that has also been embraced by many colleges of arts and science within larger universities. We certainly recognize a great deal of variation in these institutions, but we do not believe it is pertinent to our argument. When we talk about law in the liberal arts, we are making an argument about the status of legal scholarship outside of law schools and beyond the domain authority of the legal academy. Thus, the question is the degree to which a liberal education should include legal scholarship in teaching and as a focus of faculty research.

JURIDIFICATION AND THE DEMISE OF IN LOCO PARENTIS

The problem we are going to examine is often labeled juridification. By this we mean, first, the attempt to apply formal laws to situations that inherently depend on flexible, informal social interactions and, second, the tendency of these laws to be treated as reified social facts rather than moral accomplishments. Juridification is one aspect of what Weber diagnosed as the irreversible growth of bureaucratic rationality and that Habermas described as the colonization of the lifeworld by a system. Legal rules do not necessarily lead to juridification, but as we argue later in the chapter, law is inherently vulnerable to it.

In this section, we consider the rise of juridification in the post–in loco parentis college. As an example of this more general phenomenon, we look at the effects of juridification on the relation between faculty and suicidal students. We use this example because of the wide gap between the human and institutional response to this situation. The faculty member finds him or herself in a predicament in which concerned and informed care is called for, whereas the institutional directive is, in general, to refer the student to an anonymous professional. Here we see, in its starkest form, the emptying out of the moral dimension of the educational relationship and its replacement by a professionalized, legalized relation. Although we do not argue that faculty should become emotional caregivers—or therapists, heaven forbid—we suggest that education and critical engagement cannot take place within a hyperrationalized division of labor that limits the instructor's role to the formal presentation of technical expertise.

The greatest recent change in the legal environment of colleges has been the disappearance of the in loco parentis doctrine. In regard to colleges, *in loco parentis* meant that the institution had a responsibility to and authority over students similar to the responsibility and authority of a parent to a child. Before the 1960s, the courts viewed college students as children who required guidance and protection. Colleges were allowed to determine the limits of students' freedom in dress, in social behavior, and in association. The college's authority to act in place of the parent had never provided a blanket authorization for unconstitutional or immoral action. It was, however, given wide latitude. In a much-quoted decision, the Illinois Supreme Court said of Wheaton College's seemingly arbitrary rule: "Whether the rule be judicious or not, it violates neither good morals nor the law of the land and is therefore clearly within the power of the college authorities to make and enforce."[8] The court assumed that, like the relation between children and their parents, the relation between a college and its students was one that the court should only reluctantly interfere with.

The history of higher education law since the 1960s has been, as one legal scholar has written, "the gradual application of typical rules of civil liability to institutions of higher education and the decline of insulating doctrines, such as in loco parentis, which traditionally protected institutions of higher learning from scrutiny in the legal system."[9] The college has not yet entered the strict liability regime, but it is no longer in a sphere of protected autonomy.

Nevertheless, few mourn the passing of in loco parentis. In its traditional autonomy, colleges were permitted autocratic powers over students, and at least a few of them abused that power. Some of the first and most important challenges to the doctrine arose during and after the civil rights movement of the 1960s and involved the assertion of fundamental civil rights by college students. There was a series of cases in the 1960s and 1970s holding that colleges must provide basic constitutional rights to students. Most famously, the court in *Dixon v. Alabama* prevented a state college from expelling students for exercising their constitutional right to participate in a legal demonstration.[10]

In addition, there had been significant social changes within and outside the college that made in loco parentis increasingly inappropriate. Students were coming to campuses in greater numbers, and these numbers included more mature students. They were not all eighteen- to twenty-two-year-olds. Also, society's view of those in that age bracket had changed so that they were viewed as already adults. All but the youngest college students are legally entitled to vote, to sign contracts, to marry without parental approval, and to purchase firearms and, at the time, alcohol. In such a social environment, in loco parentis was no longer viable. However, despite the impossibility of returning to it, we should be clear about what has resulted from its withdrawal.

In loco parentis protected the relation between the college and the student from legal intrusion. The demise of in loco parentis created an intellectual and moral vacuum concerning college/student relations and obligations, because colleges never initiated any serious discussion involving faculty and students about alternative responses to this changing legal environment. Consequently, relations between administrators, faculty, and students began to assume legal forms defining market, rather than educational, relationships.

Recently, those defending colleges in legal and public forums have invoked the specter of in loco parentis in a way that tends to confuse the issue.[11] Attempts to hold colleges accountable for negligence through the extension of duty rules have been characterized as returning to a "new" or "hidden" form of in loco parentis. However, as Lake points out, such a characterization makes no sense:

> First, courts continue to insist that in loco parentis is dead in higher education law. Second, courts imposing legal responsibility— duty—on IHE's [Institutes of Higher Education] do not do so explicitly on *in loco parentis* doctrine. In fact, the decisions are bereft of any such reference to *in loco parentis*. And, third, it would make no doctrinal sense at all to speak of a return to *in loco parentis* because the doctrine originally existed as a protective insulating doctrine in higher education law with regards to IHE's and it was not used to create legal responsibilities of IHE's.[12]

Under current legal interpretations, the closest analogy for the relation between the college and the student is that between a business and a client, consumer, or tenant. Increasingly, courts treat colleges like other businesses, even though previous legal eras had always recognized a special relation between colleges and students. This special relation now generally means the special application of general rules of tort duty to institutions of higher learning. In essence, colleges are seen as similar to businesses but in some ways distinct from landlords, retailers, or factories. Courts have attempted to recognize the special circumstances of the college situation. Thus, the current legal approach is "both a time of mainstreaming and of tailoring."[13]

This mix of mainstreaming and tailoring has been a confusing one, however. There has been a disparate combination of three approaches: (1) the application of businesslike duties; (2) the deflection of responsibility for student misconduct, particularly around alcohol use; and (3) an assertion of the special duties of a college. It is this last item that colleges have found particularly troubling.

Under in loco parentis, the college was able to enforce encompassing rules of conduct in regard to student behavior. Along with this, the college was assumed to have a duty to protect the student. In fact, this duty to protect was often cited by the courts invoking in loco parentis as the reason for the college's power to promulgate rules. However, this duty was never clearly spelled out, and it was rarely used as the basis for a suit against the college. Lake notes that it amounted to de facto immunity from liability.

> There was never a "university" tort immunity as such: courts wove analogous immunities given to other institutions and other doctrines together to make a de facto university immunity that was similar to, but not the same as, protections given to other major societal institutions. Where appropriate, the university was immunized as a parent *(in loco parentis)*, a charity, or a government; or protected like a "social host" would be regarding alcohol use, or shielded by rules of proximate causation or by all-or-nothing affirmative defenses. The net result was minimal legal/judicial intrusion in college affairs regarding student rights and safety.[14]

Ironically, the duty that was invoked to justify the college's powers under in loco parentis appears to some to have created the new liabilities and become the basis for numerous lawsuits now that in loco parentis is gone. For example, colleges are required to minimize the risks of peer sexual and racial harassment. They have a duty to protect students from hazing if the college knows or should know of dangerous hazing activities. Colleges have a duty to exercise reasonable care in assigning student residents to housing units.[15] More important than these successful suits, the courts now rarely recognize a no-duty relation that would allow for easy and early dismissal of costly law suits.

Colleges have argued that these new duties are more difficult than those that were recognized by in loco parentis, because the duties exist with few of the previous authoritative powers. "Institutionally, colleges perceive that they must control the uncontrollable and reasonably act to do what reasonable care cannot prevent."[16] The effect of the new liability regime on the institution goes beyond the actual rulings, that is, the legal changes over the last few decades have done more than simply increase the college's formal liability. Importantly, it has meant an increase in judicial scrutiny of college affairs and parallel loss of its cherished autonomy. It is true that judicial consideration is still cautious, but even where courts have determined that there is no liability, the area has still been opened up to judicial review. This is especially relevant in a legal environment that is not stable but that is instead characterized by a trend toward increasing legal involvement in educational policy. With typical institutional caution, colleges are receiving a message of increased responsibility and legal accountability from the legal system, even where there is not (or not yet) strict liability.

Colleges have responded to this new situation with a mix of attempts to reassert paternalistic control where duty is clear and to avoid all signs that they might be assuming a duty where it is not clear. It is an example of the latter that we focus on: colleges' attempts to avoid signs of an affirmative duty in the case of student suicides, where courts have not recognized a legal duty. We argue that the incursion of the legal viewpoint into these matters has led to a juridification of the relation between the student and the college, and in particular, the professor as the college's representative.

FACULTY'S DUTY TO SUICIDAL STUDENTS

To a large extent, colleges have abandoned all but a legal responsibility for students' moral and social life. One commentator describes this new post–in loco parentis relation:

> Unable to play the role of the parent, no longer prescribing bedtimes or enforcing a moral code, the institution has effectively withdrawn from the field of morality and character formation. Even to suggest that colleges bear responsibility not only for the academic achievements but also for the character of their graduates has today a ring of anachronism and nostalgia.[17]

Professors are increasingly reluctant to promulgate moral values, even when the moral value is central to the mission of the liberal arts college, such as academic honesty. Despite indication of increased cheating among students, one study reported that most faculty members "said they would go to little or very little effort to document an incident" of academic dishonesty.[18] Gary Pavela reports that one of the reasons faculty are reluctant to pursue academic dishonesty cases is the "fear of confrontation and litigation; and the bad experiences some faculty members have had with burdensome hearing procedures."[19] In the absence of any discussion between faculty, administrators, and students about the benefits, drawbacks, and alternatives to litigation and legalistic procedures, professors tend to avoid any relation with students that might lead to legal consequences.

One particularly crucial example of this is the role of a faculty member in dealing with students with emotional difficulties, especially those that are suicidal. We have been unable to locate any research on the proper role for a college faculty member to assume in such a situation. This lack of research is itself significant. What exactly faculty should do is, of course, beyond the scope of this chapter, but we note that there is no research to support the idea that the faculty should *not* be involved or that their involvement should be limited to referring the student to professional counseling. Nevertheless, as we describe more fully later in the chapter, referring the student to professional counseling is, in most cases, the extent of the "training" that college faculty get in dealing with students with emotional difficulties. After a brief discussion of our preliminary research findings, we argue that the faculty's lack of involvement can be explained by the legal environment and its juridifying effect.

To confirm the results of our search of the relevant scholarship, we sent out a brief survey to faculty subscribing to three listserves, asking them to let us know whether they have received instruction from their college or university about how to deal with students displaying emotional difficulties, and if so, what advice, information, or instruction they received. We also did six one-on-one interviews with counseling staff and student advisers. Of course this cannot be considered in any way a systematic survey, and the results may not be representative, but the responses we received are certainly suggestive and provocative. Half of the 41 respondents said that they had never, to their knowledge, received information from their institution about how to deal with students' emotions or personal issues. The response of a professor at a small liberal arts college is illustrative.

> We take great pride in the attention we give to students—in every dimension of their lives, and it can reasonably be said that we, as professors, are expected to be attuned to more than just the academic well being of our students. That said, I cannot recall in 35 years of teaching a single time in which any formal efforts were made to educate faculty or elicit their help with severe emotional problems.
>
> If we received any of this kind of information or directive . . . it was in such a vague form that I never noticed it. We got a lot more very explicit stuff about protection of human subjects in our research, including field research and classes that have a research component. . . . We have an active office of disabilities, and it has a host of requirements for people with impairments of vision, hearing, mobility etc. and even for learning disabilities. But again, nothing that I have heard addresses emotional issues.

The other half of our respondents said that they were advised to direct students whom they thought were in emotional distress to the counseling services and/or the dean of students offices. Some faculty recalled being given this advice in a brochure for new faculty; others reported receiving such advice every once in a while along with notices of the variety of counseling and medical services available on campus. "We do receive so much instruction on so many issues [that are legally sensitive] that it is hard to keep track," more than one reported. Some faculty described the individual letters they received asking them to make academic accommodations for a particular student who had come for counseling and was experiencing emotional or medical difficulties. Also, some faculty reported that their institutions sent out seasonal reminders to take care of students' levels of stress. "Every semester around finals time we get a memo from the Dean of Students alerting us to this in case we have any students who are having difficulty." And, "each fall we get a brochure and letter through campus mail from the wellness center [reminding us about the availability of] their services and how to handle a variety of issues." The general tone of the colleges' advice giving is summarized by this comment, "on rare occasions, such as 9/11, we are entreated by the administration to be sensitive to student problems, to accommodate them in terms of relaxing academic rules, and to refer them to our fairly extensive counseling/clergy staff."

We specifically asked whether there had ever been mention of possible legal problems as a reason for their institution's recommended response to students. Here we received provocative replies that seem to corroborate our general analysis. A dozen or more faculty reported that they received information and instruction on a range of student issues about which their college/university wanted faculty to be cautious. Most often this information concerned sexual harassment or physical disabilities. However, some of the faculty responses and all of the responses we heard from the counseling and dean of students staff focused on students' rights to privacy. There seemed to be a heightened attention to this topic, and it was the first issue mentioned in a half dozen one-on-one interviews with counseling staff and student advisers.

> In 20 odd years at Z, nine of these as department chair, I have received no advice or information relating to the "handling" of the kinds of situations about which you inquire. I do recall admonitions couched in the language of students' "rights to privacy" [when I] attempted to raise specific concerns with class [counseling] deans.
> We have been made aware of legal implications in dealing with psychologically disturbed students, but in my experience it has been with respect to protecting student privacy when seeking information about them. . . . We are encouraged to get troubled students to Counseling and Psychological Services for direct intervention. Given the availability of services, it is understood that faculty should

not offer lay counseling, not because of legal concerns, but because we are not qualified to deal with serious emotional problems. I suppose there is an implicit legal admonition that to do something as foolish as intervening in place of the pros might get us sued, but the emphasis is always on getting help for the student.

Our university did tell us that if a student wants to talk to us about being sexually harassed and asks if we can keep it confidential, we have to say no and are obliged (even against the student's wishes) to report it to higher ups. (Of course, I don't know how this could be enforced.)

Notably, the one respondent out of forty-one who reported receiving "a detailed faculty referral guide" that described in full the "various common symptoms of mental/emotional health problems" was from outside the United States. Nonetheless, this and another non-U.S. respondent noted that they expected their university's policies to change and had observed signs of such change already. "There isn't the same degree of readiness to resort to litigation in Canada [as in the United States], although I am concerned we are catching up fast." A British respondent went on to describe the specific changes now taking place at his university.

I attended a briefing for supervisors of research students a couple of days ago where [verbal] reference was made to the growing "problem" of students taking legal action against universities for perceived failures of supervision, teaching, etc. and supervisors were advised to keep some kind of documentary record of all interactions with students. A photocopy of a newspaper article reporting a recent case was distributed to drive home the point. Clearly, issues of students' emotional difficulties may well play a part in such cases but that was not the primary focus of the advice. Nevertheless, it seems that juridification is making itself felt at this University, albeit still in a fairly ad hoc way, although it doesn't take much imagination, as the number of cases of litigation by aggrieved students increases, to see this as the beginning of a trend that is likely to become more formalized.

The trend, as faculty describe it, is for students and teachers to become estranged and functionally segregated so that education becomes more like training—imparting a set of specific skills—rather than cultivating capacities of mind and sensibility.

My own perception is that while the College has actually done more in recent years to attend to student emotional needs in a formal way, at the same time much of that effort has been taken away from teaching faculty and placed on other professional people in the "student life" division of the college. In that sense, our charge as faculty is more purely academic now than it was years ago. This coincides, of course, with greater demands placed on us for research/publishing.

This increasingly legalized relation constrains what the faculty can do. One faculty member described his colleagues' inability to exclude a disruptive student "who was constantly talking to his computer. . . . We were told that we could do nothing because of legal concerns. This student continued to be disruptive and very difficult to handle." In another situation, a student "with a criminal record," who was believed to be dangerous, was stalking another student. The concerned faculty were told that the "stalker" could not, by law, be prohibited from registering for classes. Where university administrations are willing to take action, they require that the faculty create a "paper trail" of warnings and notices in writing to disruptive students before taking any action. "More than anything," one professor wrote about his institution's instructions, "it implied to me that we should be thinking like attorneys; i.e. making things public, creating a type of paper trail so that it is not merely a matter of one's word against another."

Ironically, law professors seem to have less difficulty with the legal constraints than do others. One respondent described a series of interventions she made, along with help from the counseling services and the dean of students at the law school at which she teaches. She was motivated by fear that a student was suicidal and was pleased by the openness of the counseling service to her interventions with the student.

I was actually quite surprised to be let in on the details of the therapy. . . . I found it enormously helpful because I could work with the therapist and the student to figure out how the student could make up the work to graduate on time. In my 20 years of university teaching I had never seen such a case where faculty, administrators, and the mental health professionals in the counseling service worked so well together. . . . It's funny how a faculty of lawyers seems to have no fear of litigation and it never comes up explicitly. By the way, this is true of many aspects of policy where I have found far more explicitly juridicalized procedures outside of law schools than in them.

Juridicalization became so bad at one school that the faculty formally rebelled. The dean had convinced most of the faculty that the school was on the "verge of a nasty lawsuit if we didn't handle students' emotional difficulties in a very formal manner." Several members of the faculty as well as the student body "challenged this liability regime," which led to a change in the administration and deanship.

> A new Dean of Students took a far more practical attitude to the whole thing. Unless we found a case where a small liberal arts college was sued for mishandling an emotionally troubled student, we would give emotionally troubled students the same care and attention we give to all our students. In other words, we would honestly respond to their situation. We wouldn't worry about lawsuits.

These latter examples stand in marked contrast to the tenor of the majority of comments we received in response to our queries. In most cases, a suicidal student who reaches out to a faculty member that he or she knows and respects is referred to professional strangers.

The traditional role of in loco parentis has been replaced by a new legal relation. There were and are strong reasons for this replacement. The traditional relation was often discriminatory and infantilizing. However, the legal relation has lost its moral dimension, which depends on engaged discussions. Because there was no place in the liberal arts for that discussion to take place, the relation has become juridified. Relations between faculty and students are now determined by a system of laws that are viewed as background social facts rather than moral accomplishments.

THE LACK OF INSTITUTIONAL RESPONSE TO THE ROLE OF FACULTY IN DEALING WITH SUICIDAL STUDENTS

Many faculty, as discussed earlier, have their own reasons for avoiding any relation with a student that might lead to litigation or legalistic procedures. In addition, a look at the legal environment indicates the reason that most colleges avoid any training of the faculty in suicide prevention or even any mention of the faculty's role beyond that of referring the student to professional counseling.

Where the courts have recognized an affirmative duty, colleges have found themselves in a difficult predicament.[20] They feel a need to assert authoritative control in areas in which they feel both uncomfortable and ineffective. Consequently, colleges have a strong incentive to avoid any recognition of an affirmative duty. This is especially true in cases of student suicide, an area in which a number of (mainly unsuccessful) suits have already been brought against colleges and in which the stakes are high in both money and public relations.

Currently courts have rejected the idea that there is a special relationship and, consequently, duty of care between the college and a suicidal student.[21] Colleges have therefore been immune under the general doctrine that third parties are not responsible for a person's decision to commit suicide. Nevertheless, colleges have reasons to be cautious. Some courts have recognized a college's assumption of an affirmative duty where there would have been no duty if the college had done nothing. These cases have involved injuries sustained while drinking alcohol, and it is worthwhile to look in detail at a representative case to see the lessons a college might take from such a ruling.

In *Coghlan v. Beta Theta Pi Fraternity,* the court held that despite the lack of a special relation and the demise of in loco parentis, the college may be found liable if, through its actions, it has assumed an affirmative duty.[22]

Coghlan, an eighteen-year-old pledge of a university sorority, was participating in rush week and attended two sorority-sponsored parties involving alcohol—one titled Jack Daniels' Birthday Party and the other Fifty Ways to Lose Your Liver. The sorority had a protective system in place that involved a "guardian angel," a sorority sister who was supposed to look out for the pledge. However, the guardian angel deserted Coghlan, and she proceeded to the parties without her angel. In addition, university employees were assigned to monitor the party. Despite this, the freshman was served liquor. She became "intoxicated and distraught" and was later taken back to the sorority house by a sister. Later that night, Coghlan fell from the third floor fire escape and suffered serious permanent injuries.

Citing the reasoning in *Bradshaw v. Rawlings,* the trial court dismissed Coghlan's claim against the university because the university owed no duty of care to the plaintiff.[23] The Idaho Supreme Court, while agreeing that "the modern American college is not an insurer of the safety of its students," nevertheless reversed the decision. The university could still be held liable, because "it is possible to create a duty where one previously did not exist. If one voluntarily undertakes to perform an act, having no prior duty to do so, the duty arises to perform the act in a non-negligent manner." In other words, the basis for the court's decision was not in loco parentis or any other special relation between the college and the student, but the creation of an affirmative duty as a result of the steps—that is, the presence of university supervisors at the party—taken to protect the student.[24]

One can easily imagine how this doctrine might be applied to dealing with suicidal students. So long as the college does nothing, the court would not recognize any special relation that might make the college liable. However, training or encouraging faculty to attempt to care for suicidal students might create an affirmative duty and involve the university in the task of controlling the uncontrollable.

TOWARD A GENERAL THEORY OF JURIDIFICATION

The example of the relation between faculty and suicidal students reveals that juridification has at least two dimensions. On the one hand, it empties out the moral and communicative substance of personal relations, and on the other hand, it motivates the institutional response or lack of response. In the particular case of the emotionally disturbed and suicidal student, the solution seems to us to be clear. Faculty should be trained to recognize and respond to suicidal students. Of course, this training should include a recognition of the important role of professional counseling, but that should not be to the exclusion of the faculty's own role. In the absence of any research to the contrary, there is every reason to believe that a trained faculty member who has an ongoing personal relation with the student can be at least as effective in dealing with emotional problems as a professional counselor.

Juridification, however, is a general problem, and it requires more than a piecemeal solution. Indeed, the very invisibility of the problem of how faculty should deal with suicidal students—the lack of research on the proper role of faculty, the lack of training and guidelines at the institutional level, the tendency of administrators and counselors to see it as an example of professionalization rather than juridification—argues for a general theory that helps to reveal and interpret particular cases. In this section, we turn to the theories of Jürgen Habermas to help us frame a general approach to the problem of juridification in the liberal arts.

Much of Habermas's analysis of juridification is derived from Weber and the early Frankfurt school and is related to such concepts as loss of meaning, the growth of bureaucracy, alienation, and reification. To understand what is new in Habermas's theory, we need first to understand what he means by *lifeworld* and *system* because juridification is an aspect of the pathological relation between the lifeworld and system under advanced capitalism.

The division between lifeworld and system demarcates different forms through which society is achieved.[25] Put briefly, the system is that sphere in which regular and predictable social action is accomplished by interconnecting the consequences of actions of rational, self-interested individuals.[26] In contrast, the lifeworld is the sphere in which society is primarily accomplished through mutual understanding based on communication.[27] System and lifeworld are always together in practice, but a full understanding of modernity requires that they be analytically separated.[28]

The lifeworld refers to those interpretive patterns that are culturally, often interpersonally, transmitted and linguistically organized. These include the formation of group identities, collective decisions about desired goals, the acceptance of personal values, the transmission of meanings, and the development of individual personalities. All of these share the characteristic of being symbolically structured and dependent on linguistically mediated social reproduction. Such things as meaning, Habermas tells us, cannot be coerced or bought; they can only emerge out of interactive communication.[29]

Educational institutions are one of the primary examples of the lifeworld, especially when they include the types of goals—such as moral development and good citizenship—that have traditionally been identified with the liberal arts.[30] It is not simply that such education requires communication but that they require the type of communication that is oriented toward consensus—even if it is never completely achieved—and that excludes, as much as possible, the effects of power and money. Above all, liberal arts education aims to produce an individual who is open to rational persuasion, and that, for Habermas, is the essential characteristic of the lifeworld.

We should be clear about the difference between an orientation to consensus and actual consensus. According to Habermas, the lifeworld no longer simply passes on a consensus in the form of unquestioned traditions. At least since the Enlightenment, our traditions have included questioning and challenging traditions as a central tenet. One might say that our tradition is to question traditions. In addition, we now live in a society of plural heritages, and even if we should wish to return to our traditions, it is not clear which traditions they would be. This is what makes communicative action in the lifeworld so necessary and so difficult. We can no longer just accept what has always been right and must instead engage in an ongoing discussion about what is right. According to Habermas, even when any consensus about what is right is impossible, the discussion about it will require that we orient ourselves toward reaching consensus—in other words, that we are open to rational persuasion in regard to others' positions, even when we ultimately are not persuaded. It is the orientation that makes it communicative action, not the actual consensus. This, we would argue, is the traditional goal of the liberal arts education: not to produce a consensus among students but to encourage students to engage in discussions that are oriented to consensus and open to rational persuasion.

In opposition to the lifeworld, the system represents those parts of society in which social transactions and patterned action do not directly depend on communication. Instead, regularity and predictability are created by connecting the actions of anonymous individuals through the use of abstract media.[31] The primary example of a system is a free market economy. If we try to discover, for example, who sets the price of a particular commodity in an ideal free market, we soon discover that no one really does. The price of the commodity is set by functionally relating the consequences of the actions of producers and suppliers with the actions of consumers, that is, by the coordination of supply and demand. Prices go up and down, companies prosper or fail, people are hired or fired, consumers are disappointed or satisfied all because of market actions that are impossible to trace to the intent of any particular person or even group.

The lifeworld coordinates interactions primarily through mutual understanding and depends on the conscious action orientation of individuals. Systems coordinate interaction by the functional interrelation of consequences of actions and are able to (but do not necessarily) bypass the conscious intentions of individuals.[32] As the complexity of a system increases, its rationality no longer coincides with the rationality of any individual. People are able to pursue even antisocial goals that nevertheless result in the social order of the system.[33] Indeed, people's agreement on the goals of the system through rational ethical argument becomes unnecessary for social order. Actors no longer need to agree with or even understand the goals of the system in order for their actions to assume a pattern in pursuit of those goals. This is what Habermas means by the uncoupling of the system from the lifeworld.[34] The functionalist interrelations achieved through media such as money mean that the coordination of actions can be increasingly uncoupled from the lifeworld of communication and is able to work, in effect, behind people's backs.

Importantly, Habermas believes that at least some systems are necessary in a modern society, but systems become destructive when they take over functions that can be performed only by the lifeworld. If these essential parts of the lifeworld erode, social pathologies develop and manifest themselves as individual experiences of crises. Habermas calls this *colonization,* and his analysis suggests that education is especially vulnerable under modern conditions because education depends on practices of communication that are oriented to a consensus that is increasingly difficult to actually achieve.[35]

A lifeworld can be reproduced only through communication that aims at consensus. However, in the modern world, consensus no longer rests on shared cultural (for example, religious) values. Instead, consensus depends on a much more fragile, complex, and unstable process of rational discussion. Consensual agreement must be reached through discussions that often bring into question the very grounds for deciding any dispute. Consequently, agreements based on communication in a modern society are much more difficult to reach and much less stable if reached.

Because of the difficulty of reaching consensus on contestable rational grounds, communication in the lifeworld cannot possibly fulfill all the requirements of a modern society.[36] For example, when the traditional value of a commodity is no longer accepted, it is extremely difficult to set a new value for the commodity through a process of rational discussion. In our pluralistic society, it has become difficult to even imagine any way other than a system to set the prices of commodities, to decide what will or will not be produced, what companies will or will not survive, who will or will not work. Modern societies seem to need an economic system to set prices, since systems are able to coordinate actions in increasingly complex ways without the need for either binding traditions or rational consensus.

Despite the necessity of systems, Habermas argues that the current relationship between the lifeworld and the system is dangerously unbalanced. Systems have penetrated into areas, such as the socialization of children, that require a communicative coordination of action. This is colonization. For example, children are, to an increasing extent, socialized by watching television. However, the values, models, and images that appear on television are not a product of consensual discussion; instead they are decided by a market system using the media of money. Habermas argues that although such a system may be very good at setting the price of commodities sold on television, it cannot be expected to properly socialize children or to properly educate citizens. When systems assume such vital lifeworld tasks as education, unavoidable crises occur. To allow a system to invade these areas is to risk personal crises—such as schizophrenia, anomie, or suicide—that are signs of social pathology.[37]

At a practical level, this argument should feel very familiar to those involved in liberal arts education. Although not using the terms *lifeworld, system,* or *colonization,* liberal arts has always defined itself in opposition to concerns with power and money. Indeed, this has been the perennial complaint about liberal arts, that its students are sent into the world knowing so little about ways to make a living or current political trends.[38] Despite these practical drawbacks, Habermas's theory would encourage us in this effort to keep liberal arts a place of rational discussion where at least the goal, if rarely the result, is consensus and where concerns about money and power are, as much as possible, made topics, rather than determinants, of discussion.[39]

For Habermas, the law is a special case in his theoretical model, because the tension between system and lifeworld is inherent to it.[40] He therefore reserves the word *juridification* for the colonization of the law by a system.[41] Our argument is that the law is also a special case for liberal arts education and that protecting education from juridification is very different from protecting it from systems of power and money.

As traditional consensus falls apart under Enlightenment questioning and increased pluralism, the role of law in maintaining social order becomes increasingly important. Law has a role in both the lifeworld and the system. In the lifeworld, law functions as a ground for developing and legitimating whatever consensus we can reach. Where traditional consensus is now impossible to achieve, law replaces it with binding (democratically justified) decisions. For the system, law provides the "anchor" and ground for the media, such as money and power, that constitute systems.[42] Money is able to function as the mobile, abstract, and anonymous representation of the economic system because it is "legal tender."

Besides operating in both the lifeworld and the system, the law also stands between them—as the title of Habermas's book suggests, "between facts and norms." On the one hand, the law must be seen as an objective fact that stands apart from any communicative interpretation and allows actors to confidently predict its constraint on their future actions. On the other hand, the law must be seen as having moral validity and therefore a part of the lifeworld of meanings, norms, values, and identities. The law in modern society necessarily has this double aspect (the facticity of its coercive force and the capacity to develop and articulate norms) and its resulting tension.

As a social fact, Habermas argues, the law works like a system. Individuals are able to pursue egoistic and even antisocial goals within the rules of the legal system and still create social order, despite there being no intent to reach consensus.[43] This, of course, describes the adversarial process in legal proceedings. Lawyers on opposing sides are not attempting to convince each other but to win their case. Individual lawyers engaged in a particular case have little professional concern for the normative values of the legal system, such as justice or fairness, but are instead concerned with the manipulation of the law. Lawyers assume, and for the most part correctly, that even immoral, antisocial actions within an adversarial system will result in legal order so long as one stays within the system's rules.

Conversely, the law also must work like a norm. No society can maintain a legal order simply through a regime of enforcement.[44] People must be convinced of the moral validity of the system as a whole, even when they do not accept the validity of each and every law.[45] Even lawyers who are working their hardest to obtain what might be seen as an unjust outcome in the interest of their current client must believe in the ultimate justice of the system as a whole. Without that, they lose the incentive to compete according to the legal rules, and the system can no longer function. Lawyers can be immoral, they can work for injustice, and yet the system functions so long as they still follow the letter of the law. However, if they lose the moral incentive to follow the legal rules, the system falls apart.

This moral validity cannot be conferred by the system itself. Systems function or not, are efficient or inefficient. They are not, at least from the perspective of the system, moral or immoral. Judgments of morality require a lifeworld; they require communication; they require an orientation toward consensus.

Hence the law is both a fact and a norm, and the tension between the two must be maintained and managed.[46] However, just as modern capitalism tends to colonization, modern legal systems tend to juridification. In other words, they become more like systems, more like social facts, and less like a normative part of the lifeworld.

CONCLUSION:
LEGAL SCHOLARSHIP AS A DEFENSE AGAINST JURIDIFICATION

Habermas's analysis has much to say about the relation between liberal arts and the law. The liberal arts are centrally concerned with the reproduction of the lifeworld and yet also concerned with encouraging those cultural forces, such as pluralism and challenges to authority, that make a traditional consensus more difficult. Given this situation, we really are no longer in a position to simply assume traditional roles and relations. Faculty cannot pretend to be parents, nor are students any longer children. But neither can we allow roles and relations to be determined by those economic and administrative systems that cannot create or even transmit the meanings, norms, values, and identities that are the central mission of the liberal arts.

In education, to an even greater extent than in the rest of society, the law must take the place of traditions in order to achieve whatever minimal social order is necessary to the functioning of the institution. Despite the importance of keeping the liberal arts free of systems of money and power, we cannot keep it free of the law, because the law is the only viable substitute that we have for our now suspect traditions. The only alternatives to the law would be to turn the college over to the mechanizations of political or economic systems or to cynically try to retreat to some traditions that no one any longer really believes in. Either choice would betray the mission of the liberal arts.

However, the law in the liberal arts is vulnerable to juridification. The same law that has functioned as a moral force to rid the college of discriminatory traditions can easily lose its moral dimension and become a reified system. In fact, this is exactly what we have argued is happening in the relation between faculty and suicidal students. The traditional role of in loco parentis has been replaced by a new legal relation. This replacement originally came about through a moral force that took a legal form in its insistence on the civil rights of all citizens. However, the moral force of law depends on lifeworld discussions. Without that, the law loses its moral dimension and becomes a juridified system.

Because there was no place in the liberal arts for that discussion to take place, juridification is precisely what happened. The relations between faculty and students are now determined by a system of laws that are viewed as background social facts rather than moral accomplishments. The relations between faculty and students, and among groups of faculty and groups of students, are viewed through legalistic, unreasoned conceptions of the law. Rather than recognize the law as a body of rules and processes constantly in the making, we view it as a concrete set of unambiguous channels that can (and therefore should) effectively constrain action. As a result, emotionally troubled students who reach out to a professor as someone they know and respect are finding themselves referred to professional strangers.

It is significant that it was our respondent from the law faculty who reported that among his colleagues there was a greater willingness to engage students and a greater freedom of action without fear about what the law demanded or restrained. The absence of this familiarity with the law among most faculty, as well as students and administrators, leads to a legalistic invocation of rules for purposes and situations that undermine rather than promote the goals of a liberal education.

The mission of the liberal arts college requires that it be defended from juridification. The transformation of the relation between students and professors into a juridified legal relationship means the end of the singular mission of the liberal arts college. As students become consumers with implied contractual rights and professors become employees of an institution that markets socially valued qualifications, the question of moral and political education becomes personally unappealing and institutionally discouraged.

Despite its dangers, the law is necessary to the liberal arts college in modern conditions. Only law is able to replace discriminatory and suspect traditions. Only law holds any promise of staving off systems of money and power. The trick, then, is not to exclude law but to prevent its juridification—to keep the law as a moral accomplishment without it becoming an assumed social fact.

This, then, is the role of legal scholarship in liberal arts education. To prevent juridification of the law, it must be studied, interrogated, and most importantly, discussed. More than a mere collection of facts to be manipulated, the law should be the embodiment of normative commitments and visions of the good that are always open to challenge and change. Ironically, to protect the liberal arts from the law requires that law become a central concern of a liberal arts education.

NOTES

1. This chapter was prepared originally for presentation at the Conference on Legal Scholarship and the Liberal Arts at Amherst College in April 2002.

2. Richard Stull, "Liberal Arts, Our Guardian: The Pursuit of the Good Life," *Journal of Higher Education* 33 (1962): 39.

3. Here we are suggesting the traditional Aristotelian distinction between the good citizen and the good man: to whom is one loyal, to one's city or to justice?

4. We are using *fact* here in the same sense as Habermas does, as a reified, objective positivity. Jürgen Habermas, *Between Facts and Norms: Contributions to a Discourse Theory of Law and Democracy* (Cambridge: MIT Press, 1998).

5. Jerome Karabel, "Community Colleges and Social Stratification: Submerged Class Conflict in American Higher Education," in *Power and Ideology in Education*, ed. J. Karabel and A. Halsey (New York: Oxford University Press, 1977). John Marciano, *Civic Illiteracy and Education: Battle for the Hearts and Minds of American Youth* (New York: Peter Lang, 1997).

6. David Breneman, *Liberal Arts Colleges: Thriving, Surviving, or Endangered?* (Washington, D.C.: Brookings Institution, 1994), 1.

7. Max Weber, *Economy and Society: An Outline of Interpretive Sociology* (Berkeley: University of California Press, 1978).

8. *People v. Wheaton College*, 40 Ill. 186 (1866).

9. Peter Lake, "The Rise of Duty and the Fall of *in Loco Parentis* and Other Protective Tort Doctrines in Higher Education Law," *Missouri Law Review* 64 (1999): 1.

10. *Dixon v. Alabama*, 294 F.2d 150 (5th Cir. 1961).

11. E.g., G. Shur, "A Response to Professors Bickel and Lake," *Synthesis: Law and Policy in Higher Education* (1996): 543–45; or James Szablewicz and Annette Gibbs, "Colleges' Increasing Exposure to Liability: The New *in Loco Parentis*," *Journal of Law and Education* 16 (1987): 453–65.

12. Peter Lake, "The Special Relationship(s) between a College and a Student: Law and Policy Ramifications for the Post *in Loco Parentis* College," *Idaho Law Review* 37 (2001): 3.

13. Lake, "Rise of Duty," 4.

14. Ibid., 5.

15. Sexual harassment: *Lipsett v. College of P. R.*, 864 F.2d 881 (1st Cir. 1988); racial harassment: *Davis v. Monroe County Board of Education*, 526 U.S. 629 (1999); assigning student residences: *Nero v. Kansas State U.*, 861 P.2d 768 (Kan. 1993).

16. Lake, "Special Relationship(s)," 3.

17. David A. Hoekema, *Campus Rules and Moral Community: In Place of in Loco Parentis* (Lanham, Md.: Rowman and Littlefield, 1994), 19.

18. D. L. McCabe reported that academic dishonesty is prevalent and increasing. In a survey of selective schools, he found that 42 percent of students at schools with honor codes and 58 percent of students at schools without honor codes admitted "cheating on written work." In 1990, the numbers were 32 percent and 56 percent, respectively. D. L. McCabe, "New Research on Academic Integrity," *Synfax Weekly Report* (1996); D. L. McCabe, "Faculty Responses to Academic Dishonesty: The Influence of Student Honor Codes," *Research in Higher Education* 34 (1993): 343.

19. Gary Pavela, "Applying the Power of Association on Campus: A Model Code of Academic Integrity," *Journal of College and University Law* 24 (1997).

20. An affirmative duty indicates a specific duty legally required of an individual. This is in contrast to the vast majority of law, which specifies what individuals cannot do. In general, the courts have only recognized affirmative duties when there is a special relationship, such as teacher/child or caretaker/person cared for, or where an authority, such as a police officer, has indicated that he or she is in charge.

21. *Jain v. State of Iowa*, 617 N.W. 2d 293 (Iowa Sup. 2000).

22. *Coghlan v. Beta Theta Pi Fraternity*, 133 Idaho 388, 987 P.2d 300 (1999).

23. *Bradshaw v. Rawlings*, 612 F.2d 135, 139 (3d Cir. 1979).

24. In one sense, the court's decision can be interpreted as an example of an elementary idea of tort law: that one ought to pay for losses others suffer when relying on another's action. In another sense, of course, this can be seen as an example of a Hohfeldian

error, the derivation of a right from a privilege, here the right to be protected from the consequences of one's own actions as a result of the privilege of being a college student. Duncan Kennedy, *A Critique of Adjudication* (Cambridge: Harvard University Press, 1997), 84, 85, 276.

25. Jürgen Habermas, "A Reply," in *Communicative Action: Essays on Jürgen Habermas's "The Theory of Communicative Action,"* ed. A. Honneth and H. Joas, trans. Jeremy Gaines and Doris L. Jones (Cambridge: MIT Press, 1991), 215–64.

26. Habermas distinguishes between instrumental rationality and communicative rationality. The former is very similar to Weber's conception of formal rationality and denotes the selection of efficient means for a predefined end. Instrumental rationality is what we mean here by rationality in the system.

27. Jürgen Habermas, *Lifeworld and System,* vol. 2 of *The Theory of Communicative Action,* trans. Thomas McCarthy (Boston: Beacon Press, 1987), 186–87, 124.

28. Habermas, "A Reply," 255–56.

29. Ibid., 259.

30. Robert E. Young, *A Critical Theory of Education: Habermas and Our Children's Future* (New York: Teachers' College Press, 1990).

31. Habermas, *Lifeworld and System,* 154.

32. Ibid., 117.

33. This is the society prescribed by Adam Smith in *The Wealth of Nations.* Smith assumed, however, the existence and constraints of an implicit moral order, which he had earlier described in *The Theory of the Moral Sentiments.*

34. Habermas, *Lifeworld and System,* 153–97.

35. Ibid., 371.

36. Ibid., 180.

37. Ibid., 225.

38. Sidney Hook, "A Challenge to the Liberal-Arts College," *Journal of Higher Education* 10 (1939): 14.

39. It could be argued that it is education's colonization by a system that has made it so difficult to develop a new, multicultural, progressive curriculum to replace the classical canon. Instead, the current college curricula are the product of a market in which student enrollments function as the price-setting mechanism.

40. Hugh Baxter, "System and Lifeworld in Habermas's Theory of Law," *Cardozo Law Review* 23 (2002).

41. Habermas, *Lifeworld and System,* 356–63.

42. Ibid., 266.

43. Habermas, *Between Facts and Norms,* 34.

44. See Karl N. Llewellyn and E. Adamson Hoebel, *The Cheyenne Way* (Norman: University of Oklahoma Press, 1942), 20; and Abram Chayes, *The Modern Corporation and the Rule of Law* (Cambridge: Harvard University Press, 1959), 31–32.

45. Hugh Baxter, "Habermas's Discourse Theory of Law and Democracy," *Buffalo Law Review* 50 (2002).

46. This duality has been repeatedly observed, although subject to slightly different theorizations. For a recent analysis, see Patricia Ewick and Susan Silbey, *The Common Place of Law: Stories from Everyday Life* (Chicago: University of Chicago Press, 1998). Note as well the parallels that can be found in the analysis by Herbert Packer of the criminal justice system, in *The Limits of the Criminal Sanction* (Stanford: Stanford University Press, 1968), or in jurisprudence, in Robert Cover, "Nomos and Narrative," and in "Violence and the Word," *Yale Law Journal* 95, 8: 1601–29, 1986.

THE LIBERAL ARTS, LEGAL SCHOLARSHIP, AND THE DEMOCRATIC CRITIQUE OF JUDICIAL POWER

KEITH J. BYBEE

W henever I teach an undergraduate course on law and the courts, I ask students why they have enrolled. Some students respond by professing a deep interest in the subject; others praise my reputation as a teacher. Sadly, such responses are all too rare. Instead of admitting an unabashed love for the material or shamelessly flattering my vanity, most students explain their presence in class by simply saying, "I want to go to law school."

My students are not alone. Although the enrollment in law schools has fluctuated in recent years, the overall number of law students has jumped sharply since the 1960s.[1] In the 1965–66 academic year, American law schools enrolled around 55,000 students; by the 1999–2000 academic year, enrollment had climbed to over 130,000.[2] Unsurprisingly, swelling law school enrollments have led to large increases in the number of law degrees conferred and in the number of new lawyers minted. In the mid-1960s, law schools handed out a little over 11,000 J.D. and LL.B. degrees a year, and annual admissions to the bar hovered near 13,000. Thirty years later the annual yield of law degrees had risen to almost 40,000, and the annual number of bar admissions exceeded 56,000.

Since the U.S. population has increased steadily over the past several decades, one might think that the increasing number of lawyers is merely an artifact of population growth. But this is not true. The legal profession has expanded at a much faster rate than the general population, with the number of lawyers per capita more than doubling since 1960.[3] In fact, the legal profession not only has outpaced an expanding population but also has grown three times faster than the other professions as a whole.[4] In 1970, for instance, the legal and medical professions were roughly the same size; by 1995, the number of lawyers had surpassed the number of doctors by a whopping 34 percent.[5] As the Ancient Mariner might have put it, there are lawyers, lawyers everywhere, and not a drop to drink.

Of course I am not the first to take notice of these developments. Many commentators have called attention to the increasing "legalization" of the United States and debated what this trend means. Some have argued that the proliferation of lawyers is beneficial because law offers a medium of creative discourse sensitive to claims of diverse individuals.[6] Others have argued that the mushrooming legal profession is detrimental because legalized interaction is a poor substitute for the informal networks of trust on which democratic society is built.[7]

The debate between such views is important, but my concern in this essay is a bit different. Rather than directly addressing the broad issue of what the rising tide of law and lawyers portends for the American polity and its key institutions, I consider several related questions about what the waxing legal aspirations of undergraduates signify for the academic treatment of law. Should undergraduate education in law be designed to suit students' professional interests? In particular, should the law-related courses and scholarship of university professors be patterned after the work of law professors? If there is something distinctive about the study of law conducted outside of law school, what is it and why is valuable?

In this essay, I explain why the university treatment of law attempts to chart its own path more or less independently of student career plans. I begin by considering the importance of disciplinary divisions. Outside the confines of the law school, legal study is usually the province of political science, sociology, and history. I will argue that, in a broad sense, the methods and commitments of these academic disciplines distinguish the law-related work of the university, orientating it toward the advancement of scholarly knowledge rather than toward the training of legal professionals.

Broad disciplinary divisions are not, however, the only factors involved. I will argue that the requirements of liberal arts education also influence the university study of law. At one level, this influence is the result of a streak of antivocationalism. Liberal arts education, from its origins, has prized generalized instruction over specialized training in any single profession. When law is considered as a liberal art, the prospect of becoming a lawyer is subordinated to the task of cultivating the mind and instilling a sense of what it means to be human.

Beyond the pull of antivocationalism, the liberal arts shape the university treatment of law in a more specific way. I will argue that liberal arts education cultivates the individual for the sake of a particular political purpose: the goal is not just to teach the student how to lead a meaningful life in general, but to teach her how to lead a meaningful life as a free person, engaged in the practice of self-government. Liberal arts education thus steers away from narrow professional training as it moves toward the life of the citizen. In the particular case of law, liberal arts education deflects attention away from the production of lawyers and focuses instead on law's democratic uses.

Once the political orientation of liberal arts education is recognized, it becomes clear that specific conceptions of law as a liberal art depend on controversial judgments about the version of democratic self-government that one wishes to foster. Theories of democracy come in many distinct forms, each of which rests on its own set of contentious and contestable assumptions. To place legal instruction and scholarship in the service of democracy, I will argue, is thus to involve law in the ongoing debate over which theory of democracy is correct. Viewed as a whole, the distinctive task of liberal arts legal education is not only to develop political capacities in students who would otherwise pursue narrow professional goals but also to take a position in an endlessly contested debate over the meaning of democracy.

In the final sections of the essay, I present my own vision of liberal arts legal education by offering one (contestable and partial) account of what the relationship between law and democratic self-government ought to be. I will argue that the liberal art of law should cultivate a capacity for critical legal thought, providing citizens with the ability to assess the incomplete and inconsistent decisions that are frequently produced by the courts. Although ambiguous judicial decisions are conventionally dismissed as institutional failures, I contend that these decisions are actually significant judicial responses to the conditions of sharp conflict and pronounced uncertainty that often prevail in democratic politics. If liberal arts legal education is to help cultivate self-governing citizens, then it should teach students how to evaluate the muddled decisions generated as courts negotiate the diverse disputes of democratic society.

Before I proceed down the path I have described, let me underscore and clarify a few points. First, an important part of the evidence in my essay is drawn from the mission statements of liberal arts institutions. I recognize that there is usually a gap between such official institutional statements and actual institutional behavior; I would be the last to claim that an assertion is true simply because it has been made by college officials. Even so, my own experience teaching at liberal arts institutions, coupled with my reading of the broader literature on liberal arts education, persuades me that the mission statements of liberal arts institutions contain meaningful aspirations, sincerely set forth and actively pursued. Liberal arts institutions not only claim that they are trying to provide an education distinct from professional training but they also attempt to provide that education. Liberal arts institutions may fall short of their self-proclaimed goals in significant ways, as Goodman and Silbey demonstrate in the previous chapter in this volume, but the acknowledgment that liberal arts goals may not be achieved does not require the dismissal of those goals as entirely meaningless. In my view, official mission statements serve as important, yet imperfect, guides for practical action. As such, the mission statements merit study.

Second, it is important to emphasize that in describing the connection between liberal arts legal education and self-governing citizens, I am not offering a complete account of democracy's prerequisites. Liberal arts education is far from being a universal experience in the United States. Thus, to examine the democratic skills imparted by a liberal arts education is to consider the skills imparted to a small, select sector of society. This is not to say that the substance of liberal arts education is necessarily elitist. As Hartog argues in his contribution to this volume, one great strength of liberal arts scholarship is its capacity to show how law matters in the lives of ordinary people. Nonetheless, one should recognize that the large bulk of liberal arts activity, including scholarship and teaching that uncovers the informal logic of everyday life, is targeted at and largely consumed by an elite.

The educational experiences of an elite may, of course, be of great social and political significance—as the Supreme Court recently acknowledged when it upheld affirmative action in university admissions as a means for breaking down racial stereotypes among our class of future national leaders.[8] And it is possible to defend the unique education of elites on democratic grounds.[9] But it cannot be argued that the experiences of an elite tell us everything we need to know about how democracy works or why it fails.

As a final point of clarification, I stress that when I advocate a liberal art of law that helps students evaluate muddled judicial decisions, I am not claiming that law is solely a creature of the courts. Governmental actors of all stripes find themselves making, implementing, and interpreting law. Moreover, beyond the boundaries of formal government institutions, people confront a matrix of law and legal relations that shape individual strategies and self-understandings. I think that the liberal arts, as a plan of education dedicated to teaching the skills of self-government, should have something to say about the legal system in all its range and variety. My comparatively modest aim in this essay is to identify and defend one way in which the liberal arts approaches one aspect of law.

DISCIPLINARY DIVISIONS AND CATERING TO LEGAL ASPIRATIONS

At the outset, it is relatively easy to see why one might want to organize college curricula around student career plans. Higher education in the United

States is an expensive proposition. University officials may try to justify the hefty cost of college by arguing that cutting-edge faculty and state-of-the-art facilities cannot be had at bargain prices. But such a justification will not persuade all students. Shouldering the burden of high tuition, many students will understandably be more concerned with advancing their own particular interests than with bankrolling some dean's abstract vision of a good education. Indeed, one could argue that student preferences *should* trump university plans because students are the ones who ultimately foot the educational bill. If tuition-paying undergraduates want to become lawyers, then the college professor's task is to provide preprofessional legal training by mimicking the teaching methods and substantive research of the legal academy. To do otherwise is bad business.[10]

It is precisely this kind of professionally oriented, demand-driven understanding of higher education that furnishes the guiding philosophy of the University of Phoenix. Founded in 1976, the University of Phoenix is explicitly and comprehensively structured to serve the career goals of its students. "To help our students succeed in their workplace," the university's website explains, "[our] courses emphasize real-world relevance, and the application of learning on the job. Students work in learning teams that replicate the way work is done in the business world. The curriculum is also continually updated to answer the current needs of business and industry." The university exists to provide the practical training that paying students demand. The purest expression of this understanding is the University of Phoenix Online, where students can pursue a useful education on terms entirely of their own choosing: "All interaction is conducted asynchronously, like e-mail, so students participate at their convenience—in the evenings from home, during your lunch hour at work, or while traveling on business. There is no commuting. No lines. No scheduling conflicts. No wasted effort."[11]

The University of Phoenix has been phenomenally successful with its program of education. Although the university is less than thirty years old, it offers classes at more than ninety campuses in fifteen states, Puerto Rico, and Canada. The enrollment at the university's campuses tops 75,000, with an additional 12,000 students participating in the university's Internet program.[12] This colossal student body makes the University of Phoenix the largest American university by far.

Yet as successful as it has been, the University of Phoenix model has not been copied by most other colleges and universities.[13] Neither undergraduate education in general nor undergraduate legal education in particular is carried out in a strictly preprofessional mode. Undergraduates may enroll in law-related courses because they want to enter the legal profession, but such courses do not self-consciously train students to be lawyers. Thus, at many institutions of higher learning, the lawyerly aspirations of students and the substantive content of law-related courses remain mismatched. Why is this the case?[14]

As a first cut at this question, one could argue that the lack of preprofessionalism in undergraduate legal education stems from broad disciplinary divisions. Law-related undergraduate courses are typically taught in departments of political science, sociology, and history. The aim of these undergraduate courses is not to understand the law in the abstract but to represent and evaluate the law from the perspective of particular scholarly disciplines. Law schools are certainly receptive to political science, sociology, and history—and have become more so in recent decades. Even so, the general aim of law school courses is still to produce practicing attorneys, not to inculcate the specific lessons of scholarly disciplines.[15]

This difference in general aim has bred deep disdain for the law school among some university faculty. The political scientist Gerald Rosenberg has argued, for example, that law schools are essentially anti-intellectual institutions incapable of meeting the rigorous standards of any genuine academic discipline. According to Rosenberg, the weak scholarship fostered by the absence of true academic training is made worse by the desire of law professors to be perceived as authentic intellectuals capable of commenting on any topic. The punditry of legal academics comes across "at best as 'scholarship lite,' and at worst as policy preferences masquerading as neutral opinion." Judged from the perspective of actual social science, Rosenberg writes, the law school is less a locus of serious academic inquiry than a place "where arrogance meets ignorance."[16]

If one agrees with Rosenberg's view, then it simply does not make sense to gear university law courses and legal research toward the prerequisites of professional legal education. Generally speaking, the university professor grounds her legal instruction on the scholarship of her discipline, offering her students entry into an academic field of shared methodologies and pure research. And, generally speaking, this is not how lawyers are educated in law school nor how law professors pursue their scholarship. With a low opinion of what the law school does accomplish, the university professor steers her law-related teaching and research away from preprofessional preparation, responding to student dreams of a legal career with an introduction to the professor's own academic bailiwick.

THE LIMITS OF DISCIPLINARY DIVISION

The argument from disciplinary division as just outlined distinguishes the university from the law school by pointing to differences in professional practice:

university professors use the law to cultivate scholars, whereas law professors use the law to train lawyers. On this basis, the argument from disciplinary division provides answers for the questions with which I began. The argument tells us that the law-related courses and scholarship of the university do not cater to student legal aspirations because universities are dedicated to the advancement of knowledge, discipline by discipline. So long as the professional goals of students continue to be mediated by the intellectual commitments of university professors, most colleges will decide not to follow the vocational trail blazed by the University of Phoenix.

This argument is fine so far as it goes, but it is misleading in important respects. First, the argument from disciplinary division tends to exaggerate the distance between the university and the law school. University professors do indeed work within specific disciplines, but the boundaries between disciplines are porous. The academic loyalties held by university professors are not entirely exclusionary, and the work performed by university professors is not wholly unique. University professors routinely adopt the teaching techniques of the law school—for example, the Socratic method and moot court exercises—in their own law-related courses.[17] University professors also study the law by using some of the same approaches employed by legal academics; in fact, there are a number of interdisciplinary law-and-society programs around the country that explicitly import the study of law into the university curriculum. And some university professors (including myself) even teach courses at law schools. Thus, contrary to the impression given by Rosenberg, it is inaccurate to say that university professors and law professors operate on completely separate and antithetical academic planes.

It is possible, of course, to generate narrow definitions of scholarly disciplines that reduce activity in those fields to a small core of technical methods unused by most law professors. Rosenberg does this by adopting a narrow understanding of political science that effectively excludes political theory and qualitative historical study.[18] But efforts like Rosenberg's are procrustean exercises that deny the diversity of methodological commitments and substantive disputes that exist within each academic discipline. When fields like political science, history, or sociology are viewed in all their variety, the legal scholarship of the university and the legal scholarship of the law school become overlapping bodies of academic work, produced by individuals that share some of the same intellectual methods and projects.[19]

The argument from disciplinary division not only overestimates the distance between the university and the law school but also (and for my purposes, more importantly) ignores a factor that contributes to the distance that does exist. The missing factor is liberal arts education. Each political science, sociology, and history professor studies and teaches law within the context of a specific discipline. Yet it is also the case that these professors jointly examine and explain law within the context of the liberal arts.

Admittedly, the influence of the liberal arts has varied across American universities and across the history of American higher education. And some would argue that today the liberal arts ideal is in decline.[20] Even so, liberal arts education is pursued at many institutions and deserves an examination of its own.

LIBERAL ARTS AGAINST LEGAL VOCATIONALISM

To a certain extent, the liberal arts and disciplinary loyalties have a similar influence on the university treatment of law. Liberal arts education, like pure instruction in political science, history, or sociology, is pitted against vocational legal training.[21]

The antivocational orientation of the liberal arts education can be traced back to ancient Athens.[22] Among the early Greeks, *eleutherios paideia,* or "education of a free and noble person," was the highest form of education. The eleutherios paideia was a frankly aristocratic program of instruction, considered to be distinct from and superior to "the specialized training in a professional discipline by which a person [was] enabled to earn his living."[23] Over the course of the fifth century, the aristocratic Athens transformed into a more democratic society with a broader demand for the education of the eleutherios paideia.[24] A democratized eleutherios paideia subsequently emerged and was eventually formalized as the *enkuklios paideia,* the "all-around" or "in-a-circle" education.[25] But the enkuklios paideia remained at root "an aristocratic concept, intimately connected with leisure, dignified and intellectual or aesthetical pursuits, and devotion to friends and public service."[26] Although it had become more popular, higher education in the ancient world had not become more vocational.

Our own scheme of liberal arts education derives from the Athenian eleutherios paideia and enkuklios paideia, even though the differences between Greek and American educational practices initially may be more striking than their similarities.[27] Unlike the ancient Athenians, modern Americans do not maintain an aristocratic tradition that denigrates work. Indeed, Americans value work so highly that we have historically made earning a living a critical marker of social standing.[28] Unsurprisingly, American liberal arts institutions do not denigrate work either. Rather than advocating the ancient idea that work renders the individual unfree and ignoble, American liberal arts institutions are careful to connect the education they provide with the capacity to earn a living. Swarthmore College, for example, assures its applicants that a broad education in the liberal arts is ultimately practical: "It can be a little scary when you think, what am I going to do with a philosophy major after I graduate?

Business majors don't have that problem. But our society is a moving target, and if you prepare yourself narrowly to fit in a certain slot, the whole scene may have changed by the time you get there, whereas the underlying skills are always relevant."[29]

American liberal arts institutions thus gesture toward the marketplace value of their educational programs. But the gesture is faint and often symbolic. As with the ancient Greeks with their eleutherios paideia and enkuklios paideia, the central educational mission of the American liberal arts is decidedly not about earning a living.[30] The liberal arts curriculum attempts to cultivate the mind, to enrich the spirit, and to teach students how to be "cultured and versatile individuals."[31] The core components of the American liberal arts education—philosophical reflection, literary study, and the reading of history—are all designed to refine student interests and to elevate their sense of what is worthwhile. The goal is to teach what it means to be human. As Syracuse University puts it, a liberal arts education is not about how to make a living but about how to make a life.[32] Even in the United States, then, where the practicalities of earning and labor are central to national identity, liberal arts institutions provide an education whose central value is justified less by what students can do with it than by what the education does to them.

At this point, it is worth pausing to consider two objections that might be made to the antivocational portrait of the liberal arts I have presented. First, one might agree that the liberal arts stand against vocationalism yet disagree that this represents a distinctive educational philosophy. For example, James Boyd White, in this volume and in other writings, has suggested that the humanist, antivocational orientation of the liberal arts is an important component of American higher education at every level, including the law school.[33] There is some truth to White's suggestion, and it provides yet another reason for rejecting the stark division between the university and the law school asserted by Gerald Rosenberg. But if the difference between the university and the law school is not one of kind, there nonetheless remains a significant difference of degree. Some law schools may emphasize the cultivation of broad human values, but they do so within the overall context of vocational training. Liberal arts institutions, on the other hand, fear vocational training itself.[34] Contrary to White's suggestion, liberal arts institutions define their missions against the claims of job training and career advancement to an extent that law schools simply do not.

Second, and more profoundly, one might object to the antivocational account of the liberal arts that I have given by questioning whether liberal arts goals can ever be realized in the first place. Critical theorists from Foucault forward have examined the ways in which the individual subject is disciplined and constituted by systems of regulation in prisons, hospitals, schools, the market, and the administrative state.[35] From this perspective, it seems naive to expect that universities can prepare individuals for self-government when "the self" is already and everywhere being trained and shaped to suit networks of power. Free human action, to the extent it is conceivable in such a setting, can be achieved only by local and particular resistance to institutions and fields of regulation, not by submitting oneself to a particular program of education.

One response to this critique is to say that the insights of Foucault and other critical theorists must be folded into the liberal arts curriculum. Knowledge of how institutional practices have enacted and sustained social control must be considered a key lesson to be learned from the liberal arts examination of human flourishing and failing. But, admittedly, this response does not meet the Foucauldian critique at the deepest level, where the possibility of meaningful individual agency is itself called into question.

Unfortunately, to take up the debate at this deepest level would be to wander well beyond the scope of this essay. Here it must suffice to say that the liberal arts, as a pedagogical approach, rests on the notion that engaged discussion can open students up to rational suasion and create possibilities for normative judgment.[36] It is this notion of engaged discussion that would have to be elaborated and defended if the Foucauldian critique were to be adequately addressed.

THE LIBERAL ART OF SELF-GOVERNMENT

I have argued that, on the whole, the liberal arts are clearly against vocational training. Can something more specific be said about what the liberal arts are for?

We can approach this question by taking a closer look at the survival of liberal arts ideals in shifting circumstances. Why didn't the ancient Greeks simply reject the aristocratic eleutherios paideia as they became more democratic? Why have Americans, in circumstances far more hostile to aristocratic ideals than those of fifth-century Athens, continued to support the broad ideals of liberal education?

Based on the account of the liberal arts I have already given, one could respond by saying that the value placed on individual cultivation has remained constant over time. In spite of great differences in material circumstances and in cultural beliefs, different societies have all found it important to teach their members "what it means to be human" through broad exposure to accumulated knowledge.

This answer is not wrong, but it is far too general. The phrase "what it means to be human" can be given a multitude of meanings consistent with many different schemes of education. As a consequence, the claim that an ideal of cultivated humanity has sustained liberal arts education explains too little: it suggests why a commitment to some form of education has persisted across history, but it does not tell us very much that is distinctive about the survival of the liberal arts. To develop a better explanation, we must have a more specific sense of the humanity to which liberal arts education aspires.

The ancient Greeks did indeed have a specific sense of humanity in mind.[37] The noble pursuits that made up the eleutherios paideia were designed not merely to cultivate the mind outside the confines of any one occupation or profession but to cultivate the mind broadly in order to "promote political skills and political leadership."[38] Put differently, the aim of the original liberal education was not about how to lead a meaningful life in general but how to lead a meaningful life as a free person engaged in the political task of self-government. Liberal education provided aristocrats with the "skills of freedom" (e.g., the capacity for persuasive public speech; the ability to analyze problems; an understanding of history and tradition) necessary to discharge the civic duties of the worthwhile life.[39]

As Athens became more democratic, the skills of freedom were demanded by the citizenry as a whole. Like the aristocrats that preceded them, democrats believed that they required broad education in rhetoric and other arts in order to enact the preferred life of political engagement. Liberal education thus survived because Athenians understood democracy as an extension of the aristocrat's political conception of human excellence. As Kurt Raaflaub writes, the democratic ideal "was that every citizen should be enabled to do what aristocrats had always done—namely to devote most of their energy and time to politics and public service."[40] It was out such beliefs that the enkuklios paideia was born.

The connection between liberal arts education and political life has continued in the United States. The first American liberal arts colleges in seventeenth-century New England provided a broad education intended to prepare students for civic life, a plan of education that Woodrow Wilson, as president of Princeton University, once described as "the generous union . . . between the life of philosophy and the life of the state."[41] Today the avowed aim of virtually all liberal arts institutions in our country is still to create the conditions for a meaningful human life in the democratic community.[42] As Rochester Institute of Technology tells its students, using language that can be found in the mission statements of most liberal arts programs, liberal arts education instills "knowledge and critical understanding of the responsibilities and rights of living in a participatory democracy."[43] Like the ancient Greeks, we value liberal arts education not simply because it inculcates a generalized sense of humanity but because it makes individuals into good citizens effectively schooled in the art of self-government.[44]

All of this suggests that if we are to understand what it means to treat law as a liberal art, then we must recognize that liberal arts education is tied to antivocationalism as well as to self-government. We must acknowledge that law-related courses and scholarship in the university follow the twin tracks of the liberal arts as a whole, simultaneously moving away from narrow professional training and moving toward democratic practice. Unlike the legal training offered by the law school, liberal arts legal education is concerned less with litigation and the life of a lawyer than with democratic politics and the life of the citizen.

How should American liberal arts institutions structure their treatment of law in order to cultivate capacities for self-government in their students? I present my own answer to this question in the final sections of this essay. But first it is important to understand that there are many possible answers to this question and that no single answer (including my own) can be considered to be the last word on the matter.

The connection between the liberal arts and self-government is open to endless debate because democracy itself can be understood in a number of ways. The manner in which liberal arts education treats the law depends on the particular conception of self-government that the education is attempting to foster. Simply put, to understand the impact of the liberal arts on the university treatment of law, we must know which version of democracy we are promoting.

The range of competing democratic visions—and their connection to different understandings of liberal arts education—can be illustrated by considering the longstanding debate over the contemporary relevance of ancient political practices.[45] In this debate, some have argued that the Athenian brand of democratic liberty is ill suited for our times: whereas the ancients understood liberty as a collective right to be sovereign in public affairs, we moderns understand liberty as an the individual's right to pursue her own opinions, associations, interests, and beliefs.[46] Whenever modern political actors have been seduced by the ancient idea of liberty, they have crushed individuality by forcing all citizens to follow a single "best" plan of life.[47] If the dangers of ancient democracy are to be avoided, liberal arts education must instill habits of toleration and individual responsibility consistent with the modern commitment to political diversity and private choice.[48]

On the other hand, some modern thinkers have looked back admiringly at classical accounts of democracy.[49] Such thinkers do not deny the great differences in economic development and technological achievement that separate us from the ancients. But they do insist that democratic government today requires the same virtues and ideals of the good life esteemed by the great figures of the Western tradition. Without a fixed understanding of the good life to guide citizens, modern democracy devolves into a republic ruled by rank consumerism and private appetites. Far from being a dangerous threat, the pursuit of a single best life makes good self-government possible. To this end, liberal arts education must instill the wisdom of the ancients, providing citizens the "experience with things beautiful" necessary to overcome the illusions and low temptations of modern mass democracy.[50]

In one guise or another, partisans of these two visions of democracy have debated the fate of the American liberal arts education for a long time.[51] In the early decades of the twentieth century, the two camps battled over the role of empirical science in liberal arts education, with one side claiming that citizens could not intelligently negotiate the diverse choices presented by modern democratic society without some empirical training, while the other side claimed that empirical analysis necessarily raised technical questions that distracted citizen attention away from the enduring concerns of the good life.[52] In the final decades of the twentieth century, the battle between the two camps continued on new terrain, with one side arguing that the liberal arts canon of great books should be expanded to prepare citizens for the enormous diversity of modern democratic society, while the other side warned that an indispensable core of traditional wisdom would be lost if classics such as Homer's *The Odyssey* were replaced by books such as *I, Rigoberta Menchu*.[53]

In my view, there is no reason to expect that the battle between the two camps will soon subside, with universal agreement emerging on the kind of democratic government that liberal education should foster. The problem is with the idea of democracy itself. The history of political thought suggests that democracy can be rendered in a wide variety of ways, depending on the specific understandings of equality, liberty, justice, and human nature that one happens to hold. Following William Connolly, one could say that democracy is an essentially contested concept, an idea whose meaning is derived from a cluster of principles and claims that are themselves endlessly controversial.[54] No single version of democracy can be deemed all-inclusive because each version of democracy incorporates its own (controversial and contestable) sense of appropriate means and legitimate ends. Different accounts of democracy are like members of the same family: all spring from a common stock, yet each member is irreducibly different, and no member on his or her own completely or finally embodies what the family truly is.

We should therefore recognize that disagreements over the nature of democracy will always be with us in some form. It would be a mistake, however, to see such recognition as an act of resignation. To say that the argument over the meaning of democracy is enduring (and, by extension, to say that the argument over the relationship between liberal arts education and democracy is enduring) is not to say that participation in the argument is pointless.[55] Where essentially contested concepts are at stake, one cannot hope to achieve complete consensus, but one can hope to refine the terms of debate and advance discussion.[56] Although disagreements over the nature of democracy will always be with us, reasoned judgments about democracy (and the kind of liberal arts education necessary to support it) can still be made.

THE IMPORTANCE OF CRITICAL LEGAL THINKING

Where does this leave us? In the last two sections, I have made two related claims: (1) liberal arts education seeks to instill the skills of democratic self-government in students who would otherwise devote themselves to narrow preprofessional training; and (2) to decide how the liberal arts should foster self-government is to take a position in an endlessly contested debate over the meaning of democracy. Reasoned judgments about liberal arts education and the art of self-government are not impossible, but they will always be partial and open to argument.

These two related claims apply to all components of the liberal arts, including law. In its courses and scholarship, the liberal art of law attempts to prepare students for life as self-governing citizens, regardless of the particular career plans held by the students themselves. The commitment to political life not only distances the liberal art of law from professional legal training but also involves liberal arts legal education in an ongoing debate, as the question of how law may best promote self-government inevitably involves larger, enduringly controversial questions about the nature of democracy.

By highlighting the connection between the liberal arts and self-government, I do not mean to suggest that successful democracies require the entire citizenry to be liberally educated. As I have already noted, liberal arts education today, as a matter of fact, is the preserve of an elite. Although liberal arts institutions work at cultivating self-governing citizens, their program of education is not experienced by the mass of citizens who make up modern American democracy.

Although I would not deny the fact of liberal arts exclusivity, I would argue that what one makes of liberal arts exclusivity depends on which model of democracy one happens to support. For example, the limited reach of the liberal arts might be defended on Tocquevillean grounds: one could argue that for democratic society to be rescued from its own worst tendencies, it is necessary to cultivate elites who swim against the prevailing social currents, placing a brake on majoritarian impulses and critically reflecting on the broader systems of power and wealth.[57] Or the limited reach of the liberal arts might be attacked as a rank violation of popular sovereignty: one could argue that an elite whose values and beliefs fail to mirror the larger society will seek its own interests at the expense of ordinary people.[58]

My general point is that when discussing the liberal arts, debates over the structure and meaning of democracy are inescapable. In the remaining sections of this essay, I do not attempt to sort through all the competing conceptions of democracy available and the kinds of liberal arts education (legal and otherwise) that these conceptions entail. Instead, my more modest aim is to elaborate one particular view of the liberal art of law. In articulating my position, I make a series of assertions about how democracy works—assertions that bear a general resemblance to the argument that modern democracy, unlike its ancient antecedents, should be organized to reflect the enormous diversity of citizen choices and interests. Like anyone else making an assessment of law as a liberal art, I take sides in a political debate.

Let me begin with a general definition. In the broadest sense, a critical thinker is a person who can independently assess the evidence and logic supporting a position or claim.[59] A critical thinker does not accept events and decisions merely on the basis of authority or tradition. She demands that actions be supported by argument and that conclusions be justified by reasons. The critical thinker seeks explanations and judges their validity by her own lights.

Liberal arts institutions today invariably promise to teach their students critical thinking—and to do so in a specifically political way. In the liberal arts lexicon, critical thinking, like other qualities cultivated by the liberal arts, is not an attribute of the abstract or generic individual but a skill belonging to the citizen and deployed in the practice of democracy. A citizen uses critical thinking prospectively when she participates directly in the formulation of public policy, for it is the capacity for critical thought that allows policymakers to assess complex problems and to identify appropriate solutions. A citizen uses critical thinking retrospectively when she judges the actions of her chosen representatives, for it is the capacity for critical thought that permits the voter to evaluate political decisions and to hold officials responsible for results.

In short, liberal arts education envisions a citizenry schooled in critical thinking—a citizenry that reserves the authority to make its own decisions and to review the decisions others have made on its behalf. Echoing the old arguments of Walter Lippmann, liberal arts institutions insist that critical thinking is a democratic necessity.[60] They teach students to think for themselves because they believe that a "free people is one capable of thinking for itself." [61]

When law is treated as a liberal art, the connection between critical thinking and self-government remains a central concern. Consider the U.S. judiciary.[62] U.S. courts often claim to implement the people's will as expressed in statutes and in the Constitution.[63] If these courts are to be called to account for their actions, then at least some citizens must be able to understand and critique the judicial rulings made on their behalf. In legal matters, as in democratic politics more generally, free citizens must be able to think independently. Otherwise, the judiciary may speak for the people in a way that ultimately prevents the people from speaking for themselves.

Of course, it is possible to imagine institutional arrangements that keep the courts responsive to the people by means other than criticism by an informed citizenry. Where citizens tightly control the courts by directly electing judges, or where citizens simply staff the courts themselves, judicial decisions routinely reflect popular interests. Alternatively, where judges exclusively concern themselves with issues on which there is broad societal consensus and refuse to address the controversial political questions that set groups against one another, the people can be sure that judges are serving as their faithful agents.

Whether or not one thinks such institutional arrangements are feasible, it is clear that neither arrangement holds in the United States today.[64] Although many American judges are elected, the most powerful and important ones usually are not. The entire federal judiciary is staffed by judges who enjoy lifetime appointments. A significant segment of American judges thus possess independence beyond the direct influence of the ballot box.[65] One could argue that the existence of judicial independence means that judges can choose to restrict themselves to nonpolitical questions. But this is not a choice that judges have made.[66] As Tocqueville noted nearly 170 years ago, "there is hardly a political question in the United States which does not sooner or later turn into a judicial one."[67] The most cursory look at contemporary debates confirms that judges have continued to involve themselves in highly contentious political issues since Tocqueville's time.

These facts underscore the practical importance of critical legal thinking in our democracy. American judges are institutionally independent and politically active; they are not closely hemmed in by either electoral or professional constraints. If judicial power is to be effectively managed, it must be subject to public criticism. And public criticism is generated when engaged citizens understand the democratic uses of law and insist that the courts adhere to them. Lief Carter, in his widely used text on legal reasoning (a text he calls a "small version of a liberal arts education"), expresses the point well:

> Legal reasoning is the way that those with official legal authority talk about law. Hence legal reasoning describes a particularly powerful set of legal realities. In the liberal democracy we inhabit, those of us who don't hold legal power nevertheless retain the civic right and duty to decide whether we accept the realities that official law talk creates.[68]

THE DEMOCRATIC CRITIQUE OF JUDICIAL POWER: UNDER-
STANDING THE POLITICAL SIGNIFICANCE OF LEGAL AMBIGUITY

In what way, then, should liberal arts legal education cultivate critical legal thinking? What kind of judicial action should students be taught to demand? As I have already suggested, there are as many different answers to these questions as there are different understandings of democracy. I outline one conventional answer to these questions and explain why this answer is inadequate. I then put forward my own answer, using broad brush strokes to indicate one way in which law-related courses and legal scholarship can fulfill the democratic mission of the liberal arts.

Conventionally understood, judicial action is based on the clear articulation and reasoned application of general principles.[69] The origin and content of these general principles may be conceptualized along many different lines.[70] In whatever way the principles are understood, however, the conventional understanding takes rigorous reasoning on the basis of principle to be of primary importance. The idea is that judges should strive to assimilate each dispute they consider into a coherent order, articulating a framework of rules capable of justifying the decision at hand and of regulating subsequent judicial decisions.[71] In the ideal case, the principled legal order makes judicial action perfectly reasoned and predictable: every legal outcome is reached by the logical application of preexisting rules and standards to each new fact situation. Moreover, within such an ideal system, the exercise of judicial power is restrained and impartial: court decisions do not depend on the private whim or bias of the judge presiding over the case but on a known set of legal principles.

Thus, in terms of the conventional approach to judicial action, one can say that citizens sustain their power of self-government by attending to principled argument. The U.S. judiciary is independent and politically active, yet citizens nonetheless can control the courts by insisting that judges operate on the basis of clear standards and sound logic. In this view, liberal arts legal education prepares students for democratic life by teaching them to be guardians of principle, exposing them to a wide range of judicial decisions, and showing them how to evaluate these decisions as either good or bad arguments. The critical legal thinker learns how to judge the coherency of judicial action for herself, helping to ensure that courts remain reliable servants of the people.

There is an important element of truth in the conventional understanding of judicial action and the model of liberal arts legal education it suggests. Courts do draw on specific patterns of argument and principle to fashion their judgments. These patterns of argument are not iron cages; they do not rigidly dictate the content and result of judicial decisions. Even so, the way in which issues are legally framed is often of signal importance for how the judiciary ultimately acts. Legal patterns of argument and principle are meaningful resources: at any given time, judges rely on prevailing argumentative frameworks to give their actions direction and justify their authority.[72] Accordingly, liberal arts legal education must pay some attention to the coherence and rigor of judicial argumentation. If citizens do not understand that judges reason with principles, then they will be unable to call judges to account for their decisions.

Yet the conventional understanding also seems to overlook the fact that actual opinions produced by courts are often incomplete and ambiguous. Judges do indeed draw on particular funds of argument and principle, but they do not always assemble them into coherent opinions or consistent lines of decision making. Instead of being models of well-specified justification, judicial opinions often appear to be fragmented, ramshackle affairs cobbled together to dispose of the case at hand. At the level of the United States Supreme Court in particular, judicial decisions often look less like exemplars of careful justification than like the series of choices a person makes when picking out a midnight snack from whatever looks good in the refrigerator.[73] When confronted with a clear choice between several principled alternatives, members of the Supreme Court will often opt for a little bit of everything, as they have done in the case of affirmative action and in the case of abortion.[74] The citizen looking for judicial lapses in principled logic will find an embarrassment of riches.

Is the abundance of ambiguous outcomes really a significant problem for the conventional approach and the liberal arts legal education it recommends? One could argue that most ambiguous decisions are temporary and will be swept away as the judicial process advances one case at a time.[75] Moreover, to the extent that ambiguous decisions do persist, one could argue that such decisions are institutional failures. Unlike well-reasoned, principled decisions, muddled decisions do not articulate general arguments for clearly governing the judicial resolution of future cases, nor do they provide other actors with a fixed basis on which to ground their legal expectations. The existence of muddled judicial decisions thus demands renewed commitment to principled argument. Rather than seeking to explain jumbled judicial decisions on their own terms, the conventional approach should call attention to the logically consistent arguments that could have been made. In this spirit, liberal arts legal education should use judicial mistakes as the basic material for student instruction: the principled justification that ought to govern a given controversy should be discerned by looking past the muddled opinion that actually prevailed. It is by rectifying judicial error in the classroom, one could argue, that liberal arts legal education actively cultivates the capacity for critical legal thought.

I think that the pursuit of a completely coherent, coolly consistent version of law is a mistake. (My position is not unique; the essays in this volume by Constable, Hartog, and Heinzelman each in their own way call into question the presentation of law as a rigorously logical, self-enclosed system.) In my view, the depiction of jumbled judicial opinions as institutional failures is based on a misleading understanding of democracy. A more accurate understanding of democracy (and the role of courts within it) allows us to see that muddled judicial outcomes are endemic and politically significant. Given the importance of judicial ambiguity, liberal arts legal education should treat critical legal thinking less as a way of attending to principled arguments than as a capacity for skillfully handling disagreement and uncertainty.[76]

The conventional understanding of judicial action misleads because it does not recognize the centrality of conflict and uncertainty in democracy. The conventional understanding presupposes that agreement on principled judicial decisions is always possible. Yet the political disputes that give rise to important litigation, especially at the level of the Supreme Court, cast doubt on the conventional presupposition. In the litigation of hard cases, judges are confronted with sharp conflicts over principle and substantial uncertainty about practical consequences. Judges may sometimes wait for the levels of conflict and uncertainty to diminish before rendering a decision.[77] But in many other instances, judges are unwilling or unable to wait for greater consensus to emerge or better information to be gathered; they make decisions in the teeth of fragmented, fluctuating conditions. This kind of judicial engagement is necessary, because heterogeneous democratic societies constantly generate conflicts and uncertainty.[78] To wait for these conditions to pass would be to wait for a different kind of polity to come into being. If judges are to be effective within their political environment, they must work with the crooked timber that democracy offers. As Edward Levi put it, "the pretense is that the law is a system of known rules applied by a judge. . . . [Yet in] an important sense legal rules are never clear, and if a rule had to be clear before it could be imposed, society would be impossible."[79]

With conditions of conflict and uncertainty necessarily attending many important judicial decisions, the conventional aspiration for carefully reasoned legal judgment is often crowded out by the practical task of resolving disputes, as the ideal of principled judicial decision making gives way to the desire for finding acceptable settlements. Courts tend to abandon the conventional ideal in times of division and indeterminacy because judicial authority cannot be maintained on conventional terms. Under these circumstances, courts are better served by making ambiguous decisions.

To see this, consider that the basic challenge of judicial legitimacy is to ensure that disputing parties use and obey the courts. The task of securing such legitimacy is complicated by one great fact: courts are relatively resource-poor institutions that lack independent mechanisms of enforcement. As Alexander Hamilton famously put it, "[the judiciary] has no influence over either the sword or the purse; no direction of either the strength or of the wealth of society, and can take no active resolution whatever. It may truly be said to have neither FORCE nor WILL but merely judgment."[80]

Generally speaking, then, courts must attempt to maintain themselves as viable arenas of dispute resolution and must do so from a position of relative institutional weakness. How do they accomplish this feat? They have judgment, as Hamilton noted, so judgment is what they use. Courts structure the process of judicial decision making as well as the judicial decisions themselves to elicit the consent of contending parties. In other words, courts use their *practice of judgment* to legitimize their *power of judgment*. Thus, even though it is true that U.S. citizens have few direct means of controlling the courts, that is only one piece of the picture. For their part, the courts possess few direct means for exacting obedience.[81] Courts must win cooperation from citizens—citizens who in turn use their capacity for public criticism to keep the courts faithful to their interests.

It is in this vein that judicial ambiguity should be understood. Rather than being considered institutional failures, ambiguous judicial decisions should be viewed as bids for legitimacy in contentious and uncertain situations.[82] By failing to articulate the entire principled basis of a decision or by offering a compromise ruling, a court can simultaneously recognize the conflicting claims of both litigants, even as the judge ultimately rules in favor of one party over the other. The ambiguous decision is thus a many-splendored thing: even bitterly divided parties may find their claims reflected in such a decision's suggestions and silences.

No one, of course, is likely to be entirely satisfied with such a result. And considered as devices for securing deep consensus or as exercises in principled logic, ambiguous judicial decisions are rightly deemed failures. Even so, considered as a way of sustaining judicial legitimacy, ambiguous decisions have value. By leaving many dimensions of the dispute open and the principled underpinning of the opinion underdeveloped, ambiguous decisions reward victorious litigants with less than they might have won and divest defeated litigants of less than they might have lost. Both winner and loser might have done better, but they also could have done worse. Moreover, both winner and loser are left with a flexible legal framework that over time can be invoked to meet different demands and adapted to address developing disputes. Ambiguous decisions thus give contending parties reasons to rely on court judgments—and do so without placing institutionally weak courts in the difficult position of imposing settlements on recalcitrant litigants. Although these judicial outcomes lack logical elegance and rigor, a legal system in which the rules are incomplete and in flux is, as Edward Levi writes, "the only kind of system which will work when people do not agree completely."[83]

In recognition of this understanding, liberal arts legal education should not automatically consider all muddled judicial decisions to be errors that are subject to correction by critical legal thinking. Given the imperatives of judicial legitimacy, liberal arts legal education should recognize that courts will issue ambiguous decisions and do so most readily in cases involving sharp disagreement or great uncertainty. When significant conflict and poor information predominate, resource-poor courts are least likely to be able to impose broad, logically rigorous judgments on contending parties. Courts consequently will settle for ambiguous decisions that funnel disputes back into the political arena or that return disputes to the judiciary in more amenable forms. This is a political lesson that self-governing citizens should learn. Rather than always seeking out the rigorously principled holding that should have prevailed in a given case, citizens should be able to evaluate how jumbled judicial outcomes can provide a form of democratic accommodation.[84]

This is not to say that critical legal thinking has nothing to do with the quest for principled legal argument. Although many important judicial actions are incomplete and ambiguous, not all are. Courts do issue sweeping, principled decisions replete with detailed justifications.[85] The conventional emphasis on logic, coherency, and completeness is well suited to the analysis of such cases. My point is that courts also issue many inconsistent and fragmented opinions, that such opinions help sustain judicial legitimacy in a roiling sea of democratic conflict, and that citizens need the analytical tools necessary to understand and control this important political dynamic.[86]

Once liberal arts legal education recognizes muddled judicial decisions as being significant in their own right, it should not stop teaching that judicial patterns of argument and principle are important. Of course, if ambiguous decisions were simply institutional failures—unjustified breakdowns in the ordinary scheme of judicial decision making—then we would not expect such decisions to have a strong basis in inherited resources of legal argument. Yet if we consider ambiguous decisions to be part of the practice of judgment that courts use to legitimize their power of judgment, then we should expect these decisions to be fashioned from the same materials generally used to render judicial decisions. For all their inconsistency and incompleteness, ambiguous decisions are meaningful judicial actions. Liberal arts legal education should illustrate how such decisions have roots in and draw significance from past argumentative frameworks.

Finally, liberal arts legal education should recognize that the assessment of muddled decisions reserves a role for the normative critique of judicial argument. As Abramson reminds us in this volume, law often engages difficult questions of moral and political theory.[87] Indeed, law not only engages such questions but also, as Constable argues, tells us what to do.[88] Such "telling" is not always complete or clear, but it is important. Ambiguous judicial decisions invite disputing parties into an unfinished legal world and solicit their help in continuing that world's construction. The terms of participation offered by the judiciary, as fragmented and unsettled as they may be, are worth evaluating for the kind of relationships they seek to engender.

CONCLUSION

At most American universities, undergraduate legal education exhibits a basic divide: on the one hand, more students than ever enroll in law-related courses because they want to become lawyers; on the other hand, the great majority of these law-related courses (and the legal scholarship around which they are organized) are not designed to provide preprofessional training.

I have argued that the university treatment of law strays from student career aspirations for a variety of reasons. First, university faculty are educated in and committed to specific academic disciplines. As a result, their handling of law is designed to advance comprehension of a scholarly field, not to produce attorneys. Second, university faculty are educated in and committed to the liberal arts. At one level, loyalty to the liberal arts means that university faculty lean away from specialized vocational training. Law is thus studied and taught in order to convey lessons about the broad meaning of human experience, not to prepare the next generation of legal practitioners.

At another level, loyalty to the liberal arts means that university faculty share a distinct political mission: to teach students how to live as free citizens, engaged in the practice of self-government. This political mission is controversial, I have argued, because the meaning of democracy is itself enduringly controversial. Consequently, to treat the law as a liberal art is not only to examine how law may promote self-government but also to make a contestable choice about the particular conception of self-government that is to be promoted. By way of illustration, I have offered my own account of the connection between law and the liberal arts ideal of democratic self-government. I have argued that liberal arts legal education should cultivate a capacity for critical legal thought, providing students with the ability to assess incomplete and inconsistent judicial decisions. In my view, such critical legal thinking is important because ambiguous judicial decisions are a crucial part of democratic politics: in the democratic sea of conflicting interests and limited information, courts often maintain their legitimacy by muddling through. Citizens that expect only completely coherent, rigorously principled judicial decisions seek something that democratically constrained courts cannot consistently supply. In order to prepare citizens to evaluate judicial action as it actually happens, liberal arts legal education must examine how law is used for skillfully handling disagreement and uncertainty.

At the end of the day, of course, many of the students receiving a liberal arts legal education still want to be lawyers. If they succeed in realizing their career goals, these students ultimately will learn how to litigate in the interests of their clients. Yet whether or not these students become lawyers, they must, in order to be self-governing citizens, learn how the law can be made to work in the interests of all. My argument has been that law, taught and studied in the university as a liberal art, helps meet this essential political need.

NOTES

1. Rick L. Morgan and Kurt Snyder, *Official American Bar Association Guide to Approved Law Schools* (Foster City, Calif.: American Bar Association in association with IDG Books Worldwide, 2001), 454.

2. These enrollment figures are for law schools approved by the American Bar Association. Since most American law schools are ABA approved, the enrollment figures change very little when enrollment in all law schools is taken into account. See Carl A. Auerbach, *Historical Statistics of Legal Education* (Chicago: American Bar Foundation, 1997), 8–9, 13.

3. Clara N. Carson, *The Lawyer Statistical Report: The U.S. Legal Profession in 1995* (Chicago: American Bar Foundation, 1999), 1.

4. Michael DeMarco et al., "The State and Future of the Profession: A Report by the External Projects Committee," *Federal Insurance and Corporate Counsel Quarterly* 50 (2000): 401, 422–23.

5. Robert D. Putnam, *Bowling Alone: The Collapse and Revival of American Community* (New York: Simon and Schuster, 2000), 146.

6. See, e.g., Paul Schiff Berman, "Telling a Less Suspicious Story: Notes toward a Non-Skeptical Approach to Legal/Cultural Analysis," *Yale Journal of Law and the Humanities* 13 (2001): 95.

7. See, e.g., Putnam, *Bowling Alone.*

8. *Grutter v. Bollinger,* 71 U.S.L.W. 4498 (2003).

9. Alexis de Tocqueville, *Democracy in America,* ed. J. P. Mayer, trans. George Lawrence (New York: Harper and Row, 1966).

10. As Jane Smiley puts it in her novel *Moo* (New York: Alfred A. Knopf, 1995), 63, a successful university is one that caters to "customers," not one that instructs "students."

11. University of Phoenix website, http://www.phoenix.edu/ (visited May 10, 2002).

12. Ibid.

13. For a catalog of the ways in which the University of Phoenix has been criticized, see Alan Wolfe, "How a For-Profit University Can Be Invaluable to the Traditional Liberal Arts," *Chronicle of Higher Education,* December 4, 1998, B4.

14. This question presupposes that one is speaking about higher education in the United States. Other countries, such as Great Britain, provide professional legal training at the

undergraduate level, so there is no need to explain why undergraduate legal aspirations and university courses are mismatched. Although it is beyond the scope of this chapter, it would be interesting to compare the conceptions of democracy fostered by the American antivocational liberal arts ideal with the conceptions of democracy fostered by the more vocational British model.

15. J. M. Balkin and Sanford Levinson, "The Cannons of Constitutional Law," *Harvard Law Review* 111 (1998): 964.

16. Gerald N. Rosenberg, "Across the Great Divide (Between Law and Political Science)," *Green Bag* (2nd ser.) 3 (2000): 267, 272. The scorn does not flow in only one direction. Some law professors argue that academics outside the law schools are not qualified to teach law in any respect. This view stems from a "proprietary attitude" that considers "any attention by the college to conventionally legal subjects as a presumptuous infringement by self-appointed incompetents"; Brainerd Currie, "The Place of the Law in the Liberal Arts College," *Journal of Legal Education* 5 (1953): 428. In this vein, one could easily imagine that law professors might see the disdain felt by their university colleagues as simple envy. After all, law professors generally command larger salaries and enjoy higher public profiles than do most academics laboring away in the arts and sciences. It undoubtedly soothes the sensibilities of some lower-paid, less-respected university professors to envision the law school as the home of mere practitioners and intellectual poseurs.

17. Thomas R. Hensley, "Come to the Edge: Role Playing Activities in Constitutional Law Class," *PS: Political Science and Politics* 26 (1993): 64.

18. Rosenberg, "Across the Great Divide," 268.

19. For examples in political science, see Keith J. Bybee, *Mistaken Identity: The Supreme Court and the Politics of Minority Representation* (Princeton: Princeton University Press, 1998); Howard Gillman, *The Constitution Besieged: The Rise and Demise of Lochner Era Police Powers Jurisprudence* (Durham, N.C.: Duke University Press, 1993); Martin Shapiro, *Courts: A Comparative and Political Analysis* (Chicago: University of Chicago Press, 1981); Rogers M. Smith, *Liberalism and American Constitutional Law* (Cambridge: Harvard University Press, 1985).

20. Yilu Zhao, "More Small Colleges Dropping Out," *New York Times,* May 7, 2002, A20.

21. There are also points of tension between the liberal arts and disciplinary commitments. Narrow and exclusive instruction in a single discipline is vocational in the sense that it prepares one to be a professional academic. Liberal arts education stands against such instruction just as it stands against all vocational training. The conflict between disciplinary commitments and the liberal arts is just one set of competing pressures at work in higher education. For more discussion along these lines, see the chapter in this volume by Goodman and Silbey, "Defending Liberal Education from the Law."

22. Bruce A. Kimball, *Orators and Philosophers: A History of the Idea of Liberal Education,* expanded ed. (New York: College Entrance Board, 1995); Kurt A. Raaflaub, "Democracy, Oligarchy, and the Concept of the 'Free Citizen' in Late Fifth-Century Athens," *Political Theory* 11 (1983): 517; W. R. Connor, "Liberal Arts Education in the Twenty-first Century," AALE Occasional Paper in Liberal Education no. 2, 1998, available at http://www.aale.org/ (visited May 10, 2002).

23. Raaflaub, "Democracy," 529.

24. Connor, "Liberal Arts Education."

25. Raaflaub, "Democracy," 529–30; Connor, "Liberal Arts Education."

26. Raaflaub, "Democracy," 530.

27. The seven liberal arts (the medieval *quadrivium* and *trivium*) that form the core of liberal education in the Western tradition stem from the enkuklios paideia. As Connor ("Liberal Arts Education"), writes, the enkuklios paideia "included the ability to speak correctly, persuasively, and cogently—grammar, rhetoric, and dialectic as they would be called in the later *trivium*. They included enough arithmetic to keep an eye on the city's books, enough geometry to deal with surveying and land issues, and eventually enough astronomy not to be trapped in superstitious dread every time an eclipse appeared. Add harmony to arithmetic, geometry, and astronomy and you have the *quadrivium* of medieval times." For a far more detailed account of these developments, see Kimball, *Orators and Philosophers*.

28. Judith Shklar, *American Citizenship: The Quest for Inclusion* (Cambridge: Harvard University Press, 1991).

29. Swarthmore College website, http://www.swarthmore.edu/admissions/liberal arts.html (visited May 10, 2002).

30. Robert Maynard Hutchins, *The Higher Learning in America* (New Haven: Yale University Press, 1936); Eugene M. Lang, "Distinctively American: The Liberal Arts College," *Daedalus* 128 (1999): 133; Connor, "Liberal Arts Education."

31. Swarthmore College website.

32. Syracuse University website, http://www-hl.syr.edu/about/liberalartsblurb4.html (visited May 10, 2002).

33. James Boyd White, "Meaning What You Say," in this volume. See also James Boyd White, *The Legal Imagination* (Boston: Little, Brown, 1973); and White, *Justice as Translation* (Chicago: University of Chicago Press, 1990).

34. See Goodman and Silbey, "Defending Liberal Education."

35. See, e.g., Michel Foucault, *Discipline and Punish: The Birth of the Prison,* trans. Alan Sheridan (Middlesex, U.K.: Peregrine Books, 1979); and Foucault, *Power/Knowledge: Selected Interviews and Other Writings, 1971–1977,* ed. Colin Gordon, trans. Colin Gordon et al. (New York: Pantheon Books, 1980).

36. See Goodman and Silbey, "Defending Liberal Education."

37. I speak broadly here in order to make a general point. In fact, the ancient Greeks did not all agree on a single understanding of liberal education or on a single conception of humanity; for a detailed account of the range of competing conceptions, see Kimball, *Orators and Philosophers*. For my purposes, however, the nuances of the ancient debate are unimportant.

38. Raaflaub, "Democracy," 529.

39. Connor, "Liberal Arts Education."

40. Raaflaub, "Democracy," 532.

41. Quoted in Lang, "Distinctively American," 134–35. Almost all of the first American liberal arts colleges had close ties to churches—a fact that reflected not only the institutional origins of American higher education but also a widespread belief among educators in the political importance of religion. By contrast, liberal arts education today is essentially secular, even though religion remains central to the political views of many Americans. Like the commitment to antivocationalism, the secularization of the liberal arts represents a gap between liberal arts institutions and the larger society in which they operate. Although it is beyond the scope of my argument here, a full accounting of liberal arts would have to examine the changing role of religion.

42. Sidney Hook, "A Critical Appraisal of the St. John's College Curriculum," in *Education for Modern Man* (New York: New Dial Press, 1946); Lang, "Distinctively American."

43. Rochester Institute of Technology website, http://www.rit.edu/~932www/UGrad/UGradCat/colleges/cla/ (visited May 10, 2002).

44. Also like the educational institutions of the ancient Greeks, modern liberal arts institutions provide political education to only a slice of the populace. There are, of course, differences in the ancient and modern definitions of citizenship. The ancient Greeks defined the citizenry in a highly restrictive fashion, excluding women and slaves from membership in the political community. Contemporary American democracy, by contrast, prohibits slavery and does not countenance the formal political exclusion of women. As a consequence of these differences, American liberal arts education is (at least formally) available to a much larger segment of the population than the Greek enkuklios paideia ever was. Even so, American liberal arts education is, like its Greek antecedent, the education of an elite. The limited reach of American liberal arts must, as I mentioned at the outset of this essay, be kept in mind.

45. The contemporary debate over democracy's meaning is very wide ranging and includes far more than questions about the relevance of the ancients. The larger field of debate underscores the importance of attending to different varieties of democracy when discussing law and the liberal arts. Yet rather than canvassing the entire contemporary debate over democracy, I focus on the relevance of the ancients for the sake of brevity.

46. Benjamin Constant, "The Liberty of the Ancients Compared to That of the Moderns," in *Political Writings,* ed. Biancamaria Fontana (New York: Cambridge University Press, 1988).

47. Isaiah Berlin, "Two Concepts of Liberty," in *Four Essays on Liberty* (New York: Oxford University Press, 1969).

48. Lang, "Distinctively American."

49. See, e.g., Hannah Arendt, *The Human Condition* (New York: Doubleday, 1958); Alasdair C. MacIntyre, *After Virtue: A Study in Moral Theory* (South Bend, Ind.: University of Notre Dame Press, 1981).

50. Leo Strauss, "What Is Liberal Education?" address delivered at the tenth annual graduation exercises of the Basic Program in Liberal Arts for Adults, June 6, 1959, available at http://www.realuofc.org/libed/strauss/liberal.html (visited May 10, 2002).

51. This is not to say that the two visions of democracy are the only issues at stake in the debate over American liberal arts education. For a more detailed account of the liberal arts in the United States, see Kimball, *Orators and Philosophers.*

52. Empirical training: John Dewey, "President Hutchins' Proposal to Remake Higher Education," *Social Frontier* 3 (1937): 103; Dewey, "The Higher Learning in America," *Social Frontier* 3 (1937): 167; good life: Hutchins, *Higher Learning.*

53. Homer, *The Odyssey,* trans. Robert Fagles, with an introduction and notes by Bernard Knox (New York: Viking, 1996); Rigoberta Menchu, *I, Rigoberta Menchu: An Indian Woman in Guatemala,* ed. Elisabeth Burgos-Debray, trans. Ann Wright (London: Verso, 1984).

54. William E. Connolly, *The Terms of Political Discourse,* 2nd ed. (Princeton: Princeton University Press, 1983).

55. Cf. Stanley Fish, *There's No Such Thing as Free Speech* (New York: Oxford University Press, 1994).

56. Clifford Geertz, *The Interpretation of Cultures* (New York: Basic Books, 1973), 29.

57. Tocqueville, *Democracy in America.* For a similar argument, drawn from Habermas rather than Tocqueville, see Goodman and Silbey, "Defending Liberal Education."

58. This argument has a long history in the United States, beginning with the Anti-Federalists and extending through contemporary debates over race-conscious redistricting. See Bybee, *Mistaken Identity.*

59. Bruce W. Hauptli, "My View of the Nature of a Liberal Arts Education," 2001, available at http://www.fiu.edu/~hauptli/libarts.html (visited May 10, 2002).

60. Walter Lippmann, *Public Opinion* (New York: Harcourt, Brace, 1922).

61. Phillip B. Kurland, "Pre-Legal Education," address delivered at the Midwest Association of Pre-Law Advisors, Northwestern University Law School, October 14, 1984, available at http://www.cohums.ohio-state.edu/coh/alumni/value.cfm (visited May 10, 2002).

62. As I stated at the beginning of this chapter, there are many facets of the law and the legal system. In focusing on the judiciary, I call attention to only one aspect of the law that the liberal arts must address.

63. Bybee, *Mistaken Identity,* 36–48.

64. See William E. Nelson, *Marbury v. Madison: The Origins and Legacy of Judicial Review* (Lawrence: University of Kansas Press, 2000).

65. Jeffrey A. Segal and Harold J. Spaeth, *The Supreme Court and the Attitudinal Model* (New York: Cambridge University Press, 1993).

66. This is not to say that all judges have admitted as much. Many judges, like Justice Felix Frankfurter, have built their entire jurisprudence around claims of self-restraint. I am not persuaded by such arguments, mainly because I do not think that a judicial division between "nonpolitical" and "political" issues is sustainable (see Bybee, *Mistaken Identity*).

67. Tocqueville, *Democracy in America,* 270.

68. Lief H. Carter, *Reason in Law,* 5th ed. (New York: Longman, 1998), xi.

69. Terri Jennings Peretti, *In Defense of a Political Court* (Princeton: Princeton University Press, 1999), 11–35.

70. See, e.g., Herbert Wechsler, "Toward Neutral Principles of Constitutional Law," *Harvard Law Review* 73 (1959): 1; Ronald Dworkin, *Taking Rights Seriously* (Cambridge: Harvard University Press, 1977); Richard A. Posner, "Against Constitutional Theory," *New York University Law Review* 73 (1998): 1.

71. Richard A. Wasserstrom, *The Judicial Decision: Toward a Theory of Legal Justification* (Stanford: Stanford University Press, 1961), 14–22.

72. Rogers M. Smith, "Political Jurisprudence, the 'New Institutionalism,' and the Future of Public Law," *American Political Science Review* 82 (1988): 89.

73. Lief H. Carter, *Contemporary Constitutional Lawmaking: The Supreme Court and the Art of Politics* (New York: Pergamon Press, 1985), 22.

74. See, respectively, *Planned Parenthood of Southeastern Pa. v. Casey,* 505 U.S. 833 (1992); *Regents of the University of California v. Bakke,* 438 U.S. 265 (1978); and *Grutter v. Bollinger.*

75. Benjamin N. Cardozo, *The Nature of the Judicial Process* (New Haven: Yale University Press, 1921).

76. See Keith J. Bybee, "The Political Significance of Legal Ambiguity: The Case of Affirmative Action," *Law and Society Review* 34 (2000): 263; Bybee, "The Jurisprudence of Uncertainty," *Law and Society Review* 35 (2001): 501. The alternative I am recommending here should not be confused with the acceptance of judicial ambiguity found in the work of some political scientists. These political scientists view courts in general and the Supreme Court in particular as political institutions driven by the conflicting policy preferences of their members (e.g., Segal and Spaeth, *Attitudinal Model*). There is some disagreement about whether these policy preferences are expressed sincerely or strategically. See, e.g., Jeffrey A. Segal, "Supreme Court Deference to Congress: An Examination of the Markist Model," in *Supreme Court Decision-Making: New Institutionalist Approaches,* ed. Cornell Clayton and Howard Gillman (Chicago: University of Chicago Press, 1999); Lee Epstein

and Jack Knight, *The Choices Justices Make* (Washington, D.C.: CQ Press, 1998). But there is broad agreement that general legal principles, whatever their origin, are purely instrumental to the political aims of individual judges. Thus, these political scientists do not view ambiguous judicial decisions as a sign of institutional failure so much as a consequence of political conflicts on the bench. There is something to this approach. Rather than evading ambiguous decisions, these political scientists focus on explaining what courts (and especially the Supreme Court) actually do. The difficulty is that these political scientists fasten almost exclusively on political preferences and, in doing so, drain virtually all judicial argument of meaning (e.g., Segal and Spaeth, *Attitudinal Model*, 316). This leads to a peculiar result: although they want to explain what courts actually do, these political scientists typically discard a large proportion of actual judicial behavior by dismissing judicial arguments as mere rhetorical cover. This strikes me as a mistake. If the conventional understanding of judicial action can be questioned because it does not account for a common aspect of court behavior, it seems fair to question the political science approach when it sets aside most judicial action as nothing but ad hoc rationalization.

77. Alexander Bickel, *The Least Dangerous Branch: The Supreme Court at the Bar of Politics* (Indianapolis: Bobbs-Merrill, 1962).

78. See, e.g., Stuart Hampshire, *Justice Is Conflict* (Princeton: Princeton University Press, 2000); Alexander Hamilton, James Madison, and John Jay, *The Federalist Papers* (New York: Mentor, 1961); Bernard Manin, "On Legitimacy and Political Deliberation," *Political Theory* 15 (1987): 338.

79. Edward H. Levi, *An Introduction to Legal Reasoning* (Chicago: University of Chicago Press, 1949), 1.

80. Hamilton, Madison, and Jay, *Federalist Papers,* 465 (emphasis in original).

81. Gerald N. Rosenberg, *The Hollow Hope: Can Courts Bring about Social Change?* (Chicago: University of Chicago Press, 1991). Rosenberg does not include the criminal justice system in his characterization, although some scholars have argued that limited enforcement capabilities plague the courts here as well (see Shapiro, *Courts*).

82. Levi, *Legal Reasoning;* Shapiro, *Courts;* Cass Sunstein, *One Case at a Time: Judicial Minimalism on the Supreme Court* (Cambridge: Harvard University Press, 1999); Bybee, "Legal Ambiguity" and "Jurisprudence of Uncertainty."

83. Levi, *Legal Reasoning,* 104.

84. For another view of how contradiction and ambiguity provoke useful reexaminations, see Susan Sage Heinzelman, " 'Termes Queinte of Lawe' and Quaint Fantasies of Literature," in this volume.

85. Sunstein, *One Case;* and Bybee, "Jurisprudence of Uncertainty."

86. Principled decisions offer a measure of judicial legitimacy by ensuring that the exercise of court power is restrained, reasoned, and impartial. But the principled approach is not the only path to judicial legitimacy, nor is the principled approach a path that courts can follow on all occasions. The political uses of judicial ambiguity must be taken into account. For general theories of the different ways in which power may be legitimated, see Max Weber, *From Max Weber: Essays in Sociology,* ed. H. H. Gerth and C. Wright Mills (New York: Oxford University Press, 1946), 78–79, 294–301; and David Beetham, *The Legitimation of Power* (Atlantic Highlands, N.J.: Humanities Press International, 1991).

87. Jeffrey Abramson, "Teaching Civil Liberties as a Branch of Political Theory: Tolerance versus Respect," in this volume.

88. Marianne Constable, "On Not Leaving Law to the Lawyers," in this volume.

ON NOT LEAVING LAW
TO THE LAWYERS

MARIANNE CONSTABLE

I n a 1956 report on a conference, "On the Teaching of Law in the Liberal Arts Curriculum," Harold J. Berman writes:

> The quality of a civilization, and especially the quality of freedom in a civilization, is intimately dependent upon the quality of the civilization's legal system, which in turn is intimately dependent upon the extent to which a sense of law and of justice under law permeate the entire body politic. *Law*, to quote Lord Keynes' paraphrase of Clemenceau, *is too important to be left to the lawyers.*[1]

Law, Berman continues, "ranks with language, with history, with science, as one of the intellectual foundations of our faith" in civilization, its values and freedoms (29). The "two great modern threats to freedom," he adds (25), are the "growth of governmental regulation" and "greatly increased reliance upon social science research," both of which he claims are currently misunderstood and misused (30, citing Elliott Dunlap Smith, provost of the Carnegie Institute of Technology). Such misunderstanding and misuse, Berman writes, can be countered only by gaining a grip on the "reality" of law as an ordering process or by understanding that "the larger dimensions of law which relate it to justice, to equity, to social welfare, cannot easily be divorced from the technical means whereby law achieves its ends" (30). Berman argues that such understanding can only occur through the teaching of law in the liberal arts curriculum.

As a contribution to thinking about legal scholarship in the liberal arts, I consider what it means to say that law is too important to leave to the lawyers.[2] Berman uses the phrase to argue for the undergraduate teaching of law. I focus on the meaning of the phrase in the context of legal scholarship rather than teaching. In the first part of this chapter, I explore the current use of the phrase "law is too important to leave to the lawyers." Scholars in the social sciences use the phrase to justify the social scientific study of law. In the second part I analyze such use from the perspective of rhetoric, which, unlike the social sciences, is one of the seven traditional liberal arts of the medieval European university. Rhetoric shows how social science, at least as exemplified in texts that currently use the phrase "law is too important to leave to the lawyers," takes particular stances toward law and language. In the last part of the chapter, I conclude that if law is too important to leave to the lawyers, then the study of law is also too discursive to leave to the social scientists.

No doubt readers of this chapter already share some commitment to or engagement with the interdisciplinary possibilities of law and the various so-called liberal arts. Far be it from me to contest claims that law is too "enriching" of other fields,[3] or of legal practitioners, to leave to the lawyers. I grant that the intersections of law and the social sciences have been and can be enriching—intellectually, politically, academically, and otherwise—as my fellow contributors argue. I seek to draw attention, though, to the way that language and law are not only, as Berman put it, the equals of science but also irreducible to the terms of social science. In this volume, Silbey, Goodman, Bybee, and Sarat argue that the study and teaching of law in the liberal arts promote such social goods as morality and democratic politics. Insofar as morality and politics are treated as social goods, they become the subject matter of social knowledge and, as such, subject to the perspectives and limitations of social sciences. One must beware the tendency to view law—as well as morality and politics—strictly in the language and terms of the social. To allow the social sciences to lay exclusive claim to the study of law in the liberal arts is to unduly restrict the possibilities of the study of law and its language in the liberal arts.

LAW AND SOCIETY SCHOLARSHIP

The phrase "law is too important to leave to the lawyers" (or "law is too important to be left to the lawyers") has a lovely alliterative lilt to it. The sound of it immediately appeals to me, an institutionally labeled, if not quite formally certified, rhetorician (and thereby, I might add, someone whose liberal arts credentials are as impeccable as those of any grammarian, logician, musician, arithmetician, geometer, and astronomer among my readership—at least if we go by the liberal arts of the medieval university). The phrase also rings a bell; I know I have heard it before. And I suspect that like me, you've heard it—or think you've heard it—before. But what does the phrase mean?

Does it mean that *law* is too important to leave to the lawyers but that it's okay to leave some kind of non-law to lawyers? (And what might that be?) Does it mean that law is too *important* to leave to the lawyers, rather than too interesting or enriching or complicated? Does it mean that law is too important to *leave* to the lawyers, as opposed to delegating it to them or letting them borrow it once in a while? Finally, does it mean that law is too important to leave to the *lawyers,* as opposed to some others: the law professors, or judges, or legislators, or liberal artists, or scholars to whom it might otherwise be left?

When all a phrase does is ring a bell, it's hard for a nonmusician or perhaps nonarithmetician to decipher it. It has no obvious context. It's just the kind of phrase to show up in a graduation speech or a state of the union address or— wait! I've got it: Frank Munger's presidential address to the Law and Society Association (at least the version published in 2001 in *Law and Society Review*).[4] There, in a piece titled "Inquiry and Activism in Law and Society," Munger writes of the importance of communication on the part of law and society scholars

> so that we can be heard and have an effect. But the problem of communicating does not stop when we have our prose in order. Behind that concern is the still larger question of *who* we want our work to influence and *how.* The inception of the law and society field in North America, and in many other societies, was motivated by a belief in the simple proposition that *law should stand for equality and for justice.* Law and society researchers provided mounting evidence that law did not meet such high ideals. Our research appeared to have some significance in the fight for equality and justice. We agreed with Lawrence Friedman's observation that *"law is too important to be left to the lawyers."* (7–8, emphasis added)

In the context of law and society scholarship, the phrase seems to mean that law is too unequal or unjust for law and society researchers, who are committed to the fight for equality and justice, to leave to lawyers alone. Law and society scholars are motivated by belief in the ostensibly "simple proposition" that law should stand for equality and justice. Actual law does not meet the "high ideals" that law and society researchers believe law "should stand for."

In his comment on Munger's presidential address, Bob Nelson of the American Bar Foundation (ABF) writes:

> Munger at least gestures toward the need to develop theories that connect context with broader structures, as when he offers a twist on Lawrence Friedman's famous phrase that *"law is too important to be left to the lawyers"* by suggesting that "governance is too important to leave to the bankers, regulators, investors, international lawyers, and political leaders of the world."[5]

While ostensibly endorsing what has become "Lawrence Friedman's famous phrase," Nelson, in his use of "at least gestures" and "twist," implies that he endorses a slightly different meaning and emphasis than that which he attributes to Munger or Friedman. To Nelson, all the enriching and nonenriching things that corporate types—such as bankers, regulators, investors, international lawyers—do fall within the ambit of law and society research. Most important, for Nelson, is the need to theorize the connections between governance and lawyers. Like the institution of the ABF itself—a nonprofit research arm of the American Bar Association—"theories" for Nelson connect the study and research of governance in society with the broad structures of lawyers and lawyering.[6]

But let us return to Nelson's again alliterative attribution of the now-famous phrase to Friedman. No fuller citation to the phrase appears in either Munger's or Nelson's *Law and Society Review* pieces. In another article, "Mapping Law and Society," however, Munger cites Friedman's 1986 "The Law and Society Movement."[7] There, Friedman explains that although

> the law and society movement has abandoned *most* of its problem-solving emphasis, . . . [i]t simply has got to be true that policymaking is better off when it is based on a sophisticated understanding of the way the legal system actually works and *why* it works that way—better, more just, and, yes, more efficient than policymaking based on neo-Langdellian logic or on some purely abstract "theory" or "model" hatched in a book-lined office and full of "simplifying assumptions."[8]

Of course, Friedman continues, the law schools have not recognized this.

> As a consequence, the law school world is seriously impoverished. Law and society studies are not essential ingredients to make a successful lawyer; but I do not see how one can grasp the meaning of law within society except from the vantage point of social science. "Law" is a massive, vital presence in the United States. It *is too important to be left to the lawyers*—or even to the realm of pure thought. (780, emphasis added)

Friedman uses the phrase in this context (and without further attribution) to suggest that the meaning of massive and vital law is too big and alive to be left to the narrow theorizing, model building, and deadening so-called thought of lawyers, here understood as law school economists and professors. Law schools, according to Friedman, "teach people how to ferret out answers" (776).

Law school tries to empty the mind of all "extraneous" matter, the better to develop legal skills. The finest products of this process, of course, end up as teachers. Once they have emptied themselves of the extraneous, it is hard to reverse the process; and mostly they never try. (774)

If law school teachers are largely empty-headed for Friedman, lawyers are technicians:

Lawyers are inveterate problem-solvers; the legal system in general is a problem-solving system. This does not mean that it actually solves problems, in the sense that a mathematician does. It only means that trials, appeals, legislative debates, and so on must produce answers, right or wrong to the questions and issues raised. Science or philosophy can dismiss a problem as currently insoluble; the law cannot. A judge, faced with conflicting "authorities," does not abandon the case. Clients pay lawyers for answers, not for philosophical speculations and doubts. (775)

So, for Friedman, social science—or law and society scholarship—helps make policymaking better, more just, and more efficient, not because it helps with narrow problem-solving but because it "*stands for* clarity, honesty and rigor in the study of legal institutions*" (780, emphasis added). The clarity and so forth about law that Friedman values comes with law and society's emphasis on behavior, which he contrasts with non-law-and-society legal scholars' understanding of law as "norms, or language, or ideology, or rhetoric or 'consciousness,' or discourse—anything but behavior" (775).

Bold claims we have here, then, by both Munger and Friedman on behalf of both law and social science. Not leaving law to the lawyers means, for Munger, that law "should stand for" the "high ideals" of equality and justice that actual law does not meet and that law and society scholars believe in and fight for. Not leaving law to the lawyers means, for Friedman, that the law and society movement "stands for clarity, honesty and rigor" that neither speculative law school law nor lawyers' instrumentally rational policymaking can achieve without law and society scholarship. For both Munger and Friedman, law and society scholarship stands for something presumably important that lawyers' law lacks.

"STANDING FOR"

How does law and society scholarship "stand for" law and its ideals though? Both Munger and Friedman in some sense privilege social science over law.

Munger's aspirations that law and society scholarship hold law to higher standards than those to which the law holds itself, and Friedman's arguments that law and society scholarship makes policymaking better off, assert the primacy of law and society scholarship over law. Neither Munger nor Friedman cite Berman or Keynes or Clemenceau, but their claims that law and society scholarship "stands for" something allow us to reflect further on the meaning of the phrase "Law is too important to leave to the lawyers" and on the limitations of the phrase in the context of social scientific law and society scholarship.

How does social science stand for particular standards? Does it do so in the same way that Munger suggests that law should stand for equality and justice? Or in the same way that Munger's and Friedman's articles, despite their differences, stand for law and society scholarship or stand for contemporary usage of our famous phrase? Or in the way that rhetoric in this essay stands for the liberal arts?

In wondering how a body of scholarship can stand for something, one draws attention to the phrase "standing for" as a figure of speech. It seems that both Munger and Friedman take "standing for" as some sort of "representing." But there are a number of ways—not the least of which is legal—in which one thing represents another. Rhetoric names a plethora of ways in which a word or phrase can stand for something else. "Rhetoric" in this essay, for instance, functions as synecdoche for the liberal arts: a part stands for a whole.[9] But one phrase may stand for another through other relations, as when Friedman writes that law schools "empty the mind" or when Nelson writes of Munger's "twist" on Friedman's phrase. What do "empty minds" or "twists" stand for? Are these phrases representative of what they stand for? What does "standing for" stand for?

As Pierre Schlag points out in his pithy comment on Radin and Michelman, the metaphor of "stance" implies position and orientation in space.[10] "Standing for" suggests substitution or representation: one thing stands in the *place* of another. When, as for Munger, law and society scholarship stands for values that law should but does not stand for, such scholarship locates itself in the place of a higher law. It identifies itself as representative of legal interests, even as it locates actual lesser law elsewhere. In insisting on the "vantage point of social science" to grasp law, as does Friedman, law and society scholarship positions and orients itself on the side of higher, better, more just, more efficient "standards" for law. The metaphor of stance lends itself, as Schlag shows, to a taking up and defending of chosen positions—in Munger's case, to "fighting for" one's beliefs in equality and justice; in Friedman's, to championing the social scientific vantage point's standards of clarity, honesty, and rigor.

So far, so good. The previous paragraph takes no stance against anything that Munger's and Friedman's texts may be acknowledged to stand for. It emphasizes and, in some sense, even repeats the logic of Munger's and Friedman's claims. The claims of the previous paragraph thus stand neither for nor against equality, inequality, justice, injustice, clarity, murkiness, honesty, dishonesty, rigor, or sloppiness. But the claims of the previous paragraph are not, for this reason, to be dismissed as irrelevant or tangential or useless for inquiry into the relation of social science scholarship to law. That is because inquiry into the relation of social science scholarship and law need not be limited to the taking up of stances. Although the metaphor of stance, as Schlag writes, may "become a kind of closure device that works to exclude from view any intellectual activity that does not consist in stance-taking" (1061–62), other sorts of intellectual activity are possible.

Attending to figures of speech, for instance, allows one to do something other than stance taking. It provides an approach to language and to what it does that moves away from the utilization of language for representing and taking stances. Recall that behind the "problem of communicating" for Munger are strategic issues about whom to influence and how. But language is not only about communicating stances and influencing the stances of others. Exploring what language does besides communicate and influence people helps one to see "the meaning of law"—and of social science. It helps one to understand "the way the legal system actually works" and how it works that way—the very role that Friedman would grant to social science scholarship itself!

Although rhetoric and social science may resemble one another in their quest for the meaning of law, there are, of course, important differences. The rhetoric of law—like many other humanistic fields that attend to law—does not share Friedman's insistence on a strong distinction between language and behavior. For centuries before the advent of law and society (even granting Montesquieu the honor of being the first law and society scholar),[11] lawyers and humanists have known that the behavior of law (in the West) cannot be separated from its language. In contemporary parlance, lawyers and humanists have long recognized that law is both discourse and practice: a discourse that matters and a practice that involves speech.[12] From Socrates to Habermas, from Solon to the Hague, philosophers and lawyers know law to be both discursive practice and practical discourse.

For scholars and lawyers over the ages, in other words, law in some sense *tells* someone what to do. Every conception of law, whether law is conceived as text or as behavior or as something else or both, presumes that law *tells*—gestures, indicates, shows, reveals, states, describes, threatens, or commands—(to) its addressee or subject—some action or behavior to do. Parsing the rhetoric of particular laws or sets of laws or even texts about law raises constellations of issues having to do with *how* law tells the one *whom* it tells *what* to do. In any particular legal event or text, one can identify, like variations on a theme: an addressee or subject, the "one" or "ones" whom law addresses (citizens, residents, human beings, officials, Christians, moral actors, utilitarian maximizers); what to do—the character of doing that law calls for (moral action, social behavior, rule following, conscientious choice, willing, conforming, calculating); and how law presumes its addressee is to grasp the telling (by example, by cognizing statements of rules, by threats and coercion, through revelation, through moral knowledge, through legal reasoning, through deliberation or strategy).

That law "tells" addressees what to do is important for understanding law. Telling implies both speaking and acting. It suggests that whether one adopts a stance that law does its telling well or badly, the strong distinctions between action and speech or between language and behavior that some social science scholarship adopts toward law are conceptual distinctions. This does not mean that they are "only" conceptual distinctions and to be discarded. That the distinctions between speech and action, between language and behavior, are conceptual distinctions means that they are "also" rhetorical distinctions—and thus to be explored for what they presume and what their use enables one to learn, or precludes one from learning, about law.

Recognizing and investigating the rhetorical aspects of law contribute to, in Friedman's words, "a sophisticated understanding of the way the legal system actually works." Rhetorical study recognizes the inseparability of legal language, norms, and ideology from legal behavior. Having recognized such inseparability, it provides a language in which to speak of ways in which the legal system—and studies of the legal system—nevertheless sometimes insists on separating language from behavior. In some social scientific scholarship, for instance, as we have seen, scholars rely on a strong distinction between language and behavior to argue for the primacy of the standards of social sciences, which look to law in action, over the values of a legal profession that takes law as language or as "anything but behavior."[13] Law itself struggles with the distinction—as in attempts to clarify the difference between protected speech and unprotected conduct under the First Amendment, for instance.

Rhetoric considers how actions speak—as in the aphorism "louder than words," for instance—and how speech acts, drawing on the philosophy of the twentieth-century Austin, for instance.[14] Legal actions speak in the sense that the most inaudible or verbally inarticulate legal actors (or institutions or others to whom behavior is attributed), however unjust their behavior may be declared to be, lay claim to acting or behaving (and thus telling others what to do) in the "name of the law."

If legal actions speak, so too legal speech acts. Utterances (or writing or publication) of words are actions. Legal utterances involve some doing: stating, declaring, legislating, holding, ruling, promising, contracting, sentencing. What any particular utterance actually does depends on the conditions and context in which it is uttered. To count as doing something, an utterance must accord with the practice of that activity. To count as a legal doing today, for instance, an utterance must be articulated under particular conditions in particular ways—and not in others. Foucault draws attention to the way that not only law but scholarship are discursive activities or practices.[15] One can study the utterances of humanists and social scientists by asking how particular fields formulate their issues; what they presuppose; how they make, maintain, challenge, or resist particular claims. And, of course, what do their claims stand for and how?

The policy statements of journals are one way in which fields describe and circumscribe themselves. Amendments to the policy statement of the *Law and Society Review,* for instance, suggest changes in the field. Welcoming "articles and research notes by lawyers, social scientists, and other scholars which bear on the relationship between law and the social sciences," the *Review* originally announced itself in 1967 (vol. 2) as published by "the Law and Society Association, a nation-wide group, drawn primarily from the legal and social science professions, whose purpose is the stimulation and support of research and teaching on political, social and economic aspects of law."

During the next twenty-five years, the changing policy statement of the *Review* reveals the journal's broadening reach, as "work which bears on the relationship between law and the social sciences" became "work that bears on the relationship between society and the legal process" (vol. 9, fall 1974). Later the statement elaborated on the journal's scholarly breadth and suggested its openness to self-reflection and criticism. It welcomed "work bearing on the relationship between society and the legal process, including articles or notes of interest to the research community in general, new theoretical developments, results of empirical studies, and comments on the field or its methods of inquiry" (vol. 28, no. 2, 1994). From a hyphenated "nation-wide" group, the Law and Society Association merged into a nonhyphenated "nationwide group" (fall 1974), only to become "an international group" four years later (winter 1978). Its "stimulation and support of research and teaching" broadened in scope from "political, social and economic aspects of the law" (from 1967 to 1982, at least) to "cultural, economic, political, psychological, and social aspects of law and the legal system" in 1985. In 1991, the singular legal system became legal "systems." In 1994 the *Review* proclaimed that it was "broadly interdisciplinary and welcomes work from any tradition of scholarship [now leaving out teaching] concerned with the cultural, economic, political, psychological, or [!] social aspects of law and legal systems."

On its face, the policy statement of *Law and Society Review* presents an expansion of the enterprise of law and society over the past twenty-five years. But do changes in the policy statement themselves "stand for" such expansion? Or for expansion of the aspirations of the enterprise? Or of articulations of aspirations of some members of the enterprise? To what extent does the *Review* actually "stand for" the association, its membership, or their scholarship? To actually understand the meaning of the policy statement and to grasp the changes it stands for require knowing something of the role of policy statements in journals, of journals in associations, of associations in academia, as well as of the published and unpublished scholarship in the field of law and society.

Understanding the discursive activities and practices of law likewise requires knowledge of what law says in context. The rhetoric of law is neither a study in what Friedman designates the "pure thought" of the legal academy nor the "ferreting out of answers" of legal teaching, much less the "problem solving" of lawyers. Like Friedman's social science, rhetoric of law takes seriously Friedman's points: that the legal system in general is a problem-solving system, which does not mean that it actually solves problems but that it must produce answers to questions. Rhetoric of law turns to the way that law answers questions and claims to solve problems then, but not in order to solve the problems itself or to stand for better answers. Rather, rhetoric looks at how law makes its claims. Rhetoric points out how law formulates what count as legal answers against a background that has transformed problems of some sort into legally recognizable questions. What count as both questions and answers at law today presume a particular background of activity—of utterances, of actions, of events—and of institutions—of education, of lawyering, of judging—that constitute law.

In his essay on Stanley Cavell, one commentator, Dennis Des Chene, writes that "it is now part of the common sense of the humanities" that "questioning and answering presuppose a background against which the questions and answers make sense, against which an opinion counts as answering this or that question, and as agreeing with, or differing from, another."[16] Des Chene wonders whether this "truism . . . has been taken to heart." Certainly it would seem that law and society scholarship—or perhaps one should say texts that lay claim to articulating what law and society scholarship stands for—does not always seem to take such knowledge to heart. Rather, insofar as they draw strong distinctions between lawyers' concerns with law as "anything but behavior" and social scientists' interests in the behavior of law, some social scientists fail to grasp—or perhaps simply set aside—the ostensible "common sense" of the humanities and the rhetorical richness of law. Social science scholarship, like law, is itself a discursive activity or practice; its questions and answers presuppose a background against which those questions and answers make sense. Rhetoric draws attention to that background, a background in which the significance of language is all too often limited to its utilization for taking, communicating, and influencing stands.

"INTIMATELY DEPENDENT"

The reader will recall that Berman's way of not leaving law to the lawyers appears quite different from Munger's and Friedman's. Rather than appealing to what nonlawyers "stand for," Berman writes of the "intimate dependence" of the quality of law on the entire body politic and, more specifically, on the "sense" of law and justice that "permeates" such a body. Noting that social science research is misunderstood and misused, Berman does not explain what its correct understanding and use might be nor what social science stands for. Rather, he writes that "greatly increased reliance upon social science research," along with the growth of regulation,[17] is one of the two "great threats to modern freedom." The threat must be countered, he writes, by gaining a grip on the reality of law as an ordering process and understanding the "larger dimensions of law which relate it to justice, to equity, to social welfare." This in turn occurs, according to Berman, through the teaching of law in the liberal arts curriculum, a recommendation for which Berman finds support in his citation of Lord Keynes's paraphrase of Clemenceau.

What are we to make of this citation and of its relation to our understanding so far of "Friedman's famous phrase"? Clemenceau's (1841–1929) actual statement seems to have been made during the last years of World War I, when, as center-left prime minister, he represented France at the Versailles peace accords. Disagreeing with his military commander-in-chief General Foch, Clemenceau argued that only political leaders should deal with the status of the Rhineland and that political decisions must be clearly separated from military advice.[18] "La guerre, c'est une chose trop grave pour la confier à des militaires" is variously translated as "War is too important to be left to the generals" or "War is too serious a matter to leave to soldiers."[19] *Bartlett's Quotations* also attributes the statement to the French statesman and diplomat Talleyrand (1754–1838) and to Aristide Briand, a contemporary of Clemenceau's.[20]

I have not been able to find Keynes's (1883–1946) paraphrase, but student researchers and reference librarians have found numerous uses—usually without attribution—of both the war and the law phrases. The law phrase appears in an online cyberlaw article and in course syllabi about law and the humanities found on the Web. It appears in an online ad for a self-help legal text, followed by "this up-to-the-moment Law Handbook is an essential weapon in the struggle to provide justice for all."[21] Variations on the phrase have been used in the United States to the effect that "law reform is far too serious a matter to be left to the legal profession," and in Canada to the effect that "law is too serious a matter to be left exclusively to judges."[22] Variations on it have been used by academics: in his inaugural lecture at the University of Manchester, scholar of ancient religious law Bernard Jackson said, "Jewish law is too important to be left to the lawyers."[23] Variations have been used by judges: in an address on the future of the federal courts, Justice Rehnquist followed his quotation of the war phrase by "the shape of the federal court system is too important to be left to the judges."[24] Mariana Valverde quotes the phrase about war in a book review in which she writes that "philosophical questions are too important to be left to the philosophers."[25]

These citations do not move us any closer to discovering the definitive source of the quotation. A professor on the University of Massachusetts legal studies website proclaims that "John Bonsignore . . . the father of the program, of the department . . . was the first to propose that law is too important to be left to the lawyers."[26] One text attributes "If war is too important to be left to the generals, surely justice is too important to be left to the lawyers" to Robert McKay, American educator and dean of the New York University law school.[27]

This flurry of iterations does suggest some interesting things about rhetoric and law. It suggests first that "law," as the subject matter of the quotation, is being talked and written about by a good many people. It suggests second that the "importance" and "seriousness" that are attributed to law in these quotations are almost always linked to some sort of aspiration to justice. It suggests, third, the ease with which the domains of war and law are analogized to one another. Indeed one author, quoted in a 1995 article on military justice, writes of the period 1950 to 1955 that "with surprising unanimity, the common law world concluded virtually at the same moment in time that, just as war is too important to be left to the generals, so too military justice is too vital to be entrusted only to judge advocates."[28]

Fourth and finally, the multiple and disparate appearances of the phrase are suggestive of the ways that particular phrases appear and function in legal texts and legal reasoning. When, in legal reasoning, one seeks to understand the uses of language in a legal text, locating a definitive source is less important than perceiving and recognizing the many ways in which a phrase is being and has been used. So too in thinking about the meaning of the phrase "law is too important to leave to the lawyers." Only through exploring, as I do in this chapter, the meaning of the phrase in context does one begin to grasp its use and to open other possibilities. The original source of "law is too important to leave to the lawyers" remains uncertain, but the phrase now points not only to dimensions of law that social scientists claim escape the grasp of law but also to dimensions of language and of law that escape the grasp of social scientists. The larger "dimensions of law," as Berman puts it, are intimately related to justice; the larger dimensions of language, like the larger dimensions of law, cannot be left to social science scholarship about law.

Social science scholarship aspires to find the meaning of law in society. It takes its own expanding enterprise to stand for "clarity, honesty and rigor." From the vantage point of this enterprise, the behavior of law absent such enterprise fails to stand for—or achieve—standards of justice and efficiency. Such evaluations may be correct, even true, but they are dependent on language. And language, like law, does not stand still. (Law "does not just stand there to be watched," to quote a contemporary legal positivist).[29] Language, like law, does not always or exclusively stand for what a determinate speaker—whether lawyer or scholar—intends. Language implies, evokes, reveals, contradicts, inspires, and more. Law, like our famous phrase, is thus too discursive to leave to social scientists who have only limited use for language. The interminable (in Dirk Hartog's words) questioning of meaning and the unpredictable (in Martha Umphrey's words) possibilities of language and justice are what rhetoric and the liberal arts may be said to stand for in their scholarly explorations of law.

NOTES

1. Harold J. Berman, ed., *On the Teaching of Law in the Liberal Arts Curriculum* (Brooklyn: Foundation Press, 1956), 28 (emphasis added).

2. I thank Felipe Gutteriez, Austin Sarat, and participants and discussants in the Law and Liberal Arts conference for their comments. I also thank the UC Berkeley reference librarians, especially Corliss Lee, and the following students for their research assistance: Sara Kendall, Aaraon Nathan, Miah Rosenberg, Janisha Sabnani, Celene Shepard, and Jay Swallow.

3. I quote the brochure of the Conference on Legal Scholarship in the Liberal Arts, held at Amherst College in April 2002, for which this chapter was first written.

4. Frank Munger, "Inquiry and Activism in Law and Society," *Law and Society Review* 35 (2001): 7.

5. Robert Nelson, "Law, Democracy, and Domination: Law and Society Research as Critical Scholarship," *Law and Society Review* 35 (2001): 34 (emphasis added).

6. To quote from the ABF website: "Established in 1952, the American Bar Foundation is an independent, nonprofit national research institute committed to objective empirical research on law and legal institutions. This program of sociolegal research is conducted by an interdisciplinary staff of Research Fellows trained in such diverse fields as law, sociology, psychology, political science, economics, history, and anthropology.

"The American Bar Foundation is the preeminent resource of lawyers, scholars, and policy makers who seek insightful analyses of the theory and functioning of law, legal institutions, and the legal profession. The Foundation's work is supported by the American Bar

Endowment, by the Fellows of the American Bar Foundation, and by grants for particular research projects from private foundations and government agencies." American Bar Foundation website, http://www.abfsociolegal.org/ (updated June 12, 2003; cited August 7, 2003).

7. Frank Munger, "Mapping Law and Society," in *Crossing Boundaries: Traditions and Transformations in Law and Society Research,* ed. Austin Sarat et al. (Evanston, Ill.: Northwestern University Press, 1998).

8. Lawrence M. Friedman, "The Law and Society Movement," *Stanford Law Review* 38 (1986): 776–77. Harvard University dean Christopher Columbus Langdell is credited with having developed, a century or so ago, the case method of teaching in professional law schools. Students learn to abstract principles from appellate decisions, which principles they then apply in other instances.

9. Arthur Quinn, *Figures of Speech: Sixty Ways to Turn a Phrase* (Salt Lake City: G. M. Smith, 1982), 56–58.

10. Pierre Schlag, "Stances," *University of Pennsylvania Law Review* 139: 1059–62.

11. Charles-Louis Montesquieu, *The Spirit of the Laws* (New York: Hafner Press, 1949).

12. Michel Foucault, *Discipline and Punish: The Birth of the Prison,* trans. Alan Sheridan (New York: Vintage Books, 1979).

13. "Anything but" in Friedman, "Law and Society Movement," 775; for law in action versus law in the books, see early law and society literature on the "gap." Although sociolegal scholars today turn increasingly to the discourse of law, they tend to view language itself as "social" or as reducible to the terms of social investigation and analysis.

14. J. L. Austin, *How to Do Things with Words* (Oxford: Clarendon Press, 1962).

15. Michel Foucault, "The Discourse on Language," appendix to his *Archaeology of Knowledge,* trans. A. M. Sheridan Smith (New York: Pantheon, 1972).

16. Dennis Des Chene, "In Touch with Art: Cavell and His Critics on New Music," in *The Senses of Stanley Cavell,* ed. Richard Fleming and Michael Payne (Lewisburg, Pa.: Bucknell University Press; London: Associated University Presses, 1989).

17. Marianne Constable, "The Rhetoric of Community," in *Looking Back at Law's Century,* ed. Austin Sarat, Bryant Garth, and Robert A. Kagan (Ithaca: Cornell University Press, 2002) 213–31.

18. David Robin Watson, *George Clemenceau: A Political Biography* (Plymouth, Great Britain: Bowering Press, 1974), 333.

19. Georges Suarez, La Vie orguelléuse de Clemenceau (Paris, France: Éditions de France, 1886; reprint, 1930); note that *confier* means "to entrust." The first translation may be found on Lexis-Nexis by use of the quotation search function; the second at J. Hampden Jackson, *Clemenceau and the Third Republic* (London: Macmillan, 1948), 224.

20. *Bartlett's Quotations,* http://www.bartleby.com/100 (updated October 27, 1999; cited August 2003).

21. Online ad for *The Law Handbook,* in the *Guardian,* November 3, 1999, quoting Geoffrey Robertson Q.C., from the foreword to the 7th ed., http://www.cpa.org.au/garchvel/978law.html(downloaded November 19, 2002).

22. The Honorable Sir Leslie Scarman, "The Role of the Legal Profession in Law Reform," *Record of the Association of the Bar of the City of New York* 21 (1966): 12; Daniel Arthur Lapres, Case Comment, *Canadian Bar Review/Revue du Barreau Canadien* (1977), n. 35, http://www.lapres.net/html/stare.html (downloaded November 19, 2002).

23. Bernard Jackson, University of Manchester inaugural lecture, online at http://www.mucjs.org/.

24. Chief Justice William H. Rehnquist, "Address: Seen in a Glass Darkly: The Future of the Federal Courts," *Wisconsin Law Review* (1993): 1.

25. Mariana Valverde, "Money, Sex, and Speech: The Law of Speech and Law as Speech," *Texas Law Review* 79 (2001): 189 (book review of Steven Shiffrin, *Dissent, Injustice, and the Meanings of America*).

26. Marietta Pritchard, "A Civil Action—Jan Schlichtmann," *Umass Magazine* (1999), quoting Janet Rifkin, http://www.umass.edu/umassmag/archives/l999/spring_99/sp99_f_civil.html (downloaded November 19, 2002).

27. Elizabeth Frost Knappmann and David Schrager, *The Quotable Lawyer*, rev. ed. (New York: Facts on File, 1998), 217. Found through Kenneth Redden, *Modern Legal Glossary* (Charlottesville, Va.: Michie Co., 1980).

28. Jonathan Lurie, "Military Justice Fifty Years after Nuremberg: Some Reflections on Appearance v. Reality," *Military Law Review* 149 (1995): 189, quoting Frederick B. Wiener.

29. Frederick Schauer, *Playing by the Rules: A Philosophical Examination of Rule-Based Decision-Making in Law and in Life* (Oxford: Clarendon Press, 1991).

From Disciplinary Perspectives to an
Integrated Conception of Legal Scholarship*

AUSTIN SARAT

C onsider the saga of Mrs. Palsgraf and her children innocently waiting on
a railway platform for a train that would take them on a day trip to Rock-
away Beach only to have their lives turned upside down when a man running
to catch an already moving train tried to jump aboard.[1] A conductor reached
for the man and pulled him forward while a railroad employee on the platform, in some desperate contortion, pushed him from behind. Although the
unidentified man was saved by these acts, a package he was carrying dislodged
and dropped from his grasp. The package contained fireworks, which, unfortunately for Mrs. Palsgraf, exploded on contact with the rails. The explosion,
in the rather bland words of Judge Benjamin Cardozo, "threw down some
scales at the other end of the platform, many feet away. The scales struck . . .
[Mrs. Palsgraf], causing injuries."[2] Subsequently, Mrs. Palsgraf sued the Long
Island Railroad, claiming that the acts of the railroad's employees were neg-
ligent and that the railroad was responsible for her injuries. Cardozo and
the Court of Appeals of New York ruled otherwise and denied compensation
to Mrs. Palsgraf.

Such stranger-than-fiction cases regularly bring legal scholars in the liberal arts and their students face-to-face with philosophical puzzles, linguistic morasses, and soap opera–like melodramas that only the most ingenious,
or deeply perplexed, minds could invent. Confronting these puzzles, we, as
legal scholars in the liberal arts, try to help students avoid the transfixing, par-
alyzing search for legal right answers and, instead, to engage with the human
lives, as well as the intellectual challenges, hidden beneath the arcane jar-
gon and authoritative style of judicial opinions and law's other artifacts.

Poor Mrs. Palsgraf! Like many of the names without faces, the persons
whose identities become fixed and flattened by their inscription in such cases,

her fate is forever tied up with some of the most vexing ideas and complex prose ever generated in a legal decision.[3] The initial challenge of teaching about Mrs. Palsgraf and *Palsgraf v. Long Island Railroad,* the case that bears her name, is to take on such ideas—ideas about foreseeability, harm, and causation—and explain the alchemy through which they are put together to define duties that the law says we owe to one another as persons. There is, of course, also the thrill of engaging the intellectual prowess and legendary reputations of judges like Cardozo.[4]

To do this means getting students to think about Mrs. Palsgraf as something other than an unscrupulous, if unfortunate, victim of circumstance reaching for the brass ring from the opulent railroad.[5] Try as I might to get my students to suspend, at least momentarily, this hardnosed, unsympathetic reaction to poor Mrs. Palsgraf, the almost uniform "life-is-tough" attitude turns out to be less easily dislodged than the package of fireworks whose exploding contents occasioned this classic of legal education. My efforts to describe Mrs. Palsgraf in sympathetic terms evokes the gentle skepticism of those who might already see me as too liberal, too softheaded, or just not wise enough in either the ways of the world or the ways of the law.

This skepticism came alive not long ago when one student approached me after what I thought was both an illuminating rendition of the philosophical complexities of *Palsgraf* and a heartrendering description of Mrs. Palsgraf. His agitated appearance should have told me that something was not sitting right with him, but I was still off guard when he explained that he thought my rendition of the law of *Palsgraf* was probably wrong and that I should not be so sympathetic to "money-grubbing people like Palsgraf." In response I provided some further explanation of the circumstances of the case and logic of the decision, but he remained unconvinced. As he began to move away, he looked back over his shoulder, as if to shield himself, and told me that he was going to call his father to check out my interpretation. Falling into the trap, I asked whether his father was a lawyer. "He's *a law* teacher," he said in a tone that said, as between me and his father, his father was the real law teacher. "He teaches at a law school."

As a law teacher in a liberal arts college I sometimes feel, perhaps never more so than in the presence of the skepticism of the law school teacher's child, a little out of place. Law teachers, after all, really do seem to belong in law schools. At least since the beginning of the twentieth century, the authority to pronounce about things legal has been lodged with the organized profession and with the appointed guardians of its wisdom, law professors.[6] And if there is any doubt about this official placement of authority, one needs only to look at the treatment of law professors in contemporary culture. Not only do they make higher salaries than liberal arts professors do, but late-breaking developments in the Supreme Court almost inevitably lead the media to the law-book-lined office of a law professor for instant commentary rather than to one of us in a liberal arts college. Moreover, when a crisis or scandal sweeps the legal profession, law professors are called on to say the ritual incantations and staff the committees that propose needed reforms. For law teachers in liberal arts colleges, the law school thus looms as a symbol of privilege and as the reputed repository of all legal learning. There is, of course, some compensation for this life outside the law school—at least in those popular culture portrayals in which the law professor turns out to be Kingsfield, crusty master of the arcane detail of legal doctrine, while the college professor instead is Indiana Jones, venturesome hero defying professional norms by being out of place, on the wrong side of a boundary.

THINKING LIKE A LAWYER:
LEGAL EDUCATION AS PROFESSIONAL EDUCATION

One cannot, I think, understand the place of legal scholarship in the liberal arts without attending to the ways in which it differs from the conventions of professional education in law.[7]

Stated most directly, there is an important difference between teaching law to students so that they can use it as a tool in their professional lives, and teaching undergraduates about law as a social institution and about what happens when law is learned the way lawyers learn it. Legal scholarship in the liberal arts is a form of resistance to the professionalization of legal learning and its almost exclusive location in law schools.[8]

Awhile ago my Amherst College colleague Hadley Arkes recounted a story that illustrates, in vivid detail, the consequences of the professionalization of legal learning. He tells of watching the Public Broadcasting System's ten-part series *Ethics in America*, in which panels of journalists, government officials, lawyers, and other professionals went through a series of moral issues framed as hypothetical dilemmas by a series of Socratic moderators. He describes, in detail, one particular dilemma as well as the response of a well-known lawyer:

> In a case of murder . . . the killer claims that he killed reluctantly; he seeks counsel, and every lawyer extends, to this client, the protection and shield of his confidence. As [the moderator] kept turning new corners, with new, disturbing facts, the lawyers on the panel preserved their willingness to shelter their client and hold back information from the authorities. Particularly adamant here was Mr. James Neal from Tennessee. . . . The killer finally reveals to Mr.

Neal that he was responsible for yet another inadvertent killing; that another man had been convicted for his crime; and that the man who was wrongfully convicted was about to be executed. With the unpeeling of these facts, one could sense the mood altering in the room. Still, even in the face of these reports, Mr. Neal held his ground; he would not yield up information, even to save the life of an innocent man; . . . his reflex was to hide behind the "Code of Professional Responsibility." He reminded his auditors that his reactions were all quite consistent with the Code. . . . Would he really let an innocent man be executed? "Absolutely . . . people die every day. It may sound harsh, but we have values to serve."

In retelling this story, I do not mean to suggest that every lawyer would respond like Mr. Neal (indeed there is some doubt about the strength or accuracy of his interpretation of the Code of Professional Responsibility) or that his response is in any sense the product of deficiencies in his legal education.[9] Rather, I suggest that Mr. Neal's response exemplifies what it means to "think like a lawyer," and it shows the way law is most often taught in law school and the way lawyers learn the conventions of their profession.[10]

Law schools generally try hard to undo the naive, innocent impulses of their entering students, in particular their impulse to think about law in moral or political terms.[11] Much of the effort of law professors is devoted to differentiating law from moral reasoning or political argument, to focusing the mind of the would-be lawyer on the content of the positive law, and to teaching the skills of manipulating, distinguishing, and evading rules.[12] Although this is, even in law schools, contested terrain, and although many influential legal philosophers continue to press the case for connecting law to moral argument,[13] the goal of professional education remains constant—to sever the connection between the question of what is good or right and what the law permits or prohibits.

Mr. Neal's way of thinking is the antithesis of the humane judgment and political engagement that teaching law in the liberal arts should seek to cultivate. Law teaching in this setting works to reveal the very connection of the legal with the ethical and the political, which law schools try to mystify and undo.[14] Crossing the boundary from professional school to the liberal arts thus frees the legal scholar from preoccupation with techniques for manipulating rules. It provides an arena in which the complex, contingent, and varied ways in which law expresses, and/or represses, moral judgment and political position can be brought to the center of concern.[15]

In doing this, students are asked to think about how their visions of justice and the good polity can be translated from abstract commitments into a community's taken-for-granted, governing rules. They are asked to keep normative concerns perpetually at the front of their thinking and to ground them in practical efforts to create communities in which persons with different moral and political visions can live together. They are invited, if you will, into the mess of moral and political life and reminded that the just community, if it is ever to earn such a name, cannot be constructed by people with an unquestioning reverence for laws or, for that matter, any other set of rules, roles, and conventions.

There is no certainty, of course, that such teaching sticks, or even that teaching law is a particularly good way to cultivate these concerns. Indeed, from my experience teaching *Palsgraf*, sometimes I have my doubts. Moreover, I know that many of my best students will choose to make their careers in law and that some, all too eagerly, may end up speaking Mr. Neal's lines. As a result, I occasionally imagine that it would be better for everyone if students got their professional education in law first and then went to college. In that way, teaching law outside the professional school would provide a chance to engage in a little counter-socialization, to carry on a guerrilla war against the effort that law schools make to turn otherwise sensitive, decent human beings into lawyers like Mr. Neal, persons who cling so tenaciously to rule and convention that they can countenance the sacrifice of innocent life.[16]

Yet the story of law teaching inside and outside law schools is not quite as simple as the us/them narrative I have thus far presented. Law schools have lived, almost since their inception, in an ambivalent relation with the organized profession and with the universities in which they are housed.[17] That ambivalence concerns the central question of how much of law teaching could, or should, be other than an entry way into the world of legal practice; it also concerns what legal practice requires in the way of training and preparation. This is not to say that law teachers never take on law in a broader, more intellectually capacious way. Many do. It is only to say that there is a certain limiting of vision and cramping of style that come with the territory marked out by the professional school.

DISSIDENT VOICES: LIBERAL ARTS ENVY IN LEGAL EDUCATION

Despite my effort to distinguish legal scholarship in the liberal arts from professional education in law, it is, of course, important to acknowledge that some within law schools are now displaying what I might call liberal arts envy. Take, for example, Paul Kahn's *The Cultural Study of Law: Reconstructing Legal Scholarship*. Calling for the "reconstruction" of legal scholarship, pointing the way for "cultural" analysis of what Kahn sometimes labels the "rule of law" and at other times simply "law's rule," he quite rightly asks "Would a legal scholar who purports to suspend belief in law's rule—even as a program of reform—be welcome in the nation's law schools?" Advocating the development of a discipline in which law could rightfully take its place alongside philosophy, economics, or politics as a pillar of scholarly inquiry, he observes that "legal scholars are not studying law, they are doing it."[18]

The development of "a discipline of study outside of the practice of law" depends, Kahn contends, on a reorientation of the scholarly ambitions of law professors (2). Instead of focusing their attention on the project of improving the law, they should make room for a more purely academic effort to understand the place of law in culture, its power over the imagination of citizens, and its relative importance, as against politics on the one hand and love on the other, in colonizing the human imagination. In Kahn's new conception of legal scholarship, "all questions of reform—the traditional end of legal study—are bracketed" (2). Comparing the situation of legal scholarship at the end twentieth century with the situation of religious studies at the end of the nineteenth, he notes, that

> until the turn of the twentieth century, the study of Christianity was not an intellectual discipline. It was, instead, a part of religious practice. Its aim was the progressive realization of a Christian order in the world. . . . Only when the theological project became capable of suspending belief in the object of its study could a real discipline of religious study emerge. . . . Similarly, the scholar of law's rule should not be asked whether law is the expression of the will of the popular sovereign and thus a form of self-government. These are propositions internal to the systems of belief. A scholarly discipline of the cultural form approaches these propositions not from the perspective of their validity, but from the perspective of the meaning they have for the individual within the community of belief. (2–3)

"Suspending belief in the object of its study" is a wonderfully evocative phrase to describe the attitude that Kahn rightly suggests must characterize a genuinely academic discipline called law. In this suspension of belief, legal scholars can focus their attention "on the intellectual project of understanding a culture of law" (5). The central issue for such a project is, in Kahn's view, "not whether law makes us better off, but rather what it is that the law makes us" (6). "A new discipline of law," he argues, "needs to conceive its object of study and its own relationship to that object in a way that does not, at the same moment, commit the scholar to those practices constitutive of the legal order" (27).

As Kahn lays out what he takes to be the central focus of a kind of legal scholarship freed from the professional project, he compares the work of such scholarship to the work of cultural anthropology.[19] He asserts that *"the question* that defines a cultural discipline of law is: What are the conceptual conditions that make possible that practice that we understand as the rule of law?" (36, emphasis added). As he elaborates this question, he suggests that legal scholarship ought to identify the forms of understanding that "make possible the range of behaviors that we characterize as living under the rule of law" (37). The "ambition" of the new discipline that Kahn seeks to advance is to combine genealogical and architectural analyses in order to make explicit "those structures of thought by which we organize space when we live our lives under the rule of law" (65).

In issuing this call, Kahn joins an ongoing struggle over the nature and proper institutional location of legal scholarship in the extended university.[20] *The Cultural Study of Law* may very well turn out to be one of those galvanizing intellectual moments, giving voice to sentiments already present but not previously given such a striking and powerful articulation, a rallying point for an entire generation of young law professors. Indeed it would not be surprising were it to draw forth a Paul Carrington–like rebuke—"Get thee from the cathedral"—from defenders of the mainstream vision of professional legal education.[21]

THE WORK OF LEGAL SCHOLARS IN THE LIBERAL ARTS

From my vantage point, situated outside a law school, there is something odd and unsettling about Kahn's book.[22] He writes as if much of what he desires is not already being done, as if the kind of mapping of the cultural life of law for which he calls were not already a substantial component of interdisciplinary legal scholarship, as if the effort to nurture legal study in the liberal arts were not already well under way.

Legal scholars in the liberal arts have for a long time been doing what Kahn advocates, and Kahn's work tells us little about the challenges that face those who teach law in the liberal arts. The legal scholar in the liberal arts escapes the constraints of traditional legal education, constraints that Kahn so vividly portrays, only to face a different set of challenges, in particular the challenge of preprofessionalism, of students who are already primed and eager to think like lawyers or who believe that the path to the Supreme Court begins in their first year of college. Some of these students come to my classes with the view that law is to be found in some encyclopedic compilation that, if only I would produce it, would provide security, certainty, and a refuge from the confusions they find in their other classes.[23] One sees in students, at a very early stage, then, the will to have law simply be a matter of rules and to turn rule following into a way of living and the anchor of social life.

Other students, not altogether different in temperament, come to my classes with the belief that learning law is easy. For them every legal question is merely a more formal version of commonsense moral judgment. Such students generally bring with them an unarticulated sense of the nature of law's boundaries. For them the question of boundaries is, of course, not yet a question of professional identity or career; it is, instead, a question of the way moral and political judgments inform and shape legal ones, and of the permeability or resistance of law to their own sense of right and wrong. For these students, the idea that law should be connected to morals and politics is both obvious and welcome. They are, however, perplexed when they are introduced to the messiness of moral judgment and political argument, and to the complex ways in which law resists as well as incorporates such judgments and arguments.[24]

For these students and others, teaching law involves an effort to make the familiar and the seemingly easy strange and uncomfortable. One begins where they feel comfortable and goes on to make their thinking about law more complex by making the subject of law more difficult. Thus I place the nature of law's boundaries at the center of my teaching concerns and, in so doing, begin by puzzling out law's ambivalent and shifting, although undeniable, relation to morality and politics.

On the Problematic Relationships of Morality, Politics, and Law

Law's boundaries are sometimes imagined to be almost completely permeable to moral concerns. Law, at least the law of democratic societies, is thought by some to reflect judgments shared by political majorities: to be, if you will, an apt reflection of democratic preferences. For others, law is more than the reflection of such fleeting preferences. It is, when properly understood, the embodiment of fundamental and enduring ethical commitments and moral judgments. Although these views differ in identifying the source of law, they share an understanding of law as open and responsive to outside forces.

Paralleling these understandings is a somewhat different view, a belief that law respects, or should respect, the claims of individual conscience, and that it should permit, if not encourage, individuals to escape its constraints when rules conflict with conscience. One hears the voice of Antigone opposing Creon's will in the name of family, honor, and fidelity to the gods' laws; one hears Thoreau's insistence that the only life worth living is a life in which conscience is valued and followed, in which man is "thoughtfree, fancyfree, imagination-free," and in which the "only obligation which I have a right to assume is to do at any time what I think is right."[25] Law's boundaries, then, should be open.

For the teacher of law these are difficult matters. One tries to show how law both mirrors and helps to constitute our political preferences and our moral understandings. One tries to illuminate the ways law is both resistant and permissive in dealing with the claims of conscience. It is, in fact, this capacity of law to be many things at once that needs to be communicated in order to counter the view that law is the final terrain of stability and certainty and the last bastion for those seeking externally imposed answers.[26]

This requires looking at law close up; it requires literary readings of legal texts. Here another disciplinary boundary is crossed as students are invited to become familiar with the judicial opinion as both rhetorical performance and interpretable artifact.[27] Students are invited to inquire about the language of law as well as the way law constructs and understands the world beyond its boundaries.

Among the cases I teach is Yania v. Bigan.[28] Although Yania, unlike *Palsgraf*, is neither a classic of legal education nor the written product of famous judges, it provides a fine illustration of the rhetorical ingenuity of law. It seems that Yania and Bigan were both engaged in stripmining coal. As part of that business, large cuts or trenches were created to expose deposits of coal beneath the earth's surface. The trenches filled with water, which had to be pumped out regularly. One day Yania visited Bigan at his stripmining site to discuss what the Pennsylvania Supreme Court calls a "business matter." While Yania was there, Bigan asked him to help start a pump in one of the trenches. After some dispute, and apparently without explanation, Yania jumped from the bank of the trench into the water, falling approximately eighteen feet and drowning (318).

In the ensuing suit, Yania's widow sought damages for the wrongful death of her husband and claimed that

> the death by drowning of . . . [Yania] was caused entirely by the
> acts of [Bigan] . . . in urging, enticing, taunting and inveigling
> [Yania] to jump into the water. . . . After [Yania] was in the
> water, a highly dangerous position, having been induced and inveigled therein by [Bigan], [Bigan] failed and neglected to take
> reasonable steps and action to protect or assist [Yania] or extricate
> [Yania] from the dangerous position in which [Bigan] had placed
> him. (318–19)

The court, invoking the judicial equivalent of the maxim that "sticks and stones can break my bones but names can never hurt me," quickly discounted the first part of the claim by suggesting that Yania was an adult "in full possession of all his mental faculties": taunting and enticement could not in themselves constitute "actionable negligence," even where they result in demonstrable harm (319n1).

The court found the second part, concerning the failure to rescue, only somewhat more troublesome. It continued to insist that Yania had "voluntarily placed himself in the way of danger . . . [and thus] the result of his ignorance, or of his mistake, must rest with himself" (322). The court went on, however, to draw a sharp distinction between what it saw as Bigan's limited legal obligations and his more extensive moral duties. It concluded that althouogh Bigan had no legal duty in the absence of a recognized legal responsibility, he did have a moral "obligation or duty to go to [Yania's] rescue" (322). Like James Neal's insistence that his obligation as a lawyer was defined solely by the rules, and Cardozo's opinion denying compensation to the injured Mrs. Palsgraf, the court insulated Bigan from any legal duty by linking the scope of that duty to his lack of legal responsibility for placing Yania in the position of peril from which he claimed a right to be rescued.

Confronted with *Yania*, students almost instantaneously choose up sides on the question of whether there should or should not be such a solid boundary between law and morals. Some insist that the court got it right—that Bigan might be condemned for his moral obtuseness but not punished for a harm he did not bring about. Others believe that Bigan should be subject to a legal punishment for his unforgivable indifference. Instinctively, students want to say what the rule should be; they want to argue it out on grounds of morality, the place of law in society, or the requirements of fairness. It is this desire that becomes the stuff of legal education in professional schools, where it is first highlighted and then challenged in the hope of domesticating it.[29]

But there is another issue often ignored in such discussions and in the law school approach, an issue that suggests, in a direct way, the vexing quality of law's inescapable relationship to morality. This issue surfaces in the *Yania* court's own rhetorical strategy. It is that court, after all, that discusses the nature of Bigan's moral duty. The court does so even though its jurisdiction does not extend to the realm of ethics and even though the discussion is irrelevant to its own understanding of the correct legal disposition of the case. By asserting its right to make such a moral judgment, the court blurs the boundary it seems to want to create. It thus brings morality into the law even as it tries to assert its irrelevance.[30] The allegedly clear boundary between law and morals becomes less clear when one sees, in this case, that the realm of ethics is placed first outside the law, as a separate sphere of obligation, and then inside the law, making a claim that the court, I think erroneously, works to resist.

One might, of course, find that in *Yania* the court simply said too much, that it suffered from its own excesses, and that a more prudent and careful opinion could have avoided this blurring of boundaries. Perhaps. But there is more here than one court's lack of artfulness. The blurring of boundaries between the legal and the ethical is not an isolated and idiosyncratic phenomenon, a problem limited to the Pennsylvania Supreme Court. It is a historically specific but nonetheless important aspect of the life of law itself.[31]

Demonstrating the relationship of moral concerns and legal judgments, and the blurring of boundaries that arises in the very attempt to separate the two, does not of course explain the "proper" resolution of any particular case. Yet it does expand the agenda beyond lawyerlike searches for relevant precedents and existing rules of law. It opens the way to explore connections between the law's principles and broader conceptions of the good. In so doing, it brings together the study of law's rhetoric and performance with enduring questions of political and moral philosophy. It gives law teachers and undergraduate students of law the space to explore those issues, and it opens up for them the question of why law has insisted for so long on its distinctiveness and on the irrelevance of such questions. We take as our subject, then, law's own response to morality, even as we try to illuminate the way the two express themselves in each other's domain.

Language and the Law

The kind of close reading necessary to understand the interactions just described means that teaching about law inevitably raises questions about language, about the power of words to bind legal decision makers.[32] This attention to language is brought forth by judges themselves, in their denial that they need to make moral judgments, and in their insistence that judicial decisions are "compelled" by law itself.[33] Judges to this day regularly deny the role of human agency, namely, their own, in speaking the law. They act as if they have attained Thayer's version of a lawyer's paradise, "where all words have a fixed, precisely ascertained meaning; where men may express their purposes, not only with accuracy but with fullness; and where, if the writer has been careful, a lawyer, having a document referred to him, may sit in his chair, inspect the text, and answer all questions without raising his eyes."[34]

Such judges would keep our eyes fixed on the edifice of law itself, like Dorothy in the *Wizard of Oz* just before the revelation of the little man behind the smoke-blowing, noise-making, awe-inspiring visage of Oz. In so doing they command another crossing of disciplinary boundaries, this time to investigate the meaning and power of language in law; for, as Peter Pouncey put it, "the very formalization of language in legal procedures removes it from the regular give and take of daily discourse, renders it arcane, and gives it a kind of institutional force; the language of the law moves beyond verbal communication, and becomes a kind of enactment, like the recitation of a spell."[35]

The teacher of law in the liberal arts is driven to confront the vast mysteries of language itself, to engage again the play and plasticity of law's own language.[36] This is difficult for students who want to believe in the determinate meanings of words and the power of language to fix and transmit those meanings across history and cultures.[37] The rich engagement with the twists and turns of language, and with the almost infinite possibilities of shaping new meanings out of the arrangement of particular words, which may be cultivated in literary studies, is all too quickly abandoned when students confront the hard face of the law. Like Kafka's man from the country, they are transfixed, frozen, and held before law by its "possibility and impossibility, its readability and unreadability, its necessity and its prohibition."[38]

Here students need to be prodded and inveigled to reawaken their literary imagination. Here, paradoxically, teaching law in the liberal arts most resembles the job of the teacher of lawyers who imparts the following two messages to his students: first, when the law seems, on its face, to be on your side, insist that there is, and can be, one and only one meaning; second, when that language stands in your way, make it dance and insist that literal meaning has no place in this or any other universe.

Occasionally, but all too rarely, judges themselves make visible the plasticity of legal language and, in so doing, provide an antidote to the spell that law casts on young minds.[39] Occasionally they explore and explain the dangers of Thayer's fantasy as they reason their way through particular cases. Thus the California Supreme Court forcefully turned its back on such a fantasy when, in a case arising from an alleged breach of contract, it argued that contractual obligations flow only from the intentions of the contracting parties rather than from the words of the contract.[40] The court went on to explain that it is not feasible to determine intention from words alone, saying that "if words had absolute and constant referents, it might be possible to discover contractual intentions in the words themselves. . . . Words, however, do not have absolute and constant referents. . . . Judicial belief in the possibility of perfect . . . expression . . . is a remnant of a primitive faith in the inherent potency and inherent meaning of words" (38).

Judges sometimes openly display their own manipulation of legal language. For instance, Judge Jerome Frank, in a contract case involving the so-called parol evidence rule, said, "candor compels the admission that, were we enthusiastic devotees of that rule, we might so construe the record as to bring this case within the rule's scope."[41] For the law teacher, these are precious moments. When the indeterminacy of legal language is thus exposed, students confront law as something more than a system of rules. They see it as a system of human choices and moral or political judgments shaped, constrained by, and constructed out of social institutions and practices.[42]

In precipitating such a confrontation, law teachers profit from the Tocquevillean idea that legal learning is as indispensable to the cultivation of democratic citizens as it is to the practicing lawyer.[43] Although the legal learning that Tocqueville had in mind bears little resemblance to the kind of learning available to students in liberal arts colleges, a partial solution to the perplexing question of how to cross the boundary separating law schools from the liberal arts is suggested by Tocqueville's discussion of the kind of learning once associated with serving on a jury. Indeed it was on my first reading of his description of the jury "as a gratuitous public school" (364) that I could imagine what law teaching in a liberal arts college might really be about.

Tocqueville wrote about the jury and jury service to defend another boundary crossing, this time a crossing represented by the entrance of amateurs, of citizens temporarily extricated from their daily pursuits and preoccupations, into the domain of law itself. The jury, Tocqueville wrote, cannot fail to exercise a powerful influence upon the national character.

> The jury . . . serves to communicate the spirit of the judges to the minds of all citizens; and this spirit, with the habits which attend it, is the soundest preparation for free institutions. It imbues all classes with a respect for the thing judged, and with the notion of right. . . . It teaches men to practice equity; every man learns to judge his neighbor as he would himself be judged. . . . The jury teaches every man not to recoil before the responsibility of his own actions. . . . It invests each citizen with a kind of magistracy; it makes them all feel the duties which they are bound to discharge toward society, and the part they take in its government. By obliging men to turn their attention to other affairs than their own, it rubs off that private selfishness which is the rust of society. (364)

As I understand Tocqueville, he believed that what the citizen learns from his contact with the law is the discipline of judgment rather than a body of rules or doctrines. It is, after all, the "spirit" of the judges that is communicated, the spirit that understands the need to empathize with the person judged even as one accepts the responsibility of imposing judgment. The discipline of judgment requires making particular decisions by applying abstract ideas of right conduct to concrete human experiences with all of their ambiguities. Teaching law then involves teaching practical judgment, teaching the discipline of making judgments that count in the world. These judgments can result in the confiscation of property, the loss of liberty, and all too often, the sacrifice of life. Encountering law's rigors and consequences focuses the mind as no mere philosophical exercise can do.

Tocqueville's musings about the jury and his hope that it would serve as a school "to form the judgment and increase the natural intelligence of the people" (364) set a large agenda for the imagination of any teacher, young or old; for me, however, they were the key I had been looking for, a powerful statement of what it might mean to teach law outside a professional school. Nevertheless, Tocqueville's reflections do not sit well with me in all their particulars and nuances. They are a little too patrician, a little too respectful of the judges, a little too nostalgia inducing, and a little too suspicious of the intelligence of the citizens. Tocqueville was too comfortable in his assumption that citizens had something to learn rather than something to teach, too concentrated on the problems of those who must decide the fate of others, and alas, too removed from the experience of those being judged, those whose fate is being decided, who will feel the pain inflicted after law's judgments are made.[44] Crossing the boundary from law school to liberal arts is not rightly done unless and until that pain is made clear, made part of teaching law, in a way that might never happen where training lawyers is the main order of business.

Interrogating Law's Violence

Oddly enough, it is a voice from within a professional school that spoke most eloquently about the need to acknowledge this pain in our understanding of law. As Robert Cover, a professor of law at Yale, put it, the work of law always "takes place in a field of pain and death."[45] This stunning phrase is not merely rhetorical. Cover himself recognized that law's relationship to pain and death is deeply perplexing. Law deals in pain and death as a "counterpunch" to the pain and death that is done outside law. And law seems to dispense pain and deal in death with great reluctance and considerable scrupulousness, imposing on itself elaborate procedures and providing various safeguards and protections for its potential victims.

Because Cover's reminder has had a powerful effect in shaping my scholarship and teaching, I explicate it in some detail. His essay "Violence and the Word" calls for an expansion of the concerns of the legal academic, a shift in understanding, a movement away from the familiar (although by no means easy) parsing of judicial opinions toward an understanding and articulation of law from the perspective of its acts, not just its words. Cover tried to think about the doing of law as more than a problem for judges and jurors. He asked how law is given meaning by the convict sent off to await execution, by the welfare mother told she no longer qualifies for state assistance, by people like Mrs. Palsgraf, or by the homeless man who is branded as a loiterer and told to move on. As Cover put it, "the acts of judges and jurors signal and occasion the imposition of violence upon others. A judge articulates her understanding of a text, and as a result, somebody loses his freedom, his property, his children, even his life. Interpretations in law also constitute justifications for violence which has already occurred or which is about the occur. When interpreters finish their work they frequently leave behind victims whose lives have been torn apart by these organized, social practices of violence" (1601).

Cover warned that "neither legal interpretation nor the violence it occasions can be properly understood apart from one another" (1601). On the other side of the boundary separating what I teach from the education of lawyers, too little attention is paid to the violence that accompanies the interpretive act.[46] This is not to say that it is ever easy to focus attention on that violence and the pain it produces: in the liberal arts, as in professional legal education, one typically confronts students who identify themselves more easily with law's interpreters than with those who are on the receiving end of law's violence.

But that is more than a local difficulty. It is, I think, nearly impossible, here or anywhere, to convey the pain that law routinely imposes because, as Elaine Scarry reminds us,

> for the person in pain, so incontestably and unnegotiably present is it that "having pain" may come to be thought of as the most vibrant example of what it is to "have certainty," while for the other person it is so elusive that hearing about pain may exist as the primary model of what it is "to have doubt." Thus pain comes unshareably into our midst as at once that which cannot be denied and that which cannot be confirmed. Whatever pain achieves, it achieves in part through its unshareability, and it ensures this unshareability in part through its resistance to language.[47]

Despite this difficulty, one can describe the nature of law's enterprise. Here the philosopher's effort to connect law with morals and politics, and the linguist's concern to explore the interpretive conventions as well as the plasticity of legal language, gives way to an interest in the social organization of violence and law's role in it.

Law's role in the social organization of violence begins with its own effort to substitute an organized, orderly, perhaps domesticated violence for the violence imagined to exist outside the law.[48] One of the most important tasks of my teaching is to explore with students the way law constantly makes and remakes our imaginings of violence on the other side of law's boundary and keeps those images before our eyes. In making and remaking those images, law authorizes its own use of force and its own imposition of pain as gentler, or at least more rational, and thus preferable.

The story of a Hobbesian state of nature is explored not as an accurate recounting of a particular human experience or time in human history but as a lawconstructing narrative, a narrative kept alive by law itself.[49] Law by its own account saves us from "unbridled passion and atrocious crimes" by asserting its jurisdiction over us and by demanding our acquiescence.[50] This imperialistic tendency of law is exemplified in the famous opinion of Judge Baldwin in *United States v. Holmes*.[51]

Holmes was a sailor who was tried for murder because he had saved his own life by throwing some passengers overboard from an overcrowded, leaking lifeboat. Baldwin faced the question of whether Holmes's action could be justified. The claim was made that Holmes was essentially in a state of nature when he found himself adrift at sea on the verge of starvation. Baldwin refused to honor this claim and asserted that municipal law is subverted by the law of nature, but because no rule of municipal law makes homicide, in such cases, criminal. It is "the law of the land . . . that regulates the social duties of men . . . everywhere. Everywhere are civilized men under its protection, everywhere, subject to its authority" (1028). Law "everywhere," law, the indispensable ingredient of our social lives, thus explains and seeks to justify both its imperialism and its own violent nature.

It is precisely the ability of law's words to turn themselves into violent deeds, and to do so on a regular basis, that distinguishes law from philosophy or literary criticism and commands yet another crossing of disciplinary boundaries. All too often students take for granted what is essential in any legal act, the social organization and structure that turn word into deed, that take the judicial declaration of rights and duties and turn it into effective action. As Cover puts it,

> the system guarantees the judge massive amounts of force. . . . It guarantees . . . a relatively faithful adherence to the word of the judge in the deeds carried out against the prisoner. . . . I think it is unquestionably the case in the United States that most prisoners walk into prison because they know they will be dragged or beaten into prison if they did not walk. . . . The experience of the prisoner is, from the outset, an experience of being violently dominated, and it is colored from the beginning by the fear of being violently treated.[52]

As a teacher of law in the liberal arts, one also, then, must be a teacher of the sociology of law. Teaching law to undergraduates means helping them see the sociological connections between law's words and rhetoric, especially the way it portrays violence outside its boundaries, and the pain and death in which it deals. One begins by showing how law itself speaks about violence, where law's violence is made visible, and where it is kept in the shadows. In reading law, one typically finds a vivid portrait of the violence of offenders, of those like Holmes who defy law's jurisdiction. At the same time, one encounters virtual silence about the violence done by or in the name of the law. One looks in vain for even an imaginative account of what it is like to be sentenced, incarcerated, or executed in the name of the law.

Nowhere is this absence more conspicuous or more telling than in the case of *Francis v. Resweber*.[53] Willie Francis committed murder and was, as punishment, sentenced to be executed for his crime. As the court recounts the facts, "Francis was prepared for execution and on May 3, 1946 . . . was placed in the official electric chair of the State of Louisiana. . . . The executioner threw the switch but, presumably because of some mechanical difficulty, death did not result" (460). The case came to the Supreme Court of the United States when Willie Francis sought to prevent the carrying out of a "second" execution. He argued that subjecting him to such a procedure would be both a denial of due process and a form of cruel and unusual punishment.

Justice Reed, writing for the majority, carefully scrutinized the behavior of the state officials who had participated in the first "execution" and concluded that they had carried out their duties in a "careful and humane manner" (462). He then held that the Constitution permitted what he called "necessary suffering" incident even to the most humane techniques of capital punishment, and he suggested that the fact of the first attempt at electrocution would not "add an element of cruelty to a subsequent execution" (464). For Reed it was critical that there was no "purpose to inflict unnecessary pain" on Willie Francis; the state was simply attempting to carry out the order of the trial court (462).

The state could not, in Reed's view, be held accountable for what he described as "an unforeseeable accident [that] prevented the prompt consummation of the sentence" (462).[54] It is as if, for Reed, the issue was whether the state itself would be punished by being deprived of a second chance to execute Willie Francis. As a result, he worked hard to understand and describe the actions and intentions of state officials, and he conjured up a picture of diligent, even compassionate executioners frustrated by an accident "for which no man is to blame" (462).

And what of Willie Francis? He hardly even appears in Reed's opinion. We learn little about him except that he was a "colored citizen of Louisiana" (462). His absence initially seems quite unremarkable to students perhaps already conditioned by claims about law's distanced objectivity—by claims that law attends to rules, not persons. Braced subsequently by Cover's essay, however, they reconsider what it means to render Francis virtually invisible in the course of deciding his fate.

Reed does tell us that preparation for a second execution attempt placed no undue psychological strain on Francis and that he was an "unfortunate victim of this accident" (464). But the issue for Francis, of course, was not just the pain that he had already suffered; it was as much the anguish of contemplating the state's second effort to end his life and the pain he would experience when the state, with the Supreme Court's blessing, electrocuted him for the second time.

Indeed, so remote was that pain from the Court's consideration that it was only in a footnote, late in the dissenting opinion of Justice Burton, that any reference was made to what the first, unsuccessful execution attempt did to Willie Francis. There we are told that his "lips puffed out and he groaned and jumped so that the chair came off the floor" (490n2). Yet this material, taken from affidavits by witnesses to the first electrocution, was included by Burton not for its constitutional significance but simply to point out what he called "conflict of testimony" (490).

Francis illustrates Cover's argument that, in the business of doing law,

> the perpetrator and victim of organized violence . . . undergo achingly disparate significant experiences. For the perpetrator, the pain and fear are remote, unreal, and largely unshared. They are, therefore, almost never made part of the interpretive artifact, such as the judicial opinion. On the other hand, for those who impose the violence, the justification is important, real and carefully cultivated. Conversely, for the victim, the justification for the violence recedes in reality and significance in proportion to the overwhelming reality of the pain and fear that is suffered.[55]

I ask students to try to understand the perspective and position of those most concerned with justification, and the ways that concern may not be shared equally by all participants in the doing of law's business. In this way I can express my endorsement of, and discomfort with, Tocqueville's understanding of the powerful way that law is learned when one comes in contact with the "spirit of the judges." I can present what is almost always left out when law professors teach lawyer's law: the law as it is seen and experienced by the deathrow inmate, the welfare mother, Mrs. Palsgraf, or the homeless person living on the street. My students and I can explore what law would be like if we built legal theory from those experiences; we can also explore the way law's connection to moral judgment and political argument would change if those voices were made part of the conversation.

Law teaching in the liberal arts traditionally has been the prerogative of several disciplines—history, philosophy, political science—each of which takes up some aspect of the law as part of its exploration of its own distinctive disciplinary terrain. Law-related courses, such as constitutional and international law, legal and constitutional history, anthropology of law, deviance and criminology, and philosophy of law, have long been found among the offerings of social science and humanities departments. These courses cover several aspects of law and make important contributions to legal study by providing in-depth analyses of various legal phenomena.

They tend, however, to treat law merely as an example of something outside law itself and to take it apart focusing on this or that aspect of the phenomenon. For example, although legal study enriches the study of politics, much of what constitutes law (e.g., its hermeneutic and rhetorical dimensions) cannot be brought within the confines of a discipline devoted to matters political. Similarly, although philosophers may use legal materials to work out or illustrate problems in ethics or epistemology, the power and complexity of law is more than a matter of moral argument or a particular way of knowing and apprehending the world. Thus the ambition of legal scholarship in the liberal arts is often to get outside of—or to be in an unusual juxtaposition with—traditional disciplinary activities. It involves more than just another interdisciplinary venture, although it certainly draws on a variety of disciplines. Thinking about law on the other side of the boundary marked off by professional education means finding the place where moral philosophy (with its arguments about the right and the good), literary theory (with its understandings of the meanings and uses of language), and political science (with its understandings of the nature of social organization and of the harsh face of power) come together, and it means claiming that place as the space of legal scholarship itself.

Today there are signs of an emerging interdisciplinary conception of legal scholarship that moves away from professional concerns and disciplinary perspectivism and toward a new synthesis. This synthesis grounds legal scholarship in the central concerns of the liberal arts, namely, the effort to foster a general understanding of culture, history, science, and social organization and serious inquiry into normative commitments, visions of the good, and competing arguments for responding to human and natural failings. As the late A. Bartlett Giamatti wrote when he was president of Yale,

> The law is not simply a set of forensic or procedural skills. It is a vast body of knowledge, compounded of historical material, modes of textual analysis and various philosophical concerns. It

is a formal inquiry into our behavior and ideals that proceeds essentially through language. It is a humanistic study—both as a body of material wrought of words and a set of analytic skills and procedural claims involving linguistic mastery. . . . To argue, therefore, for [law in the liberal arts] is not to argue for "professional" training in college in the techniques, accumulated lore and diverse iterations of method that training for the profession also entails. It is rather to argue for philosophic, textual and historical concerns. . . . It is to argue that the medium of cohesion and conflict, ligature and litigation, that is the law, must be part of the educated person's perspective in order to appreciate one of the grandest, systematic ways of thinking human beings have developed for their survival.[56]

In the intellectual space that Giamatti marks out, legal scholarship in the liberal arts defines the study of law as more than a technical, lawyerly activity. In the rare moments when it is done right, it focuses the mind, stretches the imagination, and brings students close to an understanding of the way thought and argument are translated into social action. Here the teaching of law truly crosses boundaries and finds its real home in the liberal arts. Here the authority to interpret *Palsgraf, Yania,* and other cases, and to make Mrs. Palsgraf and Willie Francis part of the conversation about law, does not derive from the institutional authority of the law school. It derives from the moral engagement, insistent curiosity, and sympathetic imagination that the liberal arts call forth. And, finally, it allows those who teach law in the liberal arts to begin to articulate an answer to those who would challenge their credentials and their aspirations to be "real" law teachers.

NOTES

° This is a revised and expanded version of an essay first published in *Teaching What We Do: Essays by Amherst College Faculty,* ed. Peter Pouncey (Amherst, Mass.: Amherst College Press, 1991).

1. For a useful discussion of the Palsgraf case, see John Noonan, *Persons and Masks of the Law: Cardozo, Holmes, Jefferson, and Wyche as Makers of the Masks* (New York: Farrar, Straus and Giroux, 1976), chap. 4.

2. *Palsgraf v. Long Island Railroad,* 248 N.Y. 339, 341 (1928).

3. On the impersonality of law, see Noonan, *Persons and Masks.* Also Richard Danzig, *The Capability Problem in Contract Law: Further Readings on Well-Known Cases* (Mineola, N.Y.: Foundation Press, 1978).

4. On the reputation of Judge Cardozo, see Richard Posner, *Cardozo: A Study in Reputation* (Chicago: University of Chicago Press, 1990).

5. For a discussion of the social perception of tort litigants, see Neil Vidmar, "Maps, Gaps, Sociolegal Scholarship, and the Tort Reform Debate," in *Social Science, Social Policy, and the Law,* ed. Patricia Ewick, Robert Kagan, and Austin Sarat (New York: Russell Sage Foundation, 1999), 184–85.

6. See Robert Stevens, *Law School: Legal Education in America from the 1850s to 1980s* (Chapel Hill: University of North Carolina Press, 1983).

7. See Harold Berman, *On the Teaching of Law in the Liberal Arts Curriculum* (Brooklyn: Foundation Press, 1956).

8. For a further elaboration, see Austin Sarat, "Traditions and Trajectories in Law and Humanities Scholarship," *Yale Journal of Law and the Humanities* 10 (1998): 401.

9. For a different view, see William Simon, *The Practice of Justice: A Theory of Lawyers' Ethics* (Cambridge: Harvard University Press, 1998).

10. For a description of what it means to think like a lawyer, see Karl Llewellyn, *The Bramble Bush: On Our Law and Its Study* (New York: Oceana Publications, 1960). William Simon, "The Ideology of Advocacy: Procedural Justice and Professional Ethics," *Wisconsin Law Review* (1978): 29.

11. See Stuart Scheingold and Austin Sarat, "Something to Believe In: Professionalism, Politics, and Cause Lawyers," (Stanford: Stanford University Press, 2004), chap. 3.

12. For a critique of this approach, see Anthony Kronman, *The Lost Lawyer: The Failing Ideals of the Legal Profession* (Cambridge: Harvard University Press, 1993).

13. E.g., David Luban, *Lawyers and Justice: An Ethical Study* (Princeton: Princeton University Press, 1988).

14. Berman, *Teaching of Law,* 52.

15. For a discussion of this process in legal reasoning, see Duncan Kennedy, *A Critique of Adjudication: Fin de Siècle* (Cambridge: Harvard University Press, 1997).

16. For an interesting critique of this way of thinking, see Deborah Rhode, *In the Interests of Justice: Reforming the Legal Profession* (New York: Oxford University Press, 2000).

17. Stevens, *Law School.*

18. Paul Kahn, *The Cultural Study of Law: Reconstructing Legal Scholarship* (Chicago: University of Chicago Press, 1999), 2–3, 27.

19. The cultural anthropologist, Kahn claims, "suspends her ordinary beliefs and normative commitments; she does not judge the object of her inquiry . . . but pursues each proposition offered by her informants with yet another question" (ibid., 34). For other views of the role of the anthropologist, see James Clifford, *The Predicament of Culture* (Cambridge: Harvard University Press, 1988); James Clifford and George Marcus, eds., *Writing Culture: The Poetics and Politics of Ethnography* (Berkeley: University of California Press, 1986).

20. Berman, *Teaching of Law.*

21. See Paul Carrington, "Of Law and the River," *Journal of Legal Education* 34 (1984): 222, 227. Carrington argues, "When . . . the University accepted responsibility for training professionals, it also accepted a duty to constrain teaching that knowingly dispirits students."

22. For a more complete elaboration of these concerns, see Austin Sarat, "Redirecting Legal Scholarship in Law Schools," *Yale Journal of Law and the Humanities* 12 (2000): 129.

23. On the psychological origins of the search for certainty in law, see Jerome Frank, *Law and the Modern Mind* (New York: Brentano, 1930), 169–97.

24. For an example of such an approach, see Gerald Frug, "Argument as Character," *Stanford Law Review* 40 (1988): 872.

25. Sophocles, *Antigone,* trans. Michael Townsend (New York: Harper and Row, 1962). Henry David Thoreau, *Civil Disobedience* (Harrington Park, N.J.: 5 × 8 Press, 1942).

26. On law's capacity to be, or appear to be, many things at once, see Stanley Fish, "Law Wishes to Have a Formal Existence," in *The Fate of Law,* ed. Austin Sarat and Thomas Kearns (Ann Arbor: University of Michigan Press, 1991).

27. See Robert Ferguson, "The Judicial Opinion as a Literary Genre," *Yale Journal of Law and the Humanities* 2 (1990): 201.

28. *Yania v. Bigan,* 397 Pa. 316 (1959).

29. For a discussion of this process, see Richard Kahlenberg, *Broken Contract: A Memoir of Harvard Law School* (New York: Hill and Wang, 1992).

30. Fish, "Law Wishes to Have a Formal Existence."

31. Ibid.

32. See James Boyd White, "Law as Rhetoric, Rhetoric as Law: The Arts of Cultural and Communal Life," *University of Chicago Law Review* 52 (1985): 684.

33. Lawrence Douglas, "Constitutional Discourse and Its Discontents: An Essay on the Rhetoric of Judicial Review," in *The Rhetoric of Law,* ed. Austin Sarat and Thomas Kearns (Ann Arbor: University of Michigan Press, 1994).

34. James Bradley Thayer, *A Preliminary Treatise on Evidence at the Common* Law (Boston: Little, Brown, 1898), 428–29.

35. Peter Pouncey, letter to Austin Sarat, April 1990.

36. For a discussion of this play and plasticity, see Kennedy, *Critique of Adjudication.*

37. Frank, *Law and the Modern Mind.*

38. Jacques Derrida, "Devant la Loi," in *Kafka and the Contemporary Critical Performance,* ed. Alan Udoff (Bloomington: Indiana University Press, 1987).

39. This phenomena is discussed in Douglas, "Constitutional Discourse," 227–31.

40. *Pacific Gas & Electric Co. v. G. W. Thomas Drayage & Rigging Co.,* 68 Cal. 2d 33 (1968).

41. *Zell v. American Seating,* 138 F.2d 641, 644 (1943).

42. Susan Silbey, "Ideals and Practices in the Study of Law," *Legal Studies Forum* 9 (1985): 7.

43. Alexis de Tocqueville, *Democracy in America,* trans. Henry Reeve (Boston: John Allyn, 1876), chap. 16.

44. For a more complete elaboration of this point, see Austin Sarat and Thomas Kearns, "A Journey through Forgetting: Toward a Jurisprudence of Violence," in Sarat and Kearns, *Fate of Law,,* 269.

45. Robert Cover, "Violence and the Word," *Yale Law Journal* 95 (1986): 1601.

46. See Sarat and Kearns, "Journey through Forgetting."

47. Elaine Scarry, *The Body in Pain* (New York: Oxford University Press, 1985), 4.

48. Sarat and Kearns, "Journey through Forgetting."

49. Ibid.

50. See *Queen v. Dudley & Stephens,* L.R. 14 Q.B.D. 273 (1884).

51. *United States v. Holmes,* 26 F. Cas. 360 (C.C.E.D. Pa. 1842), reprinted in Joseph Goldstein, Alan Dershowitz, and Richard Schwartz, *Criminal Law: Theory and Process* (New York: Free Press, 1974), 1023.

52. Cover, "Violence and the Word," 1608.

53. *Francis v. Resweber,* 329 U.S. 459 (1947). For an interesting description of the case, see Arthur Miller and Jeffrey Bowman, *Death by Installments: The Ordeal of Willie Francis* (Westport, Conn.: Greenwood Press, 1988).

54. Indeed in the only place where Reed tries to come to terms with what the first execution did to Francis he suggests, again relying on the image of the first execution as an accident, that Francis could only have suffered "the identical amount of mental anguish and physical pain [as in] any other occurrence, such as . . . a fire in the cell block" (464). Although Reed described Francis as an "accident victim," the issue for Francis was the future as much as the past. For him what was constitutionally significant was the connection between the violence inflicted on him during the first execution and the violence that the state, with the Supreme Court's blessing, proposed to inflict on him in a second execution.

55. Cover, "Violence and the Word," 1629.

56. Ibid., quoting Giamatti.

TWO

From Technique to Moral Engagement

EXAMPLES OF LEGAL SCHOLARSHIP
IN THE LIBERAL ARTS

MEANING WHAT YOU SAY

JAMES BOYD WHITE

*Only he who knows the empire of might and how
not to respect it is capable of love and justice.*
—Simone Weil

In this essay I talk about a wide range of themes in the hope of establishing a connection among them: writing (including the teaching of writing) and what is at stake, for the writer and the rest of the world, in doing it well or badly; certain forces in our culture—hard to define and understand—that tend to reduce or trivialize human experience, indeed the very value of the human being; the conception of the human being, not trivial at all, that underlies our practices of self-government in general and constitutional democracy in particular; and the idea of justice at work, or potentially at work, in our legal system and its realization—or nonrealization—in the opinions of our courts, especially those opinions of the Supreme Court that elaborate the law of the First Amendment (which of course deals with both speech and writing). I think that these issues, or most of them, are present in every act of speech or writing, every engagement with language. As I hope to show, in each such instance it is a crucial question whether, and in what sense, the speaker or writer can be seen to mean what he is saying.

A preliminary word about the epigraph: it is taken from Simone Weil's famous article "*The Iliad,* Poem of Might," in which she reads that great poem as simultaneously defining and deeply opposing the human desire to dominate, enslave, and destroy other human beings—to use force or might to impose one's will upon them.[1] As I have just suggested, in my view this desire can be present, and destructively so, not only when people use spears and guns and bombs, but in our language, in the expectations we bring to speech and writing. One can deny humanity just as genuinely in the way one speaks as in the way one acts, and organized evil action always depends on forms of thought and speech—ideologies, habits of mind and language, ways of imagining the world—that deny or trivialize the reality and value of human beings, human experience.

I shall start with the writing of the very young, and with the teaching of writing, using some actual passages of student writing collected by David Holbrook in England during the 1960s.[2] The writers are young boys of about twelve, but the questions their writing suggests are present as well in the work of more mature writers, in many fields. Here is one passage; ask yourself how you would respond to this paragraph, and to the boy who wrote it, if you were his teacher.

> We started out on a beautiful morning with a bright sky above us and a cooling south wind. Nature was in her full glory, the air smelt sweet, birds were singing loudly, squirrels scampered up trees at our approach and rabbits' tails disappeared down burrows at our presence. Lambs jumped around friskily tormenting their mothers for nourishment. Cows lay lazily chewing their cud among the buttercups. A little foal galloped alongside her mother on its spindly legs. In another field a ploughman plodded along behind his horses furrowing the field. Butterflies fluttered from flower to flower.
>
> And so our journey went on in the presence of Nature's glory. Oh what a wonderful thing to be alive!
>
> At Langham we refueled ourselves and continued our journey.

As a teacher you would almost have to regard this as unexceptionable writing, indeed as very good: it is grammatical, clear, and full of specific detail. It has a beginning, middle, and end. It has the elegance of alliteration and manifests a certain undeniable energy. What more could you want, especially from a twelve-year-old child?

But look again. There is a sense in which this paragraph is simply a series of unelaborated clichés: beautiful morning, bright sky, cooling wind, nature in her full glory. These are phrases the writer has heard a hundred times, here replicated in their baldest form. He does nothing to make them his own. As for the details we are so eager to praise, in fact they are not organized into anything but consist rather of a list, a list of creatures—birds, squirrels, rabbits, lambs, cows—each doing what is expected of it—singing, scampering, disappearing, jumping, chewing. What relation is established among these actors and activities in this paragraph? What was the relation among them in the real world? There is no shape or sequence here, no sense of how these things actually happened, or in what order: there is no *composition*. When you try to imagine the scene, it has some of the quality of a Disney cartoon— in what other genre would rabbits' tails be constantly disappearing down burrows as the boy walked along? And how many rabbits do you think the boy actually saw, how many of them went down a burrow, and how did he know?

Likewise the lambs: how many did he see, and how many of them were "jumping friskily," how many "tormenting their mothers"? Did he in fact see the buttercups in which the cows were lying? And exactly where were the flowers between which the butterflies were fluttering? In fact, how confident are you that this boy actually took the walk he described? Maybe he just stayed home that afternoon and wrote out the paragraph before dinner.

Obviously I don't mean to pick on this twelve-year-old boy. If there is something troubling here, it is not with him but with the expectations he has been trained to meet, the ways he has been rewarded, the things he has been taught—something wrong, that is, in the world that is shaping him. But in his writing there is a quality simultaneously deeply false and deeply familiar, a quality that shows up in college essays, law school briefs and memos, official publications of all kinds, from university catalogs to EPA releases to judicial opinions, and I think it presents a danger to us all.

Look at the next to last paragraph, where the boy says that it is a wonderful thing to be alive. Of course it is, but this language invites us to ask what kind of life he reflects here: what kind of life as a walker in the woods, what kind of life as a writer? How wonderful is that? And what are we to make of the shift in tone in the very last sentence, from the self-consciously poetic to the utterly matter-of-fact—what does that imply? Has he brought his highly imitative, and in a deep sense insincere, performance to a close just a sentence too early?

Compare the following, also from a twelve-year-old boy:

> Turning the last bend we came to a halt by the river. The village at this time of the year is so unfrequented. Even so, a number of small boys were dipping jam pots into the river to catch minnows. One had caught a crayfish. We propped our bicycles by the buttress at one end of the bridge, and turned round to look at the memorial cross cut in the hill. Then riding on up the opposite side of the valley, we noticed a flock of house-martins wheeling in clusters above a farmhouse. They could not have been in England long, even though most summer visitors arrived early this year. Underneath the overhang of the farmhouse roof a row of mud nests could be seen. Some hung down limp and useless; others were inhabited by sparrows; but a few remained in a fit state for the martins. The slope from then on grew steep—so much so that we stopped for a moment at one bend and rested our bikes on the bank. We were now high above the village, and even the conspicuous white rumps of the martins could hardly be seen. Where the hill was too steep for farmland, Scots pines

were growing. On the move again we emerged from among them into the sunlight at the top of the hill.

What is the difference between these two pieces of writing, and does it really matter? One way to approach that question is to try to look through the writing to the mind of the boy producing it.

Suppose the first writer were your own son: What would you think he was doing when he wrote this? Would you be bothered by its clichéd and empty quality? Perhaps not, I imagine; he is after all succeeding in school, meeting the expectations others have of him, and doing so with great skill and apparent ease. The ability to whip off a paper that gets an A is one that, with certain transformations, will enable him to do well in college or law school, and beyond that in life. He is a successfully socialized person.

Do you have a worry that his mind is being marked by the clichés he so cheerfully uses, that it is learning to run in utterly predictable channels? This is a real question, but I think probably not, or not yet: he has learned how to write stuff he does not mean, could not mean, but, as I imagine him, he knows that perfectly well. This paper has nothing to do with what are to him the important things of life, nothing indeed to do with what happened on that afternoon, whether he took the walk or not. He may write in clichés, but that does not mean he experiences life in that way: the walk, if he took it, may have been full of interest and importance to him, the occasion for observation and reflection and questioning—as may have been whatever he did instead of taking the walk, if he in fact skipped it. The energy of the boy shines through in the exuberance with which he dishes up what his teacher will like, and he is probably in fine mental and intellectual health. The response to his situation he achieves in this writing, false as it is, may be both intelligent and sensible.

That is all true, yet there is something missing here that is present in the second passage: the capacity to write in a real way about his experience, to put on paper, out in the world where others can see it, where *he* can see it, some of the processes of mind—of observation, of feeling, of imagination and understanding—in which he actually engaged. The second writer can do some of this. You really do know something about the nature of his experience, and about his capacity to think about it as he renders it into language. "Underneath the overhang of the farmhouse roof a row of mud nests could be seen. Some hung down limp and useless; others were inhabited by sparrows; but a few remained in a fit state for the martins." You know what happened, in what order, and the position from which he observed what he saw. You know something about *him,* for he is present in his prose.

This is writing that he can mean. And the fact that he is doing it in school, under compulsion, does not keep him from creating a passage with qualities of immediacy, authenticity, and care—a passage that is of real significance to him and perhaps to others.

I have said that one cannot confidently infer from the first passage that the writer sees the world in clichés. This may be a way of talking he has learned in school, a language he must speak to succeed. Perhaps he can do it without much effort or sincerity, and hence without much consequence, beyond the important fact that he is not learning to do what the second writer achieves.[3] But consider this passage:

> On my return from school on Wednesday afternoon, my father invited me to accompany him on a visit to the Zoological Gardens. I answered in the affirmative, and we at once boarded a tramcar bound for the city. Here we caught the omnibus, and soon arrived at our destination.
>
> We had heard such a lot of talk about the new polar bear pit, we decided to visit this modern structure first of all. After a good discussion on this piece of workmanship, we made our way to the Monkey Temple. Here we had a gay half-hour watching the peculiar antics of the monkeys, who seemed almost human in some respects. We then partook of a frugal tea, and continued our tour by a visit to the noisy parrot house. This was very interesting despite the deafening shrieks of the brightly coloured birds. Next came the most exciting time of our excursion—a call at the Ape House. Alfred, an ape, and Adam, a baby chimpanzee, were the chief entertainers. On looking at the clock we saw that it was twenty minutes past seven, so we concluded our journey by viewing the humming birds.
>
> We soon arrived back at our abode, and I retired to bed, feeling that I had gleaned much knowledge during the evening.

What would you think if this were the work of your nephew say, or some other child in whose welfare you had an interest? I read it very differently from the first passage: here the boy is not simply manipulating empty forms to get his teacher off his back, but seems desperately anxious to manage forms of speech that are utterly dead. He is conforming to rigid and empty patterns, perhaps of his father, to which he has granted authority. He speaks in terms of conclusion—"good discussion," "gay half-hour," "frugal tea," "exciting time," "chief entertainers"—which he does not elaborate, does not define, by reference to his experience. We cannot know what these words mean. It is as though for him these things *must* be so. If only I can speak this way, he seems to say, I will be safe. Here there is no sense of a cheerful cynicism or manipulation but a deadly serious need to acquire rigid, dead, hopeless forms of thought and speech, and as I imagine it not only in this paper, and in school, but in life more generally. I have difficulty imagining this boy rushing out into the schoolyard after class with a joyous shout, ready to engage in life after hours of imprisonment. He is building his own prison.

Just to complete a pattern, consider the following:

> When I leave school I am going to be a comosole traveler [that is, a commercial traveler, British for traveling salesman], I would go to all sorts of shops and see what goods they want. I would go to the sweet shops espeshly. Why I would like to be a comosole traveler is because you get good money and on Sunday you can keep the car and go out to the seaside free. I have a long time to go before I leave school yet because I am only ten. My mother wants me to be a comosole traveler as well. At first my mother wanted me to be a macanicle engineer. She said you can pay up for a car weekly the boss would take it out of your wages but I would rather get a car free. If I would get the sack which I most probably will I would like to be a coal miner and dig coal from the pit. Theres one thing I would not like to happen to me or eney miner in the mine is the coal to fall in. What my mother thinks of it is too dangerous but I like using my muscles of caurse you have to have only a vest and trouses on. You get good mony on it because it is a dangrous job of course.

This writer is not in a prison of his own construction. He does as he will with his words. Neither spelling nor grammar is any restraint upon him. He expresses the run of his mind directly and authentically—this is not made up; he means it all—and it is all very attractive and appealing. As I read it, I find myself liking him, caring what happens to him, more really than any of the others.

Here we come to another aspect of the world in which all these boys are working, and one with which the first writer, for all the emptiness of the exercise, deals very well indeed. Although the last writer is not in a prison of his own imagination, of internalized expectations, he is in a prison of another kind, a social prison: unless he manages to learn how to spell, and to compose grammatical sentences, and to put it all in an order that meets the cultural demands of the classroom, he will have very limited opportunities in the world, not only in school but in the life that school can lead to. He will indeed "get the sack," as he so cheerfully and touchingly foresees. This is one reason I find the passage so affecting: here is this boy, full of life and energy, full of appeal—where will he end up?

Think of these passages now from the point of view of the teacher of writing. You need to teach your students, in law school as in elementary school, how to master the forms of speech and writing that are authorized by the culture to which you are introducing them. Yet in both cases it is common for this to be an experience for the student, and sometimes the teacher, that alienates the student from his own mind and experience as he struggles to produce a simulacrum of expression—something that looks like something he ought to write rather than something he can actually mean. He learns to produce falsity and is rewarded for it.

It may be a sign of a certain kind of psychological health that writers like the first succeed in objectifying so completely the expectations they are meeting, reducing it all to an exercise, for in this they are distancing themselves from the empty. But this boy's situation is in its way almost as tragic as that of the last student discussed, if it is true that he never learns to use language in a formal context—the class, the courtroom, the political speech, the academic article—to say what he means. Or, to put it another way: if he never gives himself a mind sufficiently engaged with life to be capable of meaning something of his own—something grounded in his distinctive experience and imagination—in the first place. He may in a sense succeed in life as a manipulator of forms, but that is its own species of lifelessness and despair.

The worst outcome, well known in college and law school and beyond, is represented in the third writer, who is so taken over by the forms that he uses that he is incapable of meaning anything except his desire to be defined by them. The consequences for him are serious indeed: a kind of emptiness of life, deadness of mind, that deprives him of what should be his birthright as a human being, namely, his capacity to use language to describe his experience and claim meaning for it, to express his own way of imagining himself and his world, to form real relations with others. He is the prisoner of the expectations that surround him, and this is in a real sense to be the prisoner of the empire of might. When speaking and thinking in such ways, he cannot be capable of love and justice, for he denies his own humanity—the reality and value of his own experience, his own mind—and this is necessarily to deny the humanity and reality of others as well. It is upon such deadness of mind and self that the propaganda of tyranny utterly depends for its force and power.

As teachers we struggle to help our students master their forms of expression so that they can turn them to their own purposes, transforming them when appropriate, placing them in constructive relation with other ways of talking, and so on, thus producing pieces of writing that are both formally correct and actually meant by the writer—and in the process acquiring a new sense of what they can mean, a new sense of the possibility of expressive and active life, indeed a new sense of the self. I sometimes sum up what I am looking for in the teaching of writing with the question "Knock! Knock! Anybody home?" If there is a person there, in the prose, we can readily deal with the problems of form and diction, the expectations of the audience, and so forth; if not, the struggle for the student is to try to change that, to find something to write that he can mean.[4]

Polonius and Hamlet

How far beyond the world of twelve-year-old English boys do the problems suggested by these passages run? Very far, I believe. Think for a moment of Polonius in *Hamlet*, who gives his famous advice to his son Laertes:

> *There; my blessing with thee!*
> *And these few precepts in thy memory*
> *Look thou character. Give thy thoughts no tongue,*
> *Nor any unproportion'd thought his act.*
> *Be thou familiar, but by no means vulgar.*
> *The friends thou hast, and their adoption tried,*
> *Grapple them to thy soul with hoops of steel,*
> *But do not dull thy palm with entertainment*
> *Of each new-hatch'd, unfledged comrade. Beware*
> *Of entrance to a quarrel; but, being in,*
> *Bear't, that th' opposed may beware of thee.*
> *Give every man thine ear, but few thy voice;*
> *Take each man's censure, but reserve thy judgment.*
> *Costly thy habit as thy purse can buy,*
> *But not express'd in fancy; rich, not gaudy:*
> *For the apparel oft proclaims the man;*
> *And they in France of the best rank and station*
> *Are most select and generous, chief in that.*
> *Neither a borrower nor a lender be;*
> *For loan oft loses both itself and friend,*
> *And borrowing dulls the edge of husbandry.*
> *This above all: to thine own self be true,*
> *And it must follow, as the night the day,*
> *Thou canst not then be false to any man.*
> *Farewell: my blessing season this in thee!*
> (*Hamlet* 1.3.57–81)

One of the main points of this speech is that Polonius does not mean it; in a sense no one could mean such a string of platitudes, all in a sense "true" but adding up to nothing. When Polonius says "Give thy thoughts no tongue," he is advising Laertes never to say anything he can mean, as he himself cannot mean this series of phrases that might have come from sixteenth-century advice books. He speaks of "friends," but what kind of friendship could be expressed or maintained in such a language, between Polonius and Laertes—or between the person he is assuming Laertes to be and anyone else? This is a world of calculation and management, all expressed in terms that have a pretended not an actual meaning. The end of the passage gives it all away, making suddenly visible the secret of what he has been saying: "to thine own self be true" is an impossible phrase in this passage, for neither Polonius nor Laertes is in this speech imagined as having a self. You would not want to be spoken to in such a way by anyone, especially I imagine your father or mother.

What is Polonius really saying about how to live life, his ostensible subject? For that you have to turn to his conduct, including his use of Ophelia as bait to test Hamlet's madness—"I'll loose my daughter to him" (2.2.161)— and this shows him to be far worse than a purveyor of platitudes. Not the genial fool he is often thought to be, Polonius represents real evil, and evil of a highly particular form: he is utterly untrustworthy because utterly incapable of trust. In the quoted passage he offers his advice to Laertes as if he were a wise and kind old man, passing on the benefit of his wisdom, such as it is, to his son; this in turn implies a certain view of his son, as capable of understanding, of remembering, of following his advice, as a person who can and will respond to what he is saying. But this view is shown to be a lie when Polonius later sends spies to follow Laertes and report upon him. The platitudes are foolish, but they mask, as platitudes often do, something much more serious, both morally and psychologically. Polonius cannot mean what he says for he is not capable of coherent meaning. You could not listen to anything he said with the attention you accord someone you respect. There is in a real sense no one there.

Whether—and how—one can mean what one says is in fact a large theme of the play as a whole, perhaps its largest theme. This is what Hamlet struggles constantly to do, and finds impossible. He can never quite find a way to imagine the world, and himself and others within it, in such a way as to make possible coherent speech or intelligible action. He compares himself to the actor who is able to express a powerful lament for Hecuba in the play he is rehearsing and asks, "What's he to Hecuba, or Hecuba to him that he should weep for her?" Think what this actor would be able to say, Hamlet goes on, if he had my real-world cause and ground for speech. But Hamlet can neither speak nor act effectively; it is not so much that there is no "objective correlative," in Eliot's famous phrase, to his internal life, as that his internal life itself has an incoherence that makes it impossible for him to ground action and speech upon it. Instead he becomes something of an increasingly despairing commentator on the events that thrust themselves upon him.

One of the major reasons for his failure is that he is surrounded by false speech: in Claudius, pretending to be a substitute father but eventually ordering Hamlet's murder; in Polonius, whom Hamlet understands and mocks with meaningless speech of his own; in Gertrude, who cannot face what she has done; and in his "friends" Rosencrantz and Guildenstern, who are the murderous agents of Claudius. He does to Ophelia what the world does to him, torturing her with inconsistent and unmeant claims, and drives her into despairing insanity. It is really only Horatio, who knows how to be silent, modest in his claims, who is solidly reliable—who can mean what he says—to whom Hamlet can speak. Our experience of this relation of trust in an untrustworthy world is, I think, the reason why Hamlet's famous closing words are so deeply touching:

> *If thou didst ever hold me in thy heart,*
> *Absent thee from felicity awhile,*
> *And in this harsh world draw thy breath in pain,*
> *To tell my story.*
>
> (5.2.333–36)

TEACHING WRITING

One question that naturally arises from a reading of the student papers about the walk in the woods ("nature in her full glory") and the trip to the zoo ("gay half hour"), and the passage from Polonius as well, is how one might help one's students, and in the process oneself, avoid such unsatisfactory forms of speech and learn to meet the dangers, for oneself and others, that they represent. In the terms I have been using, the idea would be to help our students become capable of "meaning what they say." This would require both the development of capacities of mind that would enable them to have something to say, something of their own and not merely replicative of others, and at the same time an increased understanding of the languages they use and the arts of using and transforming them. How is such an education to proceed?

There can be no easy or schematic way of talking about this—just as there cannot be about good judging, or good lawyering, or good writing, or any other valuable human activity. But it is clear that a lot of what we do, in law school and college alike, cuts the wrong way, in the direction of teaching people how to manipulate forms, meet expectations, please their audiences, without much regard to whether the student can possibly mean what she says. I do not mean that it would be good for the student, assuming she could do so, simply to dump out on the page everything that went through her mind, however empty, or vague, or clichéd; an essential part of the task is learning to think oneself to the point where one actually has something valuable to say, or do. But this is vastly more likely if from the beginning the student has some sense that it might be possible—should be possible—to say something that she means. At its best, this kind of teaching would move in the opposite direction from the forces of trivialization I have mentioned, leading to an increased and increasing sense of the value of the human being, the human mind, and human speech.

What would such teaching look like? How might one try to teach others, or to learn oneself, how to resist the clichés—the dogmas, doctrines, received ideas, unchallenged metaphors, standard phrases, hackneyed truths—that populate the mind, in their own way constituting an empire of might? How to reshape one's linguistic inheritance with the aim of achieving an individual expression or statement?

Here I offer a brief account of one especially powerful effort to engage in this kind of teaching, of which I myself had experience, namely, the famous composition course designed by Theodore Baird and taught at Amherst College in the middle years of the twentieth century.[5]

Here is the first assignment that greeted one group of freshman, a couple of years after I graduated. I hope you can see it as addressing the themes and questions of this essay:

Assignment 1:

You are now a member of a community, a social organization, or rather of a number of communities (Amherst College, the freshman class, a particular dormitory, etc.). This world is often described as artificial and secluded, an Ivory Tower. (The origin of this metaphor is obscure.) You may yourself believe, you may feel, that you have left behind the Real World. After all this is "only" a college, you are "only" a college student, this is "only" a course.

In the form of an essay deal with the following questions:

1. What is real about the Real World?
2. How do you know when you really are in the Real World?
3. If you have been in the Real World, why did you get out of it?
4. If you are outside the Real World, how do you get into it?

Finally, define "The Real World."

You can see how this works. The assignment makes the student's own language an unavoidable problem: "The 'real world'? What can *that* mean? I use that phrase all the time, but what on earth do I mean by it, does anybody mean by it? How can I use it now?" The student thus faces this part of his inheritance, which he has always used thoughtlessly, and sees it as a problem for analysis and reflection, thought of a kind he can barely imagine. At the same time, the assignment makes the student's actual experience of life a problem too: "Where actually am I when I am at Amherst College? In what community, or set of communities? And what *is* this place really—the buildings, the grounds, the people? A set of social and verbal practices? What are its boundaries? How can I possibly talk about it?" With respect to both the "real world" and his new set of communities, the "Ivory Tower," the student will find himself saying, "I thought I knew, but I don't. What can I possibly say?"

None of this will look like any paper assignment the student has ever seen before. There is nothing in it from which he can devise or figure out a set of expectations that these questions are designed to make him try to meet. There is no right answer. The student who wrote the first excerpt examined earlier ("nature in her full glory")—who can in fact stand for all of us—would have no way of dealing with such an assignment. These questions do not call for a performance of the kind the student has been trained to make; rather, in their interest, originality, and difficulty, they suggest possibilities toward which the student might direct his energies. They are amusing, full of confidence and intelligence; their function is to create a vacuum it is the student's task to fill. He is asked to speak to his reader as though he too is a person and a mind, capable of being interested and bored—as though his writing, like these questions, will achieve its completion only by the activity of reading by another intelligence. The task is to find a way to respond to the assignment with something like thought, something like an effort to mean what one says, and this is likely to seem very foreign indeed.

Here is the second assignment:

Assignment 2:
This is a genuine student's paper submitted in a writing course at Harvard in 1893.

THE PARADISE OF BOOKS
Books, I often think, are the best thing life has to offer us. No where else do we get pleasure that is so great and so lasting, that can charm us still, whatever our condition of mind and body. There we meet friends and lovers such as reality cannot acquaint us with, and adventures which furnish excitement without toil, and arouse sympathy without suffering. All the higher emotions, so incongruous

with matter-of-fact existence, may be serenely enjoyed in the realm of poetry, and all the speculative flights which transcend cold common-sense may soar undisturbed in the aether of philosophy. As long as a man has eyes to read and brain to understand, he may feel sure of one unfailing resource which can amply compensate the strokes of fortune.

We call this single paragraph a Perfect Theme. (There is also the five paragraph theme, using the structure: Introduction, Body, and Conclusion.)

[One] reader's comment on this Perfect Theme, "Simple and direct," now seems all wrong. It is not simple: look at the sentence structure and vocabulary. It is not direct: who is it who could speak in this tone of voice and yet be considered direct? Can you imagine anyone speaking these sentences to anyone else under any circumstances? Is this opposition of books and literature to reality and matter-of-fact existence and cold common sense a simple one?

What comment do you make on this Perfect Theme? What adjectives do you apply to it?

Define on the evidence of this example the Perfect Theme.

What is the alternative to such writing? How do you proceed if you are going to write really simple and direct English? Where do you begin? What models, what authors, what books, for simple and direct writing do you have in mind? What books do you think of when you think of writing in the Real World?

This assignment makes the problem of formal writing explicit: the quoted passage is in a sense perfect English, flawlessly written with complete confidence, but it is in a more important sense perfectly empty. This is an antique version of the prose the student has been taught to admire, to emulate, but here it is held out as the object of scrutiny, a problem of some sort.

How is he supposed to speak in this paper, then? In a twentieth-century version of this perfect theme? What *is* expected of him?

In the third assignment, the student's attention is drawn to the nature of his own language, the way he has learned to speak, in the following way.

Assignment 3:
This opposition between the Ivory Tower and the Real World becomes complicated when we consider how we ordinarily speak of education and of our private experience. A college, we know, protects the student from the outside world while it prepares him

for it. A student's fundamental beliefs are challenged, yet no belief ought to be offered as a substitute. Education is a purely academic endeavor, yet it also assumes a concern in those areas beyond the classroom. Student and professor join in the selfless pursuit of truth, while the aim of all our efforts is individual commitment. Education is learning how to use symbols, but the man who does not participate in the reality going on around him is uneducated. Both student and teacher pursue the ideal while they shape and are shaped by the real. And so on.

The paradoxes appear wherever we generalize. Amherst College should provide a controlled environment where inequality and competition and their inevitable disappointments do not exist, where at the same time the forces operating in the real world should have their full effect. Behavior taken for granted off the campus cannot be tolerated in our society, yet everyone has perfect freedom to follow the dictates of his own conscience. At the same time that societies are formed to make music and produce plays and take part in real politics and support particular religious organizations, everyone should be free to be himself. Team spirit is most important, yet the man we respect goes it alone.

Write an editorial, as if for the *Student*, in which you deal with this perplexing conflict. Do not be afraid of your own clichés and metaphors. The object here is to get at a vocabulary for talking about such matters. Everyone has at his command a large and useful stock of words. Give it an airing.

Here the student is asked to look simultaneously at his experience of the institution he has joined—not only Amherst College but the whole world of higher education—and at the clichés he is given by his culture as the language in which the life of that institution is to be imagined and talked about. For the lawyer it is easy to see similar questions being asked of the law, and the institutions and practices that make it up, from trial to brief writing to the idea of a court or legislature in the first place. Is one to imagine into existence an empire of might, thought about in the language of empire? What other possibility is there, and how is it to be attained?

This series of questions asks the student to begin to come to terms with what I have been calling the empire of might, in a form in which he has actually known it, namely, in the expectation that he will produce in his writing a simulacrum of something, a performance to be evaluated by how thoroughly it complies with rules of composition and grammar, of self-presentation, just as he might be judged by how appropriately he dressed or by his table manners. The collection of clichés articulated in assignment 3 is just a sample of what we all have running in our head, and the challenge of the assignment is that you think about this material and not merely deploy it as the Harvard student deployed the material of his world. The hope implied here, and reiterated every assignment for a year, is that the student can discover that he has something to say that he can mean, something he can say in his own way; that he has—that he can give himself—experience worthy of the attention of another; that he can have interests and values and a style of his own—in short that he can be a grown-up individual person, as responsible for what he says as for what he does, making himself worthy of his own respect and interest. To put it in the terms suggested by our reading of the passages with which we began: the student is invited—urged, pressed, leaned on—to discover something of his own humanity, his own capacity as a mind and person, and to be present in his writing. This—although the course never, I think, explicitly suggested it—is necessary to his recognizing the humanity of another. In such ways these assignments put into question the student's sense of his language, of his experience, of his self, of his world, of his education, calling on him to speak in a fresh way, his own way, about them.

The course asks students to write to such topics three times a week for a whole year. The bright student can of course find safe and empty things to say, time after time, but the pressure of the questions, asking you to think in ways you never thought possible, is relentless. If the course works well, you begin to speak in something like your own voice. To do that you have to know something of the empire of might, in the culture and in yourself, and how not to respect it.

THE LAW

Imagine that you are a lawyer or a litigant facing a judge who turns out to be the first writer discussed above ("nature in her full glory"), now grown up but still maintaining the same attitude toward speech and writing that he reveals in that passage. Or perhaps your judge is Polonius. How could you speak to such a mind? With what kind of honesty or authenticity? What kind of judicial opinion would you expect that person to issue? It would be a deep violation of justice to have a judge who could not, or did not, mean what he said, or one who was incapable of meaning anything, or one who did not understand the process in which he was involved, the language he was given to speak—any judge who had not made the case in an important way his own, the object of integrated thought and attention. Such a judge would unable to hear what you said, to attend to it, respond to it. Or imagine yourself as a client and ask what you want from your lawyer. Not an empty and skillful manipulator, I think, or one who thinks in conclusions, but a person with a mind of his own, one who can think about the case, in its parts and as a whole, and reach judgments of his own about it; one who can hear what you have to say and respond to it; one who can turn from that conversation to the law and find ways to use legal language, transforming it if necessary, to say what he has come to mean about your case.

It is common for people to try to learn law as if it were a set of rules to be applied more or less routinely to the facts of cases as they arise, as a simple system of commands. But as almost every law student learns, often to his or her profound discomfort, this image of the law will not work, either in law school or in practice. The lawyer and judge are typically presented with real difficulties of interpretation and harmonization of the law, in relation to facts that are themselves uncertain, all defining a set of problems through which they must think their way as independent minds.

Good legal thought and writing accordingly involve the articulation of arguments that can be made both ways—for and against the characterization of the letter as an "offer," say, which can be "accepted" and thus form a "contract"—and their arrangement in a structure that leads to a conclusion that fairly reflects the force of opposing arguments. The good judicial opinion takes the reader through the process of thought the judge herself engages in, with a fair representation of doubts, uncertainties, and the force of countering arguments. It ends with a conclusion that is not predetermined, or shaped by considerations external to the opinion, but reached by the process of thought enacted in her writing.

The good brief is both different and similar: it too leads the reader through an idealized process of thought, but this one leads to a predetermined conclusion; it also gives weight to countering arguments, plausible claims the other way, and so forth, or it will fail. The opposite of this kind of writing is what in the law we call conclusory writing, cast in terms that bury argument and thought in one's premises, reducing it all to a set of unargued assertions. The key element present in good legal writing, missing in bad legal writing, is a certain kind of life: the life of the mind, of thought and argument, that is generated by the recognition that we live in a world in which there are many valid things to say, from many points of view, with which it is the task of the legal mind to come to terms.[6]

Both in the law and out of it, then, the art required is that of finding a way to be present as a mind, a person, a voice, in a context that seems to invite the replication of standard forms, and in that context to learn what you can mean and how to express it. Think of the task of writing a note of sympathy to a friend who has lost a parent or spouse or child. What can you say? The occasion seems dominated by the language of the Hallmark card, which is not your language; what can you say that will be and sound real, written from the inside—that will be your speech? The lawyer who simply moves phrases around in his head and on the page, never really meaning anything he says—and there are plenty of them—is never actually thinking about the case, or the law, and is certainly incapable of saying something fresh or transformative. He will be thinking only about his effort at manipulation, not the merits of the question before him. I believe that once this is perceived, as it usually is by intelligent people, he will not be listened to by his audience. Why should he be? By contrast, there are lawyers who command respect and attention when they speak or write. I think one reason they do is that it is apparent that they mean what they say.

As for judges, the matter is even more crucial, for there are serious public consequences: the judge who simply articulates phrases, concepts, or ideas in an unmeaning way can likewise not be attended to, for he is not present as a mind or person. This means that his opinion cannot be read with the care and attention lawyers are trained to give authoritative texts in the law; it means, too, that he in a real way cannot be responsible for what he is doing. In some way he may in fact be seeking to avoid that responsibility by collapsing into a language of bureaucracy. This kind of writing, to use the distinction made prominent by my colleague Joseph Vining, is authoritarian, not authoritative. It is part of what Simone Weil would call the empire of might.

As an example of an argument—a kind of legal argument in fact—that is simultaneously shaped to one's audience and actually meant, consider the following exchange between Abraham and the God of Israel, as recounted in Genesis (the King James Version). The Lord is contemplating the destruction of Sodom for its grievous sins and says to Himself:

> Shall I hide from Abraham that thing which I do; seeing that Abraham shall surely become a great and mighty nation, and all the nations of the earth shall be blessed in him?
>
> For I know him, that he will command his children and his household after him, and they shall keep the way of the Lord, to do justice and judgment; that the Lord may bring upon Abraham that which he hath spoken of him.
>
> And the Lord said, Because the cry of Sodom and Gomorrah is great, and because their sin is very grievous; I will go down now, and see whether they have done altogether according to the cry of it, which is come unto me; and if not, I will know.

And the men [actually messengers of the Lord] turned their faces from thence, and went toward Sodom: but Abraham stood yet before the Lord.

And Abraham drew near, and said, Wilt thou also destroy the righteous with the wicked? Peradventure there be fifty righteous within the city: wilt thou also destroy and not spare the place for the fifty righteous that are therein?

That be far from thee to do after this manner, to slay the righteous with the wicked: and that the righteous should be as the wicked, that be far from thee: Shall not the Judge of all the earth do right?

And the Lord said, If I find in Sodom fifty righteous within the city, then I will spare all the place for their sakes.

And Abraham answered and said, Behold now, I have taken upon me to speak unto the Lord, which am but dust and ashes: Peradventure there shall lack five of the fifty righteous: wilt thou destroy all the city for lack of five? And he said, If I find there forty and five, I will not destroy it.

And he spake unto him yet again, and said, Peradventure there shall be forty found there. And he said, I will not do it for forty's sake.

And he said unto him, Oh let not the Lord be angry, and I will speak: Peradventure there shall thirty be found there. And he said, I will not do it, if I find thirty there.

And he said, Behold now, I have taken upon me to speak unto the Lord: Peradventure there shall be twenty found there. And he said, I will not destroy it for twenty's sake.

And he said, Oh let not the Lord be angry, and I will speak yet but this once: Peradventure ten shall be found there. And he said, I will not destroy it for ten's sake.

And the Lord went his way, as soon as he had left communing with Abraham: and Abraham returned unto his place. (Gen. 18:17–33)

This is a highly complex moment, for not only does Abraham find words to say what he means—"Do not destroy the righteous with the wicked"—he does so in the form of an argument, a crossexamination really, of a kind familiar to the law. He is trying to persuade the Deity to a course of action. To do that he must speak the language of the Deity, appeal to his nature and character;

he must offer Him a way of speaking to the situation that would enable Him to withhold his punishment and explain why. This is persuasive but not manipulative. Such is the effort of the modern lawyer too, at his best: to say what he means and to offer his audience something he can mean too.

One way to state what is so remarkable about this passage, and indeed about the whole relationship between the Deity and Abraham (and Moses too), is to say that it shows that Abraham can trust the Deity with the truth—the truth of his perceptions, thoughts, feelings—even though to do so is obviously risky in the extreme. Likewise, the Deity trusts Abraham with the truth of his intentions, almost as though He is asking for a response of approval or criticism. Each can say to the other what is displeasing. The one without power can speak to the One with all the power, and make claims upon Him—can make in a sense the ultimate claim, based on the character and nature of the Awesome One: "Shall not the Judge of all the earth do right?" Through the pressure of questioning, Abraham forces the Deity to recognize something about the world and Himself. Trust is the condition that makes it possible for both to speak with such frankness and honesty across the enormous gap between them, that enables them to mean what they say to each other.

THE JUDICIAL OPINION
Virginia Pharmacy Board v. Consumer Council

I now turn to an instance of modern legal writing, a passage from Justice Blackmun's opinion for the Court in *Virginia Pharmacy Board v. Consumer Council*, with what we have read in mind.[7]

First, some background. This case called into question the constitutionality (under the First Amendment) of a Virginia statute that prohibited pharmacists from advertising the price of prescription drugs. The stated reason for the statute was to protect the real and perceived professionalism of pharmacists, on the theory that price competition of the kind prohibited would lead pharmacists to work to a lower margin of profit, which would in turn lead them to take shortcuts both in the preparation of drugs and in the consultations they have with prescribing doctors and with the patients themselves. Further, it was thought that price advertising would damage the image of the profession, reducing the confidence the public has in it as a profession and not merely a business. As for any free speech interests involved, the pharmacists were free to reveal their prices when asked, and consumer groups, such as the plaintiffs here, were of course free to publish their own price surveys. All that is prohibited is price advertising by the pharmacists themselves.

As an economic regulation, this statute is of course not beyond challenge. Under its regime, drugs are sold, as one would expect, at widely differing prices in different stores in the same city, which seems to be unfair in general and to disadvantage the less sophisticated customer in particular. On the other hand, the defenders of the statute might say, price competition might itself lead to results that would be damaging to certain customers, particularly if it led to the concentration of the profession in a small number of high-volume, cut-price drugstores, which would in the nature of things be difficult and expensive for many people to reach. But that would not necessarily follow, the opponents of the statute would argue; perhaps small local drugstores would stay in business, charging more than the cut-price places but being less expensive to reach. In this way those who wanted convenience would pay for that, and those who preferred to travel for bargains would do that.

The arguments on the wisdom of the statute go back and forth in what looks like a classic case of economic regulation. But if this is how the case is regarded, the statute should almost certainly be upheld, for courts normally defer to legislative judgments about the probable real-world effects of alternative economic regimes—judgments the courts are not well situated to make or to review, depending as they do on information not readily available to the courts. The Court concedes as much.

The crucial question for the Court is thus the bearing, if any, of the First Amendment upon the case, on the grounds that the conduct regulated here takes the form of "speech." The obvious problem with this line of argument is that this speech is commercial in character, simply a way of doing business. Although there are many proposed rationales for the First Amendment, most of them conceive of it as protecting political speech, or the discovery of socially valuable truth, or the autonomy and dignity of the speaker, not purely economic processes. And, not surprisingly, when first presented with the question decades ago, the Court held that commercial speech was simply beyond the protection of the First Amendment.

Later cases complicate this picture, however, making clear that speech is not unprotected simply because money is spent to convey it, as in a political advertisement; nor because it is sold for profit, as a book or newspaper is; nor because it has a commercial subject—surely one would have a First Amendment right to complain that the anti-advertising rules in this very case were unjust, for example. Nor is it disqualified because the motives of the speaker are primarily economic, for the First Amendment protects certain forms of speech in labor disputes, not to mention forms of highly commodified speech of rather doubtful quality, from B films to television shows to romance novels. But none of these cases presents the question in its purest form, as *Virginia Pharmacy Board* does: here there is a simple proposal to engage in an economic transaction without any further artistic, ideational, political, literary, or other value. As the Court frankly says, "the 'idea' [the speaker] wishes to communicate is simply this: 'I will sell you the X prescription drug at the Y price'" (761).

The Court nonetheless holds that the First Amendment should indeed reach this form of speech, saying that the interest of the particular consumer in "the free flow of commercial information" may be "as keen, if not keener by far, than his interest in the day's most urgent political debate" (763). It expresses the core of its position in these terms:

> Advertising, however tasteless and excessive it may sometimes seem, is nonetheless dissemination of information as to who is producing and selling what product, for what reason, and for what price. So long as we preserve a predominantly free enterprise economy, the allocation of our resources in large measure will be made through numerous private economic decisions. It is a matter of public interest that those decisions, in the aggregate, be intelligent and well informed. To this end, the free flow of commercial information is indispensable. And if it is indispensable to the proper allocation of resources in a free enterprise system, it is also indispensable to the formation of intelligent opinions as to how that system ought to be regulated or altered. Therefore, even if the First Amendment were thought to be primarily an instrument to enlighten public decision-making in a democracy, we could not say that the free flow of information does not serve that goal. (765)

I do not mean to suggest that this passage, or the opinion from which it is drawn, is identical to any of the passages of student writing read earlier, but I do think that those passages may help us approach this one. The main question here, as in our earlier reading, can be put in terms of language: what kind of language does Blackmun use, and what is his relation to it?

To begin with, although this is a First Amendment case, Blackmun does not really talk in First Amendment terms. He never discusses the aims of that amendment, or the nature of the speech it is designed to protect, either as a theoretical matter or in connection with his reading of the cases.[8] What is wrong with this scheme of regulation, in his view, is not that it suppresses an independently valuable activity called speech but that it interferes with the efficiencies of the market. He might have struck the statute down on those grounds, but, as I suggested earlier, such a course would have been inconsistent with the law the Court had been making for decades concerning economic regulation. This looks like a case in which the Court disapproves of the regulation on economic grounds, but, having no way to strike it down for such reasons, reaches for the First Amendment instead. It is hard to regard Blackmun as actually meaning what he says about the First Amendment here.

In looking at Blackmun's use of economic language, we may be reminded of the young boy writing about "nature's glory" or of Polonius, each speaking as though his words were effective but without regard to whether they were meant. One might imagine market language used in a different way, metaphorically, with an awareness of its obvious difficulties—of what it leaves out—and as part of a larger vision of human life and our constitutional system. But that is not what we have here. Instead we have a dull replication of an ideology. Blackmun virtually constitutionalizes the "free enterprise system," for example, without any recognition of the fact that our economy is profoundly managed, by regulation, by taxation, and by government spending. The phrase as he uses it is really just a cliché, and much the same can be said of the rest of the formulaic language he employs. This is language that in a profound sense no one could mean.

Consider, for example, the passage already quoted in which Blackmun says that the "particular consumer's interest in the free flow of commercial information" may be "as keen, if not keener by far, than his interest in the day's most urgent political debate." You can see where this sentence comes from: a person with crippling pharmaceutical bills and little political engagement is indeed likely to focus his or her attention on the former, not the latter. But aside from the fact that many "consumers" do not fit that example, there is a deep ambiguity in the word "interest": it can mean actual engagement of attention, or even simple curiosity, on the part of an individual; or it can be the equivalent of value or worth, as in the citizen's "interest" in free elections. Although it may be factually true that some people care more about prices than politics, to say that they have a greater *interest* in "the free flow of commercial information" than in "the day's most urgent political debate" is to suggest either that the former is, as a matter of public truth, of greater worth or value than the latter, or that this is what the people in question think. The former position seems directly contrary to the choice made in the Constitution itself, which declares the primary value of "freedom of speech," with no suggestion that this value has any economic dimension. As for the second claim, the Court may be right that, if asked, many consumers would say the price of drugs is more important to them than a political debate. But under our constitutional system, our "interests" are defined not only by our present sense of need and desire but structurally, in the instrument of our government, one function of which is to make commitments for us that we do not have to make over and over again—to create, as it were, the conditions under

which we can lead our typically more selfcentered and private-valued exis-
tences. If you were to ask our citizens not whether their drug bills were a great
burden to them but whether they would like to live in a world without the
kinds of complex commitments made in an enduring way by the Constitution,
I think and hope that a great many would revise the judgment the Court attributes to them. And in any event, a judicial opinion by the United States Supreme
Court is the place above all at which the larger commitments and values of
the Constitution should be given force, especially as opposed to unsupported
judicial estimates as to the way our citizens rank their values—citizens whom
it trivializes in this context to label as mere "consumers."

Think also of the slogan "the free flow of commercial information," appearing both here and at the end of the following passage: "even if the first amendment were thought to be an instrument to enlighten public decisionmaking
in a democracy, we could not say that the free flow of information does not
serve that goal." This language too has the quality of cliché, obscuring both
thought and reality. It takes no account, for example, of the fact that the information in question is already available to anyone who makes a phone call to
the drugstore, and that, if more systematic dissemination were thought
valuable, those of the plaintiffs who are not individuals but consumer
groups could assemble the price data and communicate it to their members
or to the public. Even more significantly, it draws attention away from the fact
that the flow of information established by this decision is not really "free,"
since many of the speakers (that is, the pharmacists) presumably do not
wish to engage in the "speech" protected here. They will in fact be compelled
to speak, as a practical matter, for if one of them advertises they will all have
to do so. It is therefore not their choice that the Court is respecting but quite
the opposite; the Court is establishing a regime of effectively mandatory speech,
in the form of advertising, for the purpose of enhancing the recipients' range
of economic choices. As a way of imagining the First Amendment, the process
of speech in the world, or the reasons why speech is valuable and should be
protected by the Court, the opinion is hopeless.

True and meaningful speech, in the world and in the law, requires the living
presence of a person in the words—the person of an author, the person of a
reader. This opinion erases person, in both capacities, substituting a routine
application of dead formulae and clichés. This opinion is the iteration of an
ideology that has no distinctive place for speech in the world it imagines—
and thus cannot work as a language for thinking about a First Amendment
case—and also no significant place for speech in the world it enacts or performs, for it cannot manifest in its own composition a conception of valuable speech. Although it adheres to the forms of legal thought, and cites and

distinguishes appropriate authority, at the deepest level it lacks the most important kind of legal knowledge. Try reading the opinion as you might read the student papers with which we began, or the speech of Polonius: as holding out a promise of a world, of a life to be lived on its terms; as an invitation to join the writer in this way of thinking and imagining, this way of writing, about speech and the Constitution—how would you respond? Blackmun, like our third student writer, is in a prison of his own, defined by the language he accepts without being able to put it into question. This means that he cannot act as a responsible and independent mind, and cannot claim the authority that such action grants; it means that his writing in the deepest sense lacks the life that alone can justify its claims to power. This opinion is thus one that in a real sense he does not, and cannot, mean.

All this is not to say that the outcome in *Virginia Pharmacy Board* is necessarily wrong. The Court might evolve a doctrine of economic due process under the Fourteenth Amendment that would constitutionalize the market, at least to the extent of requiring the state to justify interferences with it by making factual showings that are here only presumed.[9] This would be especially appropriate where there is a grounded suspicion that the legislation is really designed to protect the special interests of a politically distinct and effective group, here pharmacists themselves. But such a move should be made explicitly, and on due process grounds not First Amendment ones, for only then would the case be framed and argued in appropriate terms.

There remains one more dimension of this case. It is by no means easy to do what Blackmun did not attempt to do, namely, to try to say why speech should be singled out for special protection, as it is by the First Amendment. Efforts to produce theories that describe the law of the past and shape the law of the future have not worked well, to put it mildly. This means that it is especially important to have what might be called performative or enacted definitions of the value of speech in the judicial opinion itself. If the real reason for the constitutional guarantee is to make possible serious and thoughtful deliberation on issues of public concern, for example, the Court itself can show us (or fail to show us) that kind of deliberation in action.

We are right to ask of an opinion in this field, then, not only how the Court imagines the speaking person, and the activity of speech itself, but how it *engages* in speech. Does the Court in its performance trivialize this occasion for speech, and speech more generally, or does it recognize the dignity of—or confer dignity upon—this crucial aspect of human life? Whatever the First Amendment means, it surely points in the latter, not the former, direction. Yet we can turn back to the opinion in *Virginia Pharmacy Board* and ask: how could this opinion possibly recognize what is of real value in speech, when it reduces speech to the transfer of information or a signal of a willingness to do business?

In this case Blackmun allows his mind to be taken over by a system of thought, an ideology really, in a way that leads him to slide over the issues actually presented in the case, producing a surface that does not open itself up to argument, as an opinion should, but closes it off. You either believe, as he does, in the adequacy of the language of the market to explain what is at stake here, or, like me, you do not. The consequences are especially serious because of a larger cultural fact, which is that in our world at large the ideology of the market has taken over so much of public talk and action. Obviously economics has an appropriate role as a method of thought, but its language must always be used with great care, and certainly not as a comprehensive mode of organizing life. For economic language imagines human life in an extremely impoverished way, as a set of choices designed to serve selfinterest, and it has no way to conceive of community, or collective life, except as a series of deals, and no way to imagine the natural world, upon which we depend, except as a set of resources.[10] To my mind, this is a an empty way to think of human relations, human motivation, human achievement, but it is what we live with, and for Blackmun to convert what could have been a moment for talking about the value of speech as such into another application of this ideology, which sees speech simply as an aid or adjunct to economic life, is a genuine lost moment, both for him as a writer and for us as readers.

Let me add here the important point that although the language of cliché Blackmun uses happens to be the language of economics, it would be all too possible to use the language of law in such a way, or the language of left-wing politics, or the language of religion or of human rights. The real question is whether the language and ideology in question dominate the mind and the text, or whether, by contrast, the writer finds a way to assert against such forces the presence, and the value, of his or her own mind and experience. For it is only through the assertion of the individual mind, speaking in a voice of its own, that the empire of might can ever really be resisted.

We are in fact all susceptible to the failure to which I see Blackmun succumb. This is the possibility against which we must work whenever we write and speak, knowing that at best we will succeed only sometimes, and only in part.

Thomas v. Collins

Is it possible for a judicial writer to speak differently, or is Blackmun here really an example of what we must expect? It may be useful now to look briefly at a passage of judicial prose that I think to be of quite another kind. Here is

Justice Jackson speaking in *Thomas v. Collins*,[11] a case considering the constitutionality of a Texas statute that required a labor organizer to register with a state official before soliciting memberships in a union:

> As frequently is the case, this controversy is determined as soon as it is decided which of two well-established, but at times overlapping, constitutional principles will be applied to it. The State of Texas stands on its well-settled right reasonably to regulate the pursuit of a vocation, including—we may assume—the occupation of labor organizer. Thomas, on the other hand, stands on the equally clear proposition that Texas may not interfere with the right of any person peaceably and freely to address a lawful assemblage of workmen intent on considering labor grievances.
>
> Though the one may shade into the other, a rough distinction always exists, I think, which is more shortly illustrated than explained. A state may forbid one without its license to practice law as a vocation, but I think it could not stop an unlicensed person from making a speech about the rights of man or the rights of labor, or any other kind of right, including recommending that his hearers organize to support his views. Likewise, the state may prohibit the pursuit of medicine as an occupation without its license but I do not think it could make it a crime publicly or privately to speak urging persons to follow or reject any school of medical thought. So the state to an extent not necessary now to determine may regulate one who makes a business or a livelihood of soliciting funds or memberships for unions. But I do not think it can prohibit one, even if he is a salaried labor leader, from making an address to a public meeting of workmen, telling them their rights as he sees them and urging them to unite in general or to join a specific union.
>
> This wider range of power over pursuit of a calling than over speech-making is due to the different effects which the two have on interests which the state is empowered to protect. The modern state owes and attempts to perform a duty to protect the public from those who seek for one purpose or another to obtain its money. When one does so through the practice of a calling, the state may have an interest in shielding the public against the untrustworthy, the incompetent, or the irresponsible, or against unauthorized representation of agency. A usual method of performing this function is through a licensing system.

But it cannot be the duty, because it is not the right, of the state to protect the public against false doctrine. The very purpose of the First Amendment is to foreclose public authority from assuming a guardianship of the public mind through regulating the press, speech, and religion. In this field every person must be his own watchman for truth, because the forefathers did not trust any government to separate the true from the false for us. *West Virginia State Board of Education v. Barnette*, 319 U.S. 624, 63 S.Ct. 1178, 87 L.Ed. 1628. Nor would I. Very many are the interests which the state may protect against the practice of an occupation, very few are those it may assume to protect against the practice of propagandizing by speech or press. These are thereby left great range of freedom.

This liberty was not protected because the forefathers expected its use would always be agreeable to those in authority or that its exercise always would be wise, temperate, or useful to society. As I read their intentions, this liberty was protected because they knew of no other way by which free men could conduct representative democracy. (544–45)

This passage bears on the same general question as does *Virginia Pharmacy Board*, namely, the role of the First Amendment in the area of economic activity, and it shows that in the discussion of ideas as well as facts, it is possible to engage in thought and writing that are vivid, clear, comprehensive, and deeply meant. Jackson does exactly what Blackmun does not do, which is to think of the case in First Amendment terms; more than that, he gives a kind of performative content to value of speech itself by the way he writes. He is obviously present before us in this prose, saying what he thinks and why, and doing so in way that does not trivialize the activity of thought and speech in which he is engaged but, quite the opposite, confers upon it an essential dignity.

Part of the force of the opinion lies in his recognition that he is faced not with a question simply of categorization—"Is it a 'calling' or is it 'speech'?"— but with a question of judgment in a case in which the basic principles are in tension, shading into one another at the borderlines. The undoubted power of the state to regulate professions and employment necessarily includes the power to regulate some speech. But not all speech, as he shows with his examples of the nonlawyer speaking to issues of fundamental human and legal rights, of the nondoctor urging one or another school of medical thought. How is one to draw the line? By understanding the reasons why the state has plenary power to protect the public against "the untrustworthy, the incompetent, or the irresponsible" in the practice of callings, but not against "false doctrine," where the people, and not the government, must serve as the protectors of truth.

In all of this Jackson is obviously present as a mind and person, willing to accept responsibility for his judgment, reasoning to a coherent conclusion, and demonstrating in his work how it is that we—the people—can indeed be "watchmen for truth." He is teaching us how to live with the recognition that virtually anything can be contested, often by scurrilous means, yet nonetheless to be able to speak and read and think with confidence. And this teaching is not dependent on our agreement with the particular outcome: he could have written just as good an opinion, in the sense I mean, coming out the other way. He is not in a prison either of his own construction or made by the habits of thought he adopts; he is in this sense free and responsible. This is judicial writing that is meant, and it encourages us to say what we mean, to mean what we say, as well.

The force of mind at work in this case—stating the issues, seeing the facts, defining principles, making a judgment and standing by it—is showing us a way of resisting, of not respecting, the empire of might. Jackson insists on the value of individual judgment, in him and in his reader, in the speaker and the public, for he insists that the case make sense to him, and he invites the reader to do likewise. This is not the replication of an ideology but the opposite: thought that puts into question its own methods and materials, in the interest of reaching and explaining a judgment, defined as an individual act of mind, for which he is responsible. To say this is to say that Jackson here achieves an important kind of justice.

In this essay I have tried to elaborate the claim that what Simone Weil calls the "empire of might" is not simply a matter of military force but also of language, and the use of language—a matter of writing, in short. A mind like that of our first student writer—and all of our minds share this quality more fully than we should wish—is full of a repertoire of standard moves, received ideas and images, ways of thinking and writing, that it has acquired by imitation from those whose approval matters. It is full of what I call clichés. This is not just a matter of private but public concern, as Blackmun's opinion shows, for, at least in my view, this too is full of received and unquestioned images and phrases, not thought through. And this is how the political empire of might maintains itself: through public speech that is dead and irresponsible, and through the habits of acquiescence present in all of us that make such speech effective—a willingness to talk the way we hear others talk, without testing it against our own experience, our own thought.

Writing by the manipulation of expected phrases in expected ways has the effect of distancing the writer from his or her own experience, from his or her own mind, as we saw in the first and third student writers above and I believe in Blackmun too. It closes off thought, both in the writer and in the reader, creating a false image of the world and of the mind. It creates belief in what should not be believed. And all this has political as well as personal consequences, for this is how an ideology is created and maintained—any ideology that erases the experience of others, especially the poor and weak, in our country and abroad, that makes us blind to the common humanity of all people and our common dependence on a healthy natural world.

What Weil calls "knowing the empire" consists to a large extent in knowing the ideologies, the clichés, the false languages that surround us, and knowing as well our own susceptibilities to their appeal—our susceptibilities to the pleasure and satisfaction of earning the approval of the powerful and thus having power ourselves. "Knowing how to resist it" means knowing not only where a regime may be politically vulnerable but, much more deeply, knowing how to resist the appeal of false language, false writing, to our own minds. In his own way Justice Jackson, in this rather routine case, finds a way to talk that resists the empire of might—resists it through the force of his own voice and presence, his insistence on reason, his respect for arrangements external to him and to his reader alike.[12] The temptations of acquiescence are present whenever we speak or write; resisting them means the struggle to emerge as a mind saying something true or real or valuable, something you can really mean, in the law and in the rest of life.

Without such knowledge of the empire, and how to resist it, we are as Weil says incapable of justice, for we will accept false ways of thinking and imagining and talking that obscure the reality of human suffering and cruelty and greed. We will accept talk about the "national interest" or "our friends abroad" or the "evil" of those who are different or the "rising tide that floats all boats" without examining it, or the reality it obscures. If we cannot imagine the lives of others—the half of the world's population that lives on less than two dollars a day, for example—we cannot be capable of justice toward them, for imagination is the root of justice. And if we cannot see others as they are, and understand our own role in systems of wealth and power, we certainly are incapable of love toward them too.

NOTES

1. Simone Weil, "*L'Iliade*, ou le poème de la force," first published in wartime France in *Cahiers du Sud* (December 1940–January 1941), when it was read, properly, as written against Hitler, and reprinted in *The Simone Weil Reader*, ed. George A. Panichas (Mt. Kisko, N.Y.: Moyer Bell, 1977), 153, with the quotation appearing at p. 181.

2. The first two passages are from David Holbrook, *Children's Writing* (Cambridge: Cambridge University Press, 1967), 83; the second two from David Holbrook, *English for Maturity* (Cambridge: Cambridge University Press, 1961), 148–49.

3. It is also possible that the dullness and deadness of the last sentence may express his true condition of mind. This would be far less favorable than the possibility I have been suggesting in the text.

4. For a fine book on the teaching of writing as an activity of self-creation—as a way of giving yourself simultaneously something you can mean and the capacity to express it—see William E. Coles, Jr., *Teaching Composing: A Guide to Writing as a Self-Creating Process* (Rochelle, N.J.: Hayden Book Co., 1974).

5. The course was called simply English 1–2. The questions are reprinted with permission. For accounts of the context in which it was offered, see Richard Poirer, "Reading Pragmatically: The Example of Hum 6," in *Poetry and Pragmatism* (Cambridge: Harvard University Press, 1992), chap. 4; William Pritchard, "Ear Training," in *Playing It by Ear* (Amherst: University of Massachusetts Press, 1995), chap. 1; and Pritchard, "Foreshadowings," in *English Papers* (Minneapolis: Greywolf Press, 1995), chap. 1.

6. One might resist what I have just said, insisting that lawyer and judge actually use the forms of legal discourse in purely instrumental ways, in efforts simply to persuade or to justify. On this view the whole thing is artificial, imitative, a form of manipulation, to be tested by results, not by what is said. I think this is quite wrong. It is true that the lawyer's speech situation has special features—a professional language, a set of professional audiences, and the fact that she speaks always for another—that complicate her situation in interesting ways, but in essence it is like that of the student writer discussed earlier, or any writer in fact. For everyone must speak a language that has its origins outside of him or herself, with its own limits and enablements; everyone must speak to particular audiences, defined by the expectations they bring to the occasion; and everyone has fidelities that run beyond the self, if only to the truth of the event of which he or she speaks. The lawyer and judge alike should mean what they say and say what they mean; this requires of both that they give themselves minds capable of meaning something of their own in a genuine way.

7. *Virginia Pharmacy Board v. Consumer Council,* 425 U.S. 748 (1976).

8. In some respects the Court's opinion follows the established forms of legal thought rather well: explaining clearly the grounds on which Virginia had adopted the statute, addressing the technical but important question of the standing of the plaintiffs to bring this action, and describing fairly the relevant cases the Court had earlier decided on the subject of commercial speech. But this compliance with formal expectations turns out, on closer reading, to be superficial—a bit like the similar compliance demonstrated by the first student writer discussed earlier. This is true especially in Blackmun's treatment of precedent, where he summarizes the outcomes of the earlier cases clearly and fairly enough, but does so simply in terms of rules they adopt, without seeing the judgments as motivated by competing visions and understandings of the purposes of the First Amendment, of the nature and importance of speech, and so forth. This can be seen as a kind of legalistic, not legal, thought, the reduction of purpose and reason and vision to rule. Likewise, Blackmun's basic articulation of the question before him skews his thinking: it is whether this communications is "wholly outside" the First Amendment or lacks "all first amendment protection" (748). This is one way to put the issue of course; but even if you decide that the Court should not dismiss entirely any claim of protection for this kind of speech, you need to face the question whether price advertising should be protected exactly like other forms of speech, those that are plainly central to the First Amendment concerns—like political debate, for example—or to a lesser degree, and why. The reasons and factors that had once led the Court to exclude entirely

this kind of commercial speech from protection might still have force after that position had been abandoned and lead the Court to protect advertising significantly less than speech that is more central to the aims of the First Amendment. But, apart from a few observations at the end of the opinion, Blackmun regards his task as mainly done when he has argued to the conclusion that this kind of advertising should not be entirely without protection, when in fact his main work still lies before him, namely, to explain how it should be protected, to what degree, and why.

Finally, Blackmun never really addresses the question of the relation between the Court and the legislature: he thinks price advertising desirable, the legislature thinks otherwise, both making their judgments on the basis of facts and expectations about human behavior. By what warrant does the Court substitute its judgment for that of the legislature here? There may be reasons, but Blackmun does not give them.

9. This would involve a revival of the doctrine of *Lochner v. New York*, 198 U.S. 45 (1905), which at the time of *Virginia Pharmacy Board* was thoroughly discredited.

10. For a more full explication of this point, and for treatment of economic language as a challenge to the writer, see James Boyd White, *Justice as Translation* (Chicago: University of Chicago Press, 1990), chap. 3.

11. *Thomas v. Collins*, 323 U.S. 516 (1945).

12. Or listen to the opening sentence of his dissenting opinion in *Shaughnessy v. Mezel*, 345 U.S. 206, 218 (1953), which is not without relevance for our own day: "Fortunately it is still startling, in this country, to find a person held indefinitely in executive custody without accusation of crime or judicial trial."

TEACHING CIVIL LIBERTIES AS A BRANCH OF POLITICAL THEORY

Tolerance versus Respect

JEFFREY ABRAMSON

I n this chapter, I set out one particular way of placing the study of law within the undergraduate liberal arts curriculum.[1] The approach emphasizes the interconnections between political theory and legal studies by asking students to make explicit the moral and political values that often lie implicit in legal case material.

There are dangers to this approach; it can romanticize the purity of legal reasoning and isolate the study of legal principles from the social forces that influence the power legal decision making has (or fails to have) in a society. For instance, the essays by Marianne Constable and James Boyd White in this volume persuasively unmask the rhetoric and politics behind so many seemingly neutral and high-minded legal philosophies.

Still, particularly when it comes to constitutional law and Supreme Court decisions, judges can hardly render decisions about due process or equal protection of the laws or about impairment of contracts or just compensation for takings of property without invoking *some* political theory.[2] To awaken students to the theoretical choices implicitly driving controversial cases is to awaken them as well to the indeterminacy of legal reasoning. In turn, the indeterminacy of law is the best argument for why interpretations of the law should not be left to some elite with supposed superior training but should engage citizens at large in open democratic deliberation about the ideals law seeks to embody.

A number of essays in this book come together in arguing that the core task of teaching law in the liberal arts is to uncover the moral and normative content of legal choices. Goodman and Silbey show how the tendency of American society to legalize all relations, even those on campus, trains students to regard law as an immutable social fact rather than a set of norms open to debate. Keith Bybee argues that teaching law to undergraduates is central to teaching students "how to lead a meaningful life as a free person, engaged in the practice of self-government." This essay joins the efforts of my colleagues in arguing that law is not just a professional tool belonging to lawyers; knowledge of law is central to the activity of democratic citizenship. Like other contributors to this volume, I recognize that most of my liberal arts students find their way into my courses with a "pre-law" mentality and that their nascent careerism stands in some tension with the more distancing, philosophical approach I take. But some amount of tension between students and teachers can be to the good, as they ask us to justify the detours we ask them to take from a purely preprofessional interest in the law.

For the past decade, I have had the privilege of teaching civil liberties at Brandeis University, where the introductory course in civil liberties has been a basic component of the undergraduate curriculum since the university's founding in 1948, a founding that was itself part indictment of religious discrimination in college admissions, part statement of faith in the coming tolerance of postwar America. My predecessors include some of the great commentators on and contributors to civil liberties, including Leonard Levy, Herbert Marcuse, John Roche, and Jerold Auerbach. Because the course on civil liberties is so intimately wrapped up with my university's vision of its own mission in higher education, the course readily invites students to reflect broadly on the ideals and moral purposes of law, on the one hand, and the service of law to power and the status quo, on the other hand. For these reasons, a course that explores civil liberties as a branch of political philosophy resonates with an undergraduate curriculum already centered on universities as places of social criticism and conscience.

In this essay, I concentrate on one specific philosophical theme that speaks to student curiosity about cases on freedom of religion and freedom of speech.[3] The theme contrasts two related but distinct ideals of democratic justice.[4] The first is the familiar principle of tolerance and the agreement of persons to agree to disagree. The second is the ideal of respect, an ideal that envisions a community held together by members' genuine appreciation of what they find to admire in one another. When reading cases that ask communities to be open to unpopular, sometimes disdained, religious, political, or artistic viewpoints, I ask my students to consider the grounds for First Amendment protections: how does the difference between tolerance and respect play out, for instance, in contemporary cases about hate speech, flag burning, cross burning, pornography, sodomy, Christian Scientists' refusal to accept medical treatment for their children , or the Catholic Church and the still unfolding story of clergy sexual abuse?[5] My students read the cases alongside readings in political theory that confront liberalism with reforms associated with John Rawls's great *A Theory of Justice* and with criticism from what is generally described as a "republican" or "communitarian" point of view offered in the writings of Alasdair MacIntyre, Michael Walzer, Mary Ellen Glendon, Michael Sandel, Joyce Appleby, and Bruce Ackerman.[6] The purpose of the course is to consider the pros and cons of supplementing the distant, legal posture of tolerance with the more intimate, psychological ties of respect. Over the years, I have found that my students fear any form of politics that empowers government to make moral judgments about what is in the public good. They prefer the seeming neutrality and nonjudgmental nature of the tolerance ideal. Given their starting commitments, I often find myself trying to make the case for how the obvious "judgmentalism" at stake in assigning or withholding respect from one's opponents is compatible with the openness of democratic culture.

Here is how the argument of the course develops. Tolerance of diversity (diversity of peoples as well as of ideas) is the great achievement of liberal societies, and the critics of liberalism on the reading list do not for a moment suggest any retreat from the inclusive and nondiscriminatory laws that put tolerance into practice. But when law merely constrains human behavior without changing it, then the potential for backlash is always present, especially in hard times. This is why some argue that liberal societies ought to ask more of citizens than merely to accommodate or not discriminate against others. Liberalism, according to its critics, ought to build on the habits of nondiscrimination to foster in citizens an appreciation of the contribution diversity makes to democracy.

The limits of tolerance are both practical and philosophical. Practically speaking, hard cases arise (hate speech is an example) in which tolerance may undermine rather than underwrite the equal treatment of persons as basic to democracy. The absolutism with which the principle of tolerance is often expressed leaves my students without practical guidance about where, if at all, to draw the line when it comes to tolerating the intolerant. Philosophically speaking, tolerance forms a weak social bond. Although there is much to be said for resisting the community's hold on individuals, still tolerance at times may leave individuals *too* isolated from one another. It is the ethic of strangers, a way of keeping the peace among persons who remain indifferent to and largely ignorant of cultures beyond their own. Tolerance teaches us the negative (do not discriminate against others). Respect teaches us the positive (embrace others as a way of enriching our own lives). Both are necessary.

THE TOLERANCE PRINCIPLE

Tolerance takes as its starting point what Machiavelli long ago diagnosed as the distinct condition of modernity: the arrival of "masterless men" (and women) freeing themselves from tradition, migrating within and sometimes between borders, forever pulling up anchor and moving on. For contemporary liberal societies, the mobility of individuals gives rise to a familiar pluralism or diversity of population. Citizens are largely strangers to one another, hailing from different backgrounds, professing diverse values, attending separate houses of worship, focusing on private interests. Given the heterogeneity of interests and peoples, any strong sense of community or a common good seems neither possible nor desirable.

The question arises as to what could form the basis of a stable social union in liberal democracies? What values could citizens separated by religion, national origin, culture, sometimes even language, agree upon? Belief in the inclusive spirit of tolerance is one answer to this question. Tolerant persons do not necessarily come to like one another, to respect one another's traditions, or even to know much about them. They simply agree to disagree, each unsure about where ultimate truth lies and therefore willing to accept the right of all persons to their own views.

Although tolerance is often based on skepticism about the very existence of truth, it need not require such cynicism. It would be enough to follow Mill's advice that even if truth exists, we should not trust governments to find it. Mill thought that tolerance of a wide array of views actually contributes to the emergence of truth through a process of trial and error, through competition in the marketplace of ideas that strengthens the truth by teaching persons the active spirit of inquiry necessary to discover it. Locke framed another classic argument in favor of religious tolerance: coercion may force a person to conform outwardly, but it will never bring true faith or conviction.[7]

When people share the same values, they do not need to practice the restraints of tolerance. But when we confront groups or ideas we hate, then tolerance is put to the test. Privately, one may despise skinheads, white supremacists, the Ku Klux Klan, neo-nazis, and other hate groups, yet legally one is required to grant space on the public stage to them. The strange paradox of tolerance is that it obliges us to tolerate those who would not tolerate us in return. Without necessarily respecting a particular people or a particular ideology, citizens of liberal societies accept that all groups have equal rights to express their views publicly. Of course, even liberal societies imperfectly practice the ideal that free speech gives equal voice to all citizens. Like any unregulated marketplace, the marketplace of ideas is subject to giving dominance, sometimes even monopoly, to those with money and status. The Supreme Court line of cases on money and speech dating back to *Buckley v. Valeo* has hardly helped American society deliver on the connection between free speech and democracy.[8] Still, it would be hard to imagine a working democracy that did not strive to practice tolerance of free speech. This is true not only because free speech is an instrument of democracy, giving meaning to voting and elections, but because free speech itself speaks to the equal capacity of all individuals to freely determine the content of their own minds.

Historically, tolerance has worked effectively to keep the peace and to end the religious warfare present throughout the early modernizing history of European and American states. But can tolerance deliver more than peace-keeping; can it make of the state more than a truce-keeping force between rival interests and peoples? Many endorse tolerance precisely because it minimizes the power of community over individuals. Recently, however, philosophers on both sides of the Atlantic have praised tolerance's contribution to national identity. Addressing the question of what it is that Germans can and should share, Jürgen Habermas answers that it is precisely tolerance of "the integrity of each individual, in his or her otherness" that brings Germans together into a common good.[9] The American philosopher John Rawls makes a similar point about the connection between community and tolerance in the United States. In a democracy, people voluntarily join countless different associations, some based on religion, others on work, still others on recreational interests. The national state does not aspire to replace this plurality of social unions so much as it seeks to provide the constitutional structures of tolerance that let this diversity prosper. In this sense, concludes Rawls, the tolerant state is "the social union of social unions."[10] A social union for Rawls is a community united around shared final ends that members value as good in themselves. The achievement of liberal democracy is to provide the institutions that allow for a plurality of such social unions.

THE IDEAL OF RESPECT

In my civil liberties course, I contrast the doctrine of tolerance with the alternative ethic I earlier called "respect." Respect goes beyond tolerance by prodding us not just to live with diversity, not just to "put up with it," but to find positive value in living together with persons from different walks of life. Respect comes when we affirm the worth of traditions and identities other than our own. But so long as citizens remain strangers, they rarely discover what might be of value in their neighbor's religion or their co-worker's ethnic identity. Respect therefore argues for a curriculum of civic education in democratic societies, a course of education sufficient enough to replace the distant, indifferent feelings of mere tolerance with a more intimate, knowledgeable, and sincere appreciation of other traditions. In the United States, constitutional doctrines of separation of church and state deter public schools from teaching anything "religious." This is certainly a safe course, far preferable than a public education that puts the power of the state behind one particular religion's values. But the ethic of respect suggests that democratic education needs to do a better job of teaching children what is different but important in their classmates' lives outside school.

Of course, learning about others is no guarantee that we will admire what we learn. I may find nothing to admire about fundamentalist doctrines of any religion that justify treating women as inferior. I may find nothing to appreciate about groups that preach racial and religious hatred or advocate terrorism. The more I learn about such groups, the more firmly I might conclude that tolerating their doctrines makes no contribution to democratic debate, that in fact they threaten the preconditions of treating persons with equal dignity and mutual respect upon which democratic dialogue depends. In these circumstances, the doctrine of respect will generate different political conclusions than will the doctrine of tolerance. Tolerant persons put up with even antidemocratic, antitolerant doctrines; they accept the risk that people will be converted by these doctrines in ways that misuse and even threaten the survival of tolerance. Respect abandons impartiality in favor of making substantive moral judgments about the content of a political or religious doctrine.

The German Constitution arguably alludes to the notion of respect when Article 1 makes it the "duty of all state authority" to "respect and protect . . . the dignity of man."[11] Such language implies that government must do more than end discrimination against individuals; it must take affirmative or positive steps to ensure that the personal dignity of each individual is protected against assaults from others. Consider, for instance, laws banning groups or parties that advocate race hatred. In the United States, the Supreme Court has consistently invalidated laws against hate speech, on the theory that the core principle of democracy is freedom to espouse any political idea, including hateful ideas.[12] So long as the speaker stops short of inciting imminent violence, even hate speech must be tolerated. German courts have suggested a different analysis. As important as the rights of free speech are, they are not absolute but need to be balanced against the rights of persons to live as equals in society, free from defamation and harassment on the basis of race, religion, sex, or national origin. German law is particularly sensitive on this point because of the Holocaust, and it specifically prohibits Holocaust denial as untrue statements that affront personal honor and dignity. Moreover, German law permits content-based restrictions on extremist antidemocratic speech that incites hatred or attacks the dignity of individuals or groups of a particular nationality, race, religion, or ethnicity. Other nations, including Canada and the United Kingdom, also depart from the U.S. model in balancing individual free speech rights against the collective rights of groups to reputation and dignity.[13] The position of these nations is well taken. Consider, for instance, the situation of the Roma minority in Hungary or elsewhere, long the object of vilifying speech. What kind of dignity or equality can Roma children enjoy if they walk along streets and through parks plastered with signs slandering them with the worst things that could be said of human beings? How could these children develop a sense of self-respect if government does not provide them with social respect? Democracies cherish freedom of speech because that freedom gives equal voice to all persons. But people hardly have equal voice when hate speech primes others to see them as racial and ethnic inferiors. The preaching of racial hatred is so destructive of the civility of conversation that it loses any claim on democratic tolerance.

Of course, giving governments the power to make judgments about parties and their ideologies is risky business. One of the strongest arguments for tolerance is contained in the famous metaphor of a slippery slope: once we give government the right to exclude any doctrine, we risk expansion and misuse of that power against opponents for purely partisan reasons. Far safer, then, to tolerate it all. But is it safer? On the one hand, there are risks involved in tolerating hate groups; on the other hand, suppressing them invites other risks. The ethic of respect recognizes that the risks of suppression almost always outweigh the risks of tolerance. But it would allow for the possibility that some groups are so purposely trying to foment hatreds leading to violence that democracies should run the risk of climbing even slippery slopes.

Gay and lesbian marriage is another topic that demonstrates the difference between tolerance and respect. It is one thing for society to tolerate what same-sex couples do in private; it is another to publicly recognize their partnerships as the equal of opposite-sex relations. Many persons who would not discriminate against gays nonetheless draw the line and argue that society does not have to affirmatively endorse the bond between same-sex couples, as it would were the law to permit them to marry. For instance, in an otherwise sweeping decision striking down state sodomy laws as an unconstitutional intrusion on the liberty and privacy interests of same-sex couples, the Supreme Court took pains to note that its defense of the rights of same-sex couples to be left alone did not in any way imply that government must give "formal recognition" to homosexual relationships. [14]

What is the best response to such a line-drawing argument? Gay rights groups most often rely on constitutional guarantees of equal protection of the law to argue that the prohibition against same-sex marriage *is* blatant, legal discrimination. To those worried that legal permission to marry is the same as moral acceptance of homosexuality, the gay and lesbian community assures its opponents that such is not the case. The only message of the law would be a neutral one, that persons should be allowed to choose their own marriage partners free from state-imposed orthodoxies.

Although this argument about tolerance for same-sex marriage is a strong one, it has proven legally persuasive only in Massachusetts and to a lesser degree, Vermont.[15] In reading the legal materials with my students, I suggest one reason for the failure of the tolerance ideal to win widespread popular support for same-sex marriage. The debate hinges on what the purposes of marriage are or ought to be. To the extent that the purpose of marriage is natural procreation, perhaps there would be some warrant for discriminating between gays and straights. But what about opposite-sex couples unable to conceive, uninterested in having children, preferring adoption, or trying in vitro fertilization? No state denies marriage licenses to such persons, not even if they are on their deathbeds, as the Massachusetts Supreme Judicial Court wryly noted. When it comes to opposite-sex relationships, the law amply recognizes that the institution of marriage gives public recognition to a couple's love, not its procreative capacity.

If this is so, the question is whether same-sex partners marry for love every bit as much as opposite-sex couples do. Legal argument based on tolerance seeks to avoid this question, to bracket it and say that the state need not get into questions like this, that it should simply let people make their own choices about love and marriage. As the Massachusetts Court wrote, the state constitution protects persons from "unwarranted government intrusion into . . . [w]hether and whom to marry, how to express sexual intimacy, and whether and how to establish a family."[16] Legal and political argument based on the ethic of respect takes a different tack. It seeks to justify same-sex marriage by educating the majority straight community about gay love—and through educating them, changing political attitudes on the basis of respect for the sincerity of love and the reality of exclusive relationships in the gay community. Perhaps this overstates the educational mission. Perhaps the goal is more modestly getting all to see that same-sex and opposite-sex couples marry for lots of reasons, from love to money to raising children. The very sameness of the motives is what the law should respect and recognize.

The Massachusetts decision authorizing same-sex marriage and Vermont law on civil unions prove to be especially rich material for law courses in a liberal arts curriculum. Both force students to confront why states regulate marriage at all and what the public interests are in encouraging marriage in the first place. To the extent that students see marriage in material terms, as a way the state extends certain tangible benefits to couples, they tend to be satisfied with the equality given same-sex couples in Vermont by a system of civil unions that extends them benefits equal with those offered to opposite-sex couples in officially recognized marriages. But to the extent that students think there is some nonmaterial benefit attached to public and legal recognition of marriage, they tend to agree with the Massachusetts court in rejecting Vermont-style civil unions as a perverse kind of "separate but equal" arrangement that refuses to same-sex couples the symbolic meaning of the marriage title.[17]

One of the attractions of tolerance is that it seems such a neutral and impartial principle. Tolerance strips government of jurisdiction over individual life choices, so long as those choices threaten no harm to others. Instead of delivering official judgment about the worth of a group or its ideas, the tolerant government simply frees us to pursue "our own good in our own way," in the famous phrase of John Stuart Mill.[18]

But is tolerance truly neutral? I ask my students to consider again Mill's dictum that the state is neutral because it places top value on freeing persons to choose their own good in their own way. But why should we accept that freedom of choice has this sovereign value, that living life as a questioning individual is such a good way to live, better for instance than a life lived in loyalty to inherited traditions and customs? Clearly, Mill's statement of tolerance rests on an unspoken preference for the "voluntarist" lifestyle of the dissenter over the involuntary lifestyle of the devout. This does not make Mill's argument necessarily wrong: perhaps democracy does depend on the habits of mind instilled in a person by exercising personal freedom of choice. But it means that the doctrine of tolerance itself rests on implicit moral assumptions about which lifestyles are most worthy of respect.

U.S. law on abortion is often cited as an example of the moral neutrality achieved by tolerance, but any course on civil liberties needs to raise doubts about this claim. In *Roe v. Wade,*[19] the U.S. Supreme Court stated that it would not take a position on the controversial question of when life begins, that it would simply agree to let Americans disagree. But precisely because Americans are divided on the ultimate moral questions surrounding abortion, the Court argued that law should be neutral and permit women to make the decision themselves as to whether to abort or carry a fetus to term. By making "pro-choice" the law of the land, the Court concluded, government itself was an impartial bystander, giving equal legal protection to the different choices different women would make.

Even for those (like me) who agree with this decision, it hardly seems neutral. Legalizing abortion clearly accommodates the views of those who think abortion is a morally acceptable choice. But it does not at all accommodate the views of those who believe that abortion is murder because life begins at conception. The Supreme Court was wrong to claim it could resolve the legal dispute over abortion without taking a side on the moral dispute about whether the fetus is a person. To tolerate lawful abortion is to reject the views of those who think there is no moral difference between infanticide and abortion. It is to side with those who argue that the freedom of women to control their own bodies is the guiding value to respect in this area.

What is true about the abortion case is true of many difficult legal controversies: practicing tolerance does not somehow let us avoid taking a position on underlying moral disputes. Neutrality is simply impossible, and decisions require courts to make a substantive, moral argument in favor of one set of values or the other.

RISK, RESPECT, AND TOLERANCE AFTER SEPTEMBER 11

Tolerance and respect each contribute to the equality of persons without regard to race, religion, or national origin. Tolerance is more modest in what it demands of citizens, asking us simply to accommodate other persons and views, regardless of what we think of them. Beyond accommodation, respect ties peoples together in mutual appreciation of their differences.

After September 11, the need to combine tolerance and respect is more urgent than ever. The terrorists who attacked the World Trade Center and the Pentagon fit a definite ethnic (Middle Eastern) and religious (Muslim) profile. Not only the United States but all its allies have good reason to fear more terror from Middle Eastern sources. (It may be that domestic terrorist groups are operating as well, but this does not lessen the danger of attacks from the Qaeda network.) The aftermath of the war in Iraq only complicates the picture and, beyond Al Qaeda, adds to Middle Eastern sources of attack against U.S. interests. When danger of grave proportions is so clear and present and tied to a particular ethnic minority, the majority population may be tempted to think it necessary in the fight against terrorism to encroach on the civil liberties of any and all who share ethnicity with the terrorists. Of course, the claim of necessity has a hollow ring to it when restrictions on civil liberties are the first resort proposed rather than the last resort. The so-called USA Patriot Act, passed by Congress in the immediate aftermath of September 11, makes it easier than before to detain and to search immigrants suspected of ties to terrorist organizations, with ambiguous definitions of what constitutes a "terrorist" entity.

Some law enforcement agencies suggest that normal bans on racial profiling and random stops do not apply in our current situation. Whereas racial profiling is morally objectionable when no crime has occurred but suspicions fall only on the likelihood of criminal behavior in a certain group, these agencies point out that racial profiling of Arab nationals (for instance) may well be justified where crimes of terror have already occurred, and where the intent and capacity to commit further crimes are clear.

Would it be safer to target all Muslims and Middle Eastern persons for special surveillance? Perhaps, although scapegoating Muslims at home might well prove counterproductive to U.S. efforts to enlist Muslim regimes abroad in the fight against terror. But let us suppose that protection of equal civil liberties for all is risky, more dangerous than at least residents in the United States knew before September 11. The real issue is whether citizens of liberal democracies find the maintenance of open and diverse societies worth the risk.

Here is where the psychology of respect becomes crucial. The more the majority sees a potential terrorist in every Middle Eastern face, the greater the risks they will see in civil liberties for the suspect population. Of course, the majority population knows better. They know that Muslims worked and died alongside non-Muslims in the World Trade Center. They know that few Muslims are terrorists, no greater a percentage of the Muslim population than IRA terrorists are of the Catholic population. But although they know all these truths abstractly, the majority know little about the actual doctrines of Islam, less about how their Muslim fellow citizens actually practice their religion. This ignorance did not jeopardize tolerance in the good old days before September 11, but it puts tolerance on shaky psychological ground today.

In the immediate weeks after the attacks, President Bush commendably attended a prayer service at a Washington, D.C., mosque. The president also invited an Islamic clergyman to participate in a national prayer service alongside Christian and Jewish clergy. Perhaps President Bush took these steps for expedient or political reasons, as a show for the world. Still, how often had a president gone to a domestic mosque before? At a time when some were holding the Islamic religion responsible for the making of terrorists (this would be like blaming Christianity for the Ku Klux Klan), paying public respect to a minority religion was the right thing for the president to do.

Tolerant persons do not ever have to enter one another's houses of worship, schools, parks, or homes. But the accommodations of separate cultures that hold in good times are strained during crises. Democratic diversity finds firmer footing when citizens cross over to other sections of town, daring to learn and appreciate firsthand the "otherness" of others. It is this transition from tolerance to respect that events of September 11 force upon liberal societies, with still uncertain results.

By raising questions for students about the difference between tolerance and respect, I hope to lead them back to the case material with a deepened interest in sorting out exactly what we must defend as central to a democratic way of life, even when that defense involves risk.

TEACHING CONSTITUTIONAL LAW
AS A BRANCH OF POLITICAL THEORY

In this essay, I have tried to show how one particular line of cases on tolerance and hate speech raises fundamental questions about the ties that do or do not bind democratic citizens together: do we share merely the constitutional protections that allow us to differ and to live in peace with persons whose cultures we neither know nor respect or do we aspire to share a stronger sense of community, with all the perils to dissent that loyalty to a common good portends?

This is hardly the only point of political theory raised by legal cases. In his essay in this volume, James Boyd White shows the competing views of democracy at stake in the Supreme Court's decisions to recognize commercial speech as worthy of First Amendment protection.[20] The entire line of cases, dating back to *Buckley v. Valeo*, equating money with speech, raises similar questions about free speech and democracy.

The deep connection between political theory and constitutional law is apparent in so many Supreme Court decisions. Cases on redistricting and the Voting Rights Act turn on the meaning of representation in a democracy and how to give effective weight to the vote of racial minorities.[21] Cases on the jury as a "representative cross-section of the community" require us to ask in what sense we wish to encourage jurors to be "representatives" and whether juries perform the same representative functions as legislatures are assigned.[22] Cases on congressional power under the commerce clause to this day find justices struggling to articulate their understanding of federalism and state autonomy within a federal system.[23] The line item veto provoked reflections on the doctrine of separation of powers and its contributions to freedom from tyrannical government.[24] Welfare rights cases find the Court being presented with arguments that the Fourteenth Amendment's equal protection clause essentially enacts John Rawls's difference principle into law.[25] For the better part of a half century, judges have argued about whether "free exercise of religion" is best promoted by a strict policy of religious neutrality on the part of government or by affirmative steps taken by the government to exempt the religious from obligations (the military draft, for instance) that secular citizens must shoulder.[26] Affirmative action finds justices offering competing conceptions of the contribution that diversity makes to good education, the extent to which universities are or ought to be meritocracies, and the differences between giving preference to athletes, musicians, North Dakotans, sons and daughters of alumni(ae), and racial minorities.[27]

This list is hardly exhaustive but should suffice to convince that political theory and constitutional law are subjects yoked to one another. As compared with course offerings a generation ago, even law schools have adjusted their curricula to acknowledge the normative choices driving constitutional law. But it is not enough that future lawyers be trained to participate in the ongoing arguments about how best to interpret the meaning of free speech or free exercise of religion or privacy. It is our job as teachers of the liberal arts to make as many students as possible literate in the law. Literate in science, math, art, and technology as well, but literate in the law for the special reason that law is the language of democracy, or at least it is when the broad body of citizens not only hears the law pronounced from on high but gets to speak up as the law is democratically interpreted in the first place. I leave for another essay just how to reconcile traditional notions of judicial review with this argument that law should involve the citizenry at large in democratic debate. But even this hanging question leads back to my main point in this essay, that we can hardly debate law in the liberal arts without simultaneously debating the struggle of constitutional democracies to reconcile the twin ideals of the rule of law and the rule of the people.

In *The Trial*, Franz Kafka has a priest tell a parable about the law to a prisoner awaiting execution. In the parable, a man from the country comes "before the Law," to the door of the Law itself to beg admission. But he meets a doorkeeper who tells him it is not possible to admit him at the moment. The man from the country waits—and he waits. He tries bribery, he considers storming the door, but in the end he waits until his death. As he is dying, the man asks the doorkeeper why no one else in all these years has come to the door of the Law. The doorkeeper replies that this door was meant for the man from the country alone and now he will close it.

What went wrong? Was the man from the country too passive, too cowardly? Why did he even believe in the image of a "Law" hiding behind a door? And what about the doorkeeper, was he faithful to the Law or was he the culprit rather than the Law itself? Like many other teachers of undergraduate legal studies courses, I assign this parable to my students.[28] I have no particular agenda, and some years the students get into it, some years they do not. But when they do get excited, it is because the simplicity of the parable forces them to explore their own tendency, like that of the man from the country, to treat the law as a "thing," as a finished vessel that contains authority precisely because of its mysterious status as a holy relic guarded by doorkeepers. To begin reflecting on the power bestowed by this imagery (but on whom—the doorkeepers or the law itself?) is the beginning of the liberal arts odyssey into the law.

NOTES

1. An earlier draft of this essay was presented at the Conference on Legal Scholarship in the Liberal Arts in April 2002 at Amherst College. The author thanks participants in that conference for helpful suggestions. The author also thanks Anja Karnein for her research assistance in preparing this essay.

2. See, e.g., Jeffrey Abramson, "Ronald Dworkin and the Convergence of Law and Political Philosophy," *Texas Law Review* 95 (1987): 1201–32.

3. For further development of my views on the philosophy of free speech, see Jeffrey Abramson and Elizabeth Bussiere, "Free Speech and Free Press: A Communitarian Perspective," in *New Communitarian Thinking*, ed. Amitai Etzioni (Charlottesville: University of Virginia Press, 1995), 218–33.

4. For an elaboration on these two ideals of democratic justice, see Jeffrey Abramson, "Two Ideals of Democratic Justice," in *The End of Tolerance*, ed. Susan Stern (London: Nicholas Brealey, 2002), 98–109. Some of this essay has been adapted from that earlier article.

5. See, e.g., *R.A.V. v. St. Paul*, 505 U.S. 377 (1992) (hate speech); *Texas v. Johnson*, 491 U.S. 397 (1989) (flag burning); *Virginia v. Black*, 123 S.Ct. 1536 (2003) (cross burning); *American Booksellers v. Hudnut*, 771 F.2d 323 (7th Cir. 1985) (pornography); *Lawrence v. Texas*, 123 S.Ct. 2472 (2003) (sodomy); Caroline Fraser, "Suffering Children and the Christian Science Church," *Atlantic*, April 1995, 105–20.

6. John Rawls, *A Theory of Justice* (Cambridge: Harvard University Press, 1971); Alistair MacIntyre, *After Virtue: A Study in Moral Theory* (South Bend, Ind.: University of Notre Dame Press, 1997); Michael Walzer, *Spheres of Justice: A Defense of Pluralism and Equality* (New York: Basic Books, 1984); Mary Ann Glendon, *Rights Talk: The Impoverishment of Political Discourse* (New York: Free Press, 1991); Michael Sandel, *Liberalism and the Limits of Justice* (Cambridge: Cambridge University Press, 1982); Joyce Appleby, *Liberalism and Republicanism in the Historical Imagination* (Cambridge: Harvard University Press, 1992); Bruce Ackerman, *Social Justice in the Liberal State* (New Haven: Yale University Press, 1981).

7. John Stuart Mill, *On Liberty* (Indianapolis: Hackett Publishing, 1978), chaps 1–2. John Locke, *Letter on Toleration* (Indianapolis: Hackett Publishing, 1983), 27.

8. *Buckley v. Valeo*, 424 U.S. 1 (1976).

9. Jürgen Habermas, *A Berlin Republic: Writings on Germany*, trans. Steven Rendall (Lincoln: University of Nebraska Press, 1997).

10. Rawls, *Theory of Justice*, 527.

11. Art. 1 (F.R.G.), translated in *The Constitution of the Federal Republic of Germany: Essays on the Basic Rights and Principles of the Basic Law with a Translation of the Basic Law*, ed. Ulrich Karpen (Baden-Baden: Nomos, 1988), 227.

12. *R.A.V. v. St. Paul;* but cf. *Virginia v. Black* (upholding Virginia law banning cross burnings as intentional acts of intimidation).

13. For an excellent analysis of the difference between German and U.S. law on hate speech, see Michel Rosenfeld, "Hate Speech in Constitutional Jurisprudence: A Comparative Analysis," *Cardozo Law Review* 24 (2003): 1523, 1548–55, 1542–48.

14. *Lawrence v. Texas*, 123 S. Ct. 2472 (2003).

15. On November 18, 2003, the Massachusetts Supeme Judicial Court ruled that the state constitution granted same-sex couples an equal right with opposite-sex couples to obtain civil marriage licenses. *Goodrich v. Dept. of Public Health*, 440 Mass. 309 (2003).For a summary of Vermont law recognizing civil unions between same-sex couples, see Deborah L. Markowitz, "The Vermont Guide to Civil Unions," http://www.sec.state.vt.us.

16. *Goodrich v. Dept. of Public Health*, 440 Mass. 309.

17. In February 2004, the Massachusetts High Court issued an advisory opinion to the state legislature specifically rejecting a proposed civil union law as sufficient to meet the equal protection guarantees of the state constitution. I wish to thank Tamara Metz, a graduate student in political theory at Harvard University writing a dissertation on marriage, for pointing out to me the symbolic importance attached to official public recognition of marriage.

18. Mill, *On Liberty*, 12.

19. *Roe v. Wade*, 410 U.S. 113 (1973).

20. For Supreme Court doctrine on commercial speech, see *Virginia Board of Pharmacy v. Virginia Citizens Consumer Council,* 425 U.S. 748 (1976).

21. See, e.g., *Shaw v. Reno,* 509 U.S. 630 (1993); *Shaw v. Hunt,* 517 U.S. 899 (1996) (discussing the permissibility of using race as a factor in drawing the boundary of congressional districts so as to create districts in which a minority achieves majority voting power).

22. See *Taylor v. Louisiana,* 419 U.S. 522 (1975) (Sixth Amendment guarantee of trial by an impartial jury requires the petit criminal jury to be drawn from a representative cross-section of the population). For a discussion of the jury as a representative body, see Jeffrey Abramson, *We, the Jury: The Jury System of the Ideal of Democracy* (Cambridge: Harvard University Press, 2000).

23. See, e.g., *New York v. United States,* 505 U.S. 144 (1992); *Printz v. United States,* 521 U.S. 898 (1997).

24. *Clinton v. New York,* 524 U.S. 417 (1998).

25. See, e.g., Frank Michelman, "Foreword: On Protecting the Poor through the Fourteenth Amendment," 83 *Harvard Law Review* (1969): 699.

26. Cf. *Sherbert v. Verner,* 374 U.S. 398 (1963), with *Employment Div. v. Smith,* 494 U.S. 872 (1990).

27. Cf. *Gratz v. Bollinger,* 123 S.Ct. 2411 (2003) (undergraduate admissions procedures that automatically award bonus points to applicants of certain races declared unconstitutional), with *Grutter v. Bollinger,* 123 S.Ct. 2325 (2003) (law school admissions program that considers minority race as one factor among many in assessing candidates individually declared constitutional).

28. In fact, Kafka's parable gives its name to a textbook widely used in undergraduate legal studies courses, *Before the Law: An Introduction to the Legal Process,* 7th ed., ed. John J. Bonsignore et al. (Boston: Houghton Mifflin, 2002).

ROMANCING THE QUOTATION

HENDRIK HARTOG

L ike other interdisciplinary legal scholars of my generation, I have staked a career on finding the right example, the right story, the right quotation. For me, it has often seemed as if knowledge about law lay in the production and reproduction of what was "there": in the archives, in the case files, in the sources. Although I am and have been naive in this enterprise, I am not that naive. I have always known that what I saw and found and wrote about was predetermined by presumptions—theories—that guided me. And sometimes I wrote as if I were participating in scholarship about legal theory or about the historiography of law. But what really moved me was the thought that I engaged with the voices, the words, the texts of dead people in conversations about law. And that out of those (imaginary) conversations came a capacity to tell or reveal or reproduce the stories of those dead people. Sometimes the point of the stories was to show those dead people as real "makers" of law (as against the judges and other legal authorities of the law school imagination). Sometimes the point was to show the coercive power of law over real people leading real lives, or to show the relatively absent power of law over real people leading real lives. Often the point was to fit the contradictions and conflicts within "law" into the lives of real people living within a changing and multiple American culture. Always it was the particular story (which sometimes might be a case, but always meant, in effect, a collection of odd and revealing quotations) that seemed to offer the hope of scholarly success and the romantic possibilities—the hope of love—that make scholarship happen.

This then is an essay about my particular romance with one peculiar "liberal arts" way to gain understanding about law. That way goes by many titles: in legal anthropology, it has long been identified with the study of the "case of trouble," the trouble case.[1] In late twentieth-century historiography, the way is marked by the shift from social history to cultural history, as exemplified in the works of Natalie Davis or Carlo Ginzberg or LeRoy Ladurie, and also by "the return of storytelling."[2] Bakhtin and other literary theory references are also important for some portrayals of the way.[3] But equally crucial have been long-standing challenges to positivistic and systematic and structuralist forms of knowledge production (or better, knowledge revelation), as well as a growing sense that the odd and the apparently idiosyncratic will, when properly examined, be at least as revealing, and certainly more interesting and more lovable, than a "routine" or "ordinary" that seems today both oppressive and fictional (an illusion).

Were I able to accommodate Austin Sarat, who asked me to go "meta," a number of moves would follow that would allow exploration of the big themes raised in the enterprise of writing about law from within history and anthropology: epistemologically, dilemmas of how particulars join to become generalizations, singulars become plurals and explanations; historically, or genealogically, how cultural history, legal history, cultural anthropology, legal anthropology, and literary theory all converged at a particular historical moment; ethically, about the use and manipulation of dead voices to satisfy present needs and desires (necrophilia); and jurisprudentially, about the relative significance of nonstate legal actors in narratives about the evolution of law and the uses of the trouble case as offering access to the underlying order or the culture of a society, or as offering access to counterhegemonic or nonstate-identified conceptions of legality.

But here I refuse such opportunities. Instead I explore my romance with "stories" and "quotations," by telling a story about "stories" and "quotations." I think the story raises themes that are central to this volume. But, to be honest, the story came first, my accommodation to the aims of this volume second. I came across the story about six months ago, and I realized that the story connected to an anxiety that I had been feeling for some time. The story has obsessed me since then (why that is so might be a subject for therapy, but not here), and so I offer it as a poisoned gift and in the hope that doing so will help free me from my obsession. I hope that writing this will help me elucidate a bit of the significance that I sense lies beneath. But I confess further that, at this moment, I have no idea if that is actually the case. As always, I write here out of the faith (blind and stupid) that the story contains the knowledge, the meaning, that will be revealed, in discussion, if not in this essay.

One more warning: the story is not exactly about law, although it is very definitely about scholarship in the liberal arts. And the story does not come to a clear conclusion. Like many "real" stories, it drifts off.

It is a story with two finished parts. In the first act we watch the anthropologist David M. Schneider recount a serious quarrel he had with his wife, Addie Schneider, between 1966 and 1968. The second act rehearses Schneider's imagined argument with Clifford Geertz (and other interpretive anthropologists). I also include the beginning of a third act, one that plays out my imagined dialogue with Schneider: why I think his position needs to be taken seriously, even though everything in my training and disciplinary orientation tells me he is and was wrong.

ACT ONE

In 1968, the anthropologist David M. Schneider published *American Kinship,* a work that remains today inescapable for anyone who wants to understand modern American family law and family history.[4] For Schneider, American culture distinguished between two realms of kinship: a realm of law and a realm of blood. These two realms were joined together by the fertile and sexual magic of heterosexual marriage. Now, at the moment of its creation, this conceptualization was "wrong," and it was quickly becoming more "wrong." There were, as Schneider himself later acknowledged, many groups in American society whose kinship structures were inconsistent with his portrait (121—23). More important, the legal and cultural centrality of heterosexual marriage was being dethroned at the very moment that he was positing a model dependent on its regnant presence. And few (perhaps no one) today would write in the structuralist idiom that Schneider took on and defended. Yet, Schneider's book remains a breakthrough, a transformative moment, in the history of scholarship on kinship and family roles, in part because of its single-minded insistence on viewing kinship as a single cultural system of symbols and meanings.

I say that it is an inescapable book. Yet I confess that it had long escaped me, though I have been writing about family law and family history for more than fifteen years. I always knew of its existence, but I had not read it until last summer. I did so, when I did, because I am now involved in a research project in which questions about who is kin to whom have become crucial, and as I began to read in the recent anthropological literature on kinship, I realized that everyone who wrote on the subject still wrote in the shadow of Schneider.

This story, however, is not at all about Schneider's scholarly significance, not even about his scholarly significance for me, although it is very definitely about the writing of the book on which much of his significance rests.

American Kinship is an abstemiously and ascetically framed little book. Although Schneider's introduction describes the research project—the interviews and samplings—that he conducted before beginning to write the book, Schneider insists from the beginning that he is not describing anything, certainly not any particular living family or kin grouping. He intends the book to offer "an account" of American kinship as a "cultural system."

In a reconsideration of the work, added as a final chapter to the second edition (1980); Schneider responded at length to the criticism (he doesn't name the critic) that the book made no use of data or quotations, that it was entirely lacking in description thick or thin. Schneider's response took the following form: there is no way to distinguish between "fact" and "analysis." Data, when gathered, are already a selection, chosen by way of the presuppositions of the gatherer. "A set of facts or body of data is simply some empirical statement made within the framework of a conceptual scheme or theory, however inexplicit this remains." He did not "deny" that there existed six thousand pages of typed interview material, and he acknowledged that that "material" was "not quite the same thing as this book." Still, the relationship between the 6,000 pages of notes and the 117 pages of the first edition of the book was "intimate and determinate": the book constituted generalizations, whereas the field notes were "specific instances" shaped by the same "apprehension, comprehension, and presuppositions" as the book. There was no way to understand the field notes as existing prior to and independent of the argument developed in the book. As a result, he chose not to offer extended examples drawn from the notes to illustrate claims made in the book, since those examples proved nothing, as they only existed as data because of those claims (123).

Schneider then offered a "useful" bit of "history." At the time he was writing, "a close associate" took the field notes and found "a veritable treasure trove," an "embarrassment of riches," of quotations from informants and observations by field workers that "supported" almost every statement he made. But, relying on "the well known rule that 'no good deed goes unpunished,'" Schneider rejected the gift. Because data and analysis are inextricably intertwined, quotations and observations prove nothing. And to include them might have been easily misunderstood as confirming the analysis. His work did not need to be "pepped up" with illustrations. He had often felt offended by other social scientists' willingness to allow readers to suppose that generalizations were "proven" or "supported." Not he. He would hold on to a "pious" refusal to "cheat." "Needless to say," he concluded, "my associate disagrees and has not forgiven me to this day" (123–24).

Fourteen years later, in 1994, in the course of a book-length interview about his life as an anthropologist, Schneider expanded that useful bit of history.[5] The close associate was, of course, revealed as his wife, Addie. In 1966, two years before *American Kinship* appeared, Schneider had moved with her for what they thought would be only six months, from the University of Chicago to the Center for Advanced Study in the Behavioral Sciences at Stanford. Schneider was going there to write the first draft of the book; his wife was going to take classes in French in San Francisco. He had promised her that they would use the second half of his leave year to travel in France. He took with him the six thousand pages of interview data that he had accumulated over the previous few years.

As they drove across the country, he used the time to think through the argument of the book. But before they reached California, in Coeur d'Alene, Idaho, his wife discovered a lump in her breast. She had breast cancer. In California, she had a mastectomy, and with all their plans "upset," once "she began to get back on her feet," she turned to his interview notes. Trained as a historian, she believed claims ought to be grounded in archival evidence. She examined the archives (his notes), and she found the evidence. And she presented him with the quotations that would strengthen his book.

Her doing so, Schneider claimed in 1994, led him to formulate his position that such evidence was "a lot of baloney."[6] Addie was furious. He had spent other people's money and his time collecting this information. How could he not use it? He replied that he didn't want to pretend that it was "evidence" that proved something. She reminded him that in the introduction to the manuscript, he claimed the authority of having conducted the study and reported to his readers his possession of all those pages of notes. He conceded the point: "It's not a lie. It's just—it's like—what would you call it? Flim-flam. Ornamentation. It's the sort of thing you have to put in a monograph." And in any event, NSF wanted to know that he had done the work. She became "livid," accused him of dishonesty. On the one hand, he wouldn't use the quotations to support statements he had made. On the other hand, he allowed people to get the impression that what he had written derived from the interviews and the study and all the fieldwork. Meanwhile, he was telling her that he knew exactly how the work was going to come out before he had even begun.

The interviewer then asked Schneider how she responded to the fact that he dedicated the book to her. Schneider replied: by never mentioning it, never acknowledging it. And she went back to the room in which she had put together her pile of quotations, and she took two days to destroy every single piece of paper on which she had written anything. "At that point we were having a pretty serious war with each other" (209–12).

Schneider then shifted the 1994 conversation to what he regarded as the fallacious assumption of postmodernists who insisted on the centrality of ethnography. And he concluded: "It isn't ethnography, it isn't fieldwork, that is the sine qua non. It is the study of culture, period" (217).

ACT TWO

Fourteen years earlier, in the final chapter of his 1980 edition of *American Kinship,* his argument with Addie, his "close associate," had led directly to his consideration of two paragraphs from Clifford Geertz's famous essay on "thick description"[7]:

Culture is most effectively treated, the argument goes, purely as a symbolic system (the catch phrase is, "in its own terms"), by isolating its elements, specifying the internal relationships among those elements, and then characterizing the whole system in some general way—according to the core symbols around which it is organized, the underlying structures of which it is a surface expression, or the ideological principles upon which it is based. . . . this hermetical approach to things seems to me to run the danger (and increasingly to have been overtaken by it) of locking cultural analysis away from its proper object, the informal logic of actual life.

Behavior must be attended to, and with some exactness, because it is through the flow of behavior—or more precisely, social action—that cultural forms find articulation. They find it as well, of course, in various sorts of artifacts, and various states of consciousness; but these draw their meaning from the role they play (Wittgenstein would say their "use") in an ongoing pattern of life, not from any intrinsic relationships they bear to one another. (17)

Geertz's first paragraph contained a critique of efforts, like those of Schneider's in *American Kinship*, to describe "culture" as an isolated symbolic system. This approach, Geertz wrote, "seems to run the danger . . . of locking cultural analysis away from its proper object, the informal logic of actual life." The second paragraph made the positive claim that "cultural forms find articulation" in behavior and crucially "in an ongoing pattern of life, not from any intrinsic relationships they bear to one another."

For Schneider, those two paragraphs raised "a veritable mare's nest of problems," and they challenged directly what he had tried to do in *American Kinship*. And so, in turn, Schneider worked to contradict Geertz's claims. Much of the imagined debate Schneider conducted with Geertz is beside the point of this essay, locked as it is in the twists and turns of social science debates of the period 1960 to 1980. There is a lot of dancing on Talcott Parson's grave, a good bit of Saussure and Lévi-Strauss. At bottom, Schneider worked in this part of the 1980 edition to defend the enterprise of exploring "the systematic features of culture." He distinguished the study of "the culture as constituted," which is what he was interested in, from what people actually do, what their actual patterns of action are. Geertz had insisted that meaning was not to be found in the specifications of relationships among symbolic elements but only in descriptions of actual behavior. Schneider disagreed. The specification of symbolic elements did not deny the next move, which would be to explore how culture (that is to say, those symbolic elements) would be articulated in social action. And he conceded that without that next move, "all the rest is empty." But still, the specification was both prior and necessary. "There is a system of signs and meanings which everyone has to learn as a child and must continue to learn even as an adult, and this is not simply an edict of any individual actor."[8]

How does one identify, how does one find, "the systematic features of culture"? Where should one look for evidence, say, about kinship as culture? At the beginning of *American Kinship* (13–14), and again in his 1994 interview, Schneider gave special, although unclear, weight to his own status as a relatively expert "informant," because he was himself an American living in America. In other words, it might be, as his wife had suggested, that he had asserted solipsistic authority prior to coming to the sources, that he already knew what he was looking for, and then he found it. And at various points in both texts he came close to conceding her point. Here, though, in his 1980 one-sided debate with Geertz, he moved in a different direction, along the way resuscitating the six thousand pages of field notes that he had effectively killed off a few pages earlier.

The "very first step," he writes, "is to deal with the 'flow of social action' and 'actual behavior' as much as possible, or, what is the next best thing, to report what people say about what they are doing, and what they think they are doing, and why they are doing what they are doing, and above all, how they define and understand what they are doing." Out of this material—here the six thousand pages—symbols and meanings are abstracted. And the real question is whether the process of abstraction has been performed properly (127).

As Schneider wrote about Geertz, so I might write of Schneider: that a veritable mare's nest of problems lurk in this passage. Here, suddenly, the research has been re-created as standing prior to and independent from the scholarship. At its simplest and most defensible, he seems to be saying that he is engaged in a particular process of abstraction in which the product—a theory of culture—that he is after derives from but remains rhetorically and conceptually distant from the "evidence" collected and analyzed. One would then reframe the Geertz–Schneider argument as between Schneider, who believes in a three-step process—case or archive or fieldwork, followed by abstraction toward a structural theory of culture, followed by inquiries back into how culture is articulated in social action (as in the stories, anecdotes, and quotations found in the case or archive or fieldwork), and Geertz, who would short-circuit that roundabout way of proceeding (and insist that the only culture worth talking about is in the stories). There is a difference in procedure and, presumptively, in product. But Schneider's way depends, as Geertz's does, on the work in the field.

But then why respond as he did to Addie, as if evidence were infinitely manipulable and meaningless, and why continue, as he did in the 1994 interview, to insist on the insignificance of fieldwork?

I'm not sure of an answer. Again, one could distinguish the problem Addie's collected quotations raised for him from the problem Geertz sets up. That is, we can distinguish the problem of the indeterminacy of any one piece of evidence, any particular story, from the necessity of collecting evidence and collecting stories. Thus, to go to my own little backyard of work: one could insist that no individual case about domestic violence can prove anything either about the history of marriage or about coverture as a cultural form; yet, at the same time, we might agree that one should read many such narratives and cases in order to abstract a theory of coverture. Something, actually quite a lot, seems wrong with that formulation. But I have to admit that it seems wrong to me largely because I am so committed to the notion that the enterprise of doing a cultural history of law is, in the first instance, about "uncovering" (discovering, construing, finding words that approximate) the "informal logic of actual life," to use Geertz's famous phrase. And that may be simply to say that I am generationally (temporally and by temperament) a poststructural-ist, whereas Schneider was definitely, and in the end defiantly, a structuralist.

The problem, at least as presented in his 1994 rendition, is that Schneider did not draw the distinction I just made up for him to solve his Addie problem and his Geertz problem. Instead, he wrote: "I do not believe that anything more than minor alterations or emendations or ornamentations in my basic presuppositions arose either from the interview material or from the discussions from the interviewers that in some way changed my picture of what the hell was happening, what the schema was like" (209). Schneider then went on to claim that he never really looked at the interviews and other field materials at all while he was writing the book. And the clear implication of his words was that the whole process of gathering interview material—the six thousand pages—had been a waste of time. The interviewer challenged him: "One of the great virtues of anthropology is going out into the world and talking to people and looking at situations. It's not exactly that we go out to test hypotheses, but the field situation does offer a resist-ance to our preconceptions, and our theorizing comes out of our engagement with that situation." I'm not sure if Schneider was simply tired, or if he was tired of challenging the conventional wisdom of his interviewer, but at that point, he agreed. And in the last few pages of the interview he suggested, with a "nod to Geertz," that really fieldwork, research, is "doing the interpretation" as one is "doing it" [the research]. But that then led him back toward a general critique of work that ascribes any particular significance to fieldwork (212–17).

ACT THREE

Now I enter into the story, at least momentarily. If Clifford Geertz was a stand-in for Schneider's wife, so Geertz and Addie Schneider stand in for me, at least in my legal historical identity. Let me frame the problem as sharply as possible: everything about the historical enterprise to which I have committed my life leads me to want to identify with Addie Schneider and Clifford Geertz, in their real and imagined arguments with David Schneider. I have always been captured by a yearning for access to the "informal logic of actual life." I have long believed in the power of quotations and the independence and priority (and partial unassimilability) of stories, anecdotes, and quotations drawn from archives (field notes). I have an inveterate skepticism of large theories—systems—particularly when they seem disconnected from direct engagement with evidence. And if we are going to understand law as we (liberal arts scholars) would like to understand it, as a part of what Carol Greenhouse calls "the impossible goal of trying to find a way to write about actual people," then we will do so with continuing attention to stories and quotations and the other ephemeral leavings that offer us our only access to that understanding of law.[9]

Yet those commitments carry anxieties, both about intellectual honesty (who am I fooling, and how am I fooling them when I tell a story or mobilize a quotation or an anecdote?) and about the meaningfulness of the enterprise.

On the first anxiety: In my book *Man and Wife in America: A History*, I wrote about the treatment of domestic violence by courts (lower and appellate) and treatise writers in early nineteenth-century America. I gathered quotations that demonstrated that these voices all took issue with the common understanding (then and now) that male violence was ordinarily unregulated within the home.[10] These quotations played a crucial role in my portrayal of a legal system dedicated to distinguishing the legitimate from the illegitimate uses of male power. And they left the impression, one I worked somewhat in the text to challenge, that the law actually operated as a restraint on male power.

I don't mean to qualify the argument I made there. I think I presented material accurately and honestly. But those quotations lend apparent weight to the argument, without fully conceding the selectivity inherent in the presentation. A different set of concerns would surely have produced a different presentation. All those quotations could have been repackaged in a narrative about the continuity of private power or about the meaninglessness of legal language. I could have written about them with an ironic or a winking voice, inviting the reader to explore the bad faith or the blindness of the writers to the real wrongs going on around them. If I had not been so convinced that their import was coherent with other features of the practices and rules (the system) of marriage law during the first half of the nineteenth century, I might have portrayed them as outliers or the random leavings of a historical process that never presents us with a representative sample of voices.

Or, on the second anxiety: I talk about stories and practices, but I know I mean structures. And I look for working rules, which often become, in the telling, abstracted and dyadic categories and principles. It is, of course, wrong to imagine that law ever is "a system of signs and meanings which everyone has to learn as a child." But I write to create order, not to reproduce chaos, and so, like Schneider, I would love "to abstract from that ongoing flow of life certain regularities."

Thus, to offer one last anecdote, at a recent workshop at Yale on how the historiography of family law has changed in recent years, Laura Edwards described her current research. She has found (the lure of the archive) a large body of cases throughout the early nineteenth-century South in which local judges and prosecutors affirmed the right of wives to sue their husbands for abuse. Meanwhile, she has also traced the more familiar story of the largely impenetrable barriers appellate courts seemed to place against such suits. And then she told us about how in South Carolina, and perhaps elsewhere, the same judges who were accepting prosecutions on behalf of wives against husbands in lower courts were also sitting on the appellate courts, where the formal rules against such prosecutions were being articulated.

At that moment, the legal historian Robert Gordon challenged both Edwards and myself (we were the discussion leaders) by asking whether there was any systematic explanation, any systematic structural description, that could accommodate both the local and the elite/appellate stories within them. He thought trying to do so was a useless task. He might have said, "Why bother?" Or perhaps, what he said was more like, give up on the fantasy. But both Edwards and I disagreed with him. As with one voice, both of us said yes, we do believe in the search for the systematic explanation that would join local and elite together, although neither of us had the words or the theories or the categories to suggest how it all worked together, in the moment. Yet if that is what I believe, how can I avoid structural "abstractions," along lines not so very different as those that David Schneider argued for. As I think back through my imagined conversations with the dead David Schneider, I want to concede to him that the capacity to talk about how things work together—our ability to suggest how the local and the elite/appellate come together—will only come after we have "abstracted" from the particular, moved on to a plane of structures quite separated from the noise and jumble of the stories.

Like Molière's *bourgeois gentilhomme*, am I speaking structurally in spite of myself?

Yet I would still insist that one humanistic task for those of us who are not of (or who have separated ourselves from) the law school world is to reconstruct and play out the meanings and tonalities located in the stories, quotations, and anecdotes that offer us primary access to the ways women and men work through and think about their relationships to law. Greenhouse's impossible goal is, for those of us who share it in legal studies and legal history, compounded by the additional weirdnesses of trying to figure out how law mattered in the lives of real people and, more oddly still, of trying to write about real people by the use of legal sources from the past. We are captured by the romance of the project. Along the way, I would also affirm my still vibrant romantic attachment to "the archives," to the possibility of learning things one never expected (better, never completely expected), about a world to which we have radically incomplete access (other minds, other people).

NOTES

1. Karl N. Llewellyn and E. Adamson Hoebel, *The Cheyenne Way: Conflict and Case Law in Primitive Jurisprudence* (Norman: University of Oklahoma Press, 1941), 27–29.

2. Natalie Z. Davis, *The Return of Martin Guerre* (Cambridge: Harvard University Press, 1983); Carlo Ginzburg, *The Cheese and the Worms: The Cosmos of a Sixteenth-Century Miller* (Baltimore: Johns Hopkins University Press, 1980); Emmanuel LeRoy Ladurie, *Montaillou* (New York: Penguin, 1980); Lawrence Stone, "The Revival of Narrative: Reflections on a New Old History," *Past and Present* 85 (1979): 3–24; James Goodman, "For the Love of Stories," *Reviews in American History* 26, 1 (March 1998): 255–74.

3. M. M. Bakhtin, *The Dialogic Imagination: Four Essays,* ed. Michael Holquist, trans. Michael Holquist and Caryl Emerson (Austin: University of Texas Press, 1981).

4. David M. Schneider, *American Kinship: A Cultural Account* (Chicago: University of Chicago Press, 1968; 2nd ed., 1980). See Barbara Yngvesson, "Negotiating Motherhood: Identity and Difference in 'Open' Adoptions," *Law and Society Review* 31, 1 (1997): 31–80; Janet Carsten, ed., *Cultures of Relatedness: New Approaches to the Study of Kinship* (Cambridge: Cambridge University Press, 2000); Sarah Franklin and Susan McKinnon, eds., *Relative Values: Reconfiguring Kinship Studies* (Durham, N.C.: Duke University Press, 2001).

5. David M. Schneider and Richard Handler, *Schneider on Schneider: The Conversion of the Jews and Other Anthropological Stories* (Durham, N.C.: Duke University Press, 1995).

6. It might be noted then that in this case his generalization did follow from a confrontation with evidence.

7. Clifford Geertz, *The Interpretation of Cultures: Selected Essays* (New York: Basic, 1973), 3–30, quotation at 17. Geertz and Schneider had been colleagues both at the University of Chicago and at Berkeley, although evidently their relationship soured in the 1960s. In his 1994 interview, Schneider accused Geertz of having maintained inappropriate government connections, whereas Geertz, like many others, was upset over the "politicization" of the university. Schneider and Handler, *Schneider on Schneider,* 189.

8. Schneider, *American Kinship,* 125–36.

9. The Greenhouse quotation occurred in conversation.

10. Hendrik Hartog, *Man and Wife in America: A History* (Cambridge: Harvard University Press, 2003), 103–5.

"TERMES QUEINTE OF LAWE" AND
QUAINT FANTASIES OF LITERATURE

SUSAN SAGE HEINZELMAN

Quaint: OFr. cointe (quointe, cuinte, etc.), queinte:—
L. cognitum: known. Of persons and things: know-
ing, canny, cunning; Of speech: full of fancies or
conceits; Of the woman's body: ingeniously wrought,
uncanny, genitalia (vulgar: cunt).

        —Oxford English Dictionary

The occasion for this collection is to reflect, once again, on the relationship between law and the humanities, a relationship grounded in a set of shared assumptions about the importance of inquiring into our culture's philosophic foundations and a recognition that such an inquiry is both an investigation in and through language.[1] This linguistic emphasis explains, in part, the etymological epigraph ("Quaint") to this essay.

The authors of this volume were invited to consider a "new synthesis" of legal scholarship and liberal arts, but in this essay I suggest that we should consider a new version of an old synthesis. Indeed, when we glance at the text that prompted this volume—Harold Berman's account of a symposium at the Harvard Law School in 1954—we find that he too is calling for a new way of thinking about the law. He quotes from an AALS report of 1953, which argues that the "law needs other disciplines. . . . It needs constantly recurring guidance from the outside, whether it be in the matter of fundamental values to which philosophy and history and literature may contribute, or in the matter of means in a particular environment in which the social sciences are coming to give enlightenment."[2] Berman's reflections are themselves rooted in previous claims by legal scholars such as Blackstone and Burke, that a complete education implies knowledge of the law as well as the study of the humanities. One could go on tracing this regressive narrative, as Berman does, back at least to the fourteenth century.[3] My point here is simply to note the powerful nostalgia that informs these reflections, a nostalgia for that original time when law and humanities were not separated but rather inextricably united, one discipline, one body of knowledge, such that people instinctively knew how to live in a state of harmony with one another and with the world around them. Such nostalgia is not, of course, peculiar to the modern era; Peter Goodrich cites Cicero's complaint that legal rhetoric separated from poetics produces not merely "ineloquence" but injustice. And Peter Fitzpatrick cites Freud's "purely fictive account of the origin" of civilization, wherein this ideal harmony between law and poetics is "achieved in [the] imagination [of] the first epic poet."[4]

Depending on whom you believe, the Enlightenment either delivered us from the monsters of ignorance that flourished when this Edenic world was lost or it ensured that those monsters continued their relentless "slouching toward Bethlehem."[5] For French philosopher Bruno Latour, however, both versions of this intellectual history suffer from the mistaken belief that what defines the Enlightenment is the separation of the scientific, the political, and the aesthetic. For Latour, knowledge has always been represented both in its separate, disciplinary forms—what he calls purification—and, simultaneously, in the interdisciplinarity that we identify as one of the forms of postmodernism—what Latour calls hybridity. The Enlightenment, argues Latour, is not a rupture from a previous system of belief but rather a renaming of that system: the first Enlightenment thinkers "no longer saw anything in the hybrids of old but illegitimate mixtures that they had to purify by separating natural mechanism from human passions, interests or ignorance. . . . The obscurity of olden days, which illegitimately blended together social needs and natural reality, meaning and mechanism, signs and things, gave way to a luminous dawn that cleanly separated material causality from human fantasy."[6] For those who were "enlightened," a longing for a world of hybrids seemed merely retrograde and primitive.

Rejecting this pre-Enlightenment appreciation of the intimate relations between the natural and the human world was one way for post-Enlightenment thinkers to distinguish themselves from their more "primitive" predecessors, one way to insist on a progressive ideology by which they "naturally" embodied the modern. This continuing insistence by our culture on the inevitably primitive quality of that which invokes the nonrational shadows much feminist criticism, marking it as dangerous in its subversion of the apparently rational consensus of post-Enlightenment Western civilization. But the act of imagination that feminist critic Maria Aristodemou proposes—that is, to reconstitute a time " 'before the law,' before representation, before logos"— is surely no more regressive or antirational than Freud's imaginative reconstruction of the origins of civilization in an act of parricide, from which an elaborate psycho-social system has developed. Linking the nostalgia for an ancient harmony and balance with an overt feminist critique of the "modernist and masculinist model of justice and rights," critics like Aristodemou and Goodrich, among others, lament the effort to exclude poetics from law, especially the gendered and hierarchical nature of that exclusion. The repression of the aesthetic and the emotional in law is "an attempt to deny . . . the presence of 'a feminine genealogy within the ancient constitution, a feminine unconscious to the doctrines of the common law.' "[7]

As inhabitants of a postlapsarian world, we acknowledge that within each discipline, certain kinds of knowledge will be (temporarily and conditionally) privileged. These representational hierarchies are unstable, however, and so although the relationship of poetics to law may be represented between disciplines as the relationship of the feminine to the masculine, poetics nevertheless performs as masculine within its own disciplinary protocols. We must therefore acknowledge that our conversation about interdisciplinarity is always already fraught with the implications and values of those disciplines from which we speak and that their values, and the ones of those disciplines we investigate, are volatile and relative to our particular historical moment and the perspective we assume. My own reading of two tales from Chaucer's *Canterbury Tales,* which I offer here as an allegory of the relationship between law and literature, exemplifies this relativity, speaking as I do from the perspective of one trained formally in literature. Moreover, my historical gesture replicates those that I noted earlier in the essay; I too turn back to canonical texts to explore the relationship of legal scholarship and the liberal arts in the contemporary construction of disciplinary knowledge. I do not do so, however, in the belief that I will find there the certainty and stability that the present lacks.

AN ALLEGORY OF INTERDISCIPLINARITY: THE MAN OF LAW AND THE WIFE OF BATH

For the purposes of this essay, I have read the text of the *Canterbury Tales* in ways that scholars of Chaucer might find both historically and theoretically problematic. I have not, for example, engaged with the critical debate over the relationship between the character of the pilgrim and the suitability of his or her tale, nor with the various theories about the order of the tales, and I have not drawn out the implications of Chaucer's authorial relationship to his characters, specifically the Man of Law and the Wife of Bath.[8] (In the character of the Wife, for example, we have a case of cross-gendered ventriloquism.) Although I recognize that both tales are fictional constructs, that both tellers are fictional subjects (and, as "creations" of the fictional narrator, fictional objects), I speak about the Man of Law and the Wife of Bath *as if* they were real individuals, ignoring for the time being the fact that both are "voiced" by a narrator, who is himself voiced by Chaucer. This essay is not the place to unravel the implications of these narrative complications. I have taken the tales at face value so that, paradoxically, they might perform metaphorically and illustrate how law and literature, or what we might call, using Chaucerian terms, authority and experience, is represented as gendered and hierarchical. I undertake my allegorical reading in two ways: first, in terms of the tensions between legal and literary discourse manifest within each tale, and then, in terms of the relationship implied between these two tales. Such readings suggest the complexities we face when integrating law and liberal arts, and they are themselves an articulation of that practice.

The play of competing discourses—familiar and foreign, popular and aristocratic, customary and formal, Christian and pre-Christian, material and spiritual—is ubiquitous in the *Canterbury Tales,* but the Man of Law and the Wife of Bath offer us two precise and gendered versions of this discursive contest. As two of the twenty-nine pilgrims identified in the "General Prologue" journeying from London to the shrine of the martyred Saint Thomas à Becket in Canterbury Cathedral, the Man of Law and the Wife of Bath enact, both in their persons and through their particular tales, a contest between the growing centralized and professional face of the law and what Clifford Geertz calls "the informal logic of actual life." It was a contest familiar to Chaucer's audience and even now provides fertile ground to scholars such as Hendrik Hartog, who, "doing a cultural history of the law," seek to uncover and thereby convert into narrative ("romance") those occasions when law bumps up against the lives of real people.[9]

The Man of Law's Tale of Custance

According to the narrator's account in the "General Prologue," each pilgrim has agreed to tell a story to pass the time on the journey, and the one who, in the opinion of the judge—the Host of the tavern where they begin their pilgrimage—"telleth in this caas / Tales of best sentence and moost solaas" ("tells in this way, tales of best significance and most comfort") will be rewarded with a prize (A 798). The Host invites the Man of Law to fulfill the terms of the contract and begin the contest. "Biheste is dette" ("A promise is a debt") responds the lawyer, for whom "the act of tale-telling is all in a day's work,"[10] claiming his status as a professional teller of tales about authority and the law, "oure text" (B 41, 45).

The Man of Law is a sergeant-at-law ("servientes ad legem"), one of the king's legal servants, who "had exclusive rights to plead cases in the Court of Common Pleas." They were "selected from barristers of sixteen years' standing. From their number [the Order of the Coif] were chosen the judges of the King's courts and the chief baron of the Exchequer. . . . They were few in number—about twenty when Chaucer wrote—and the most eminent members of the profession."[11] As a practitioner of the common law, the Man of Law is part of that tradition of English common law that might be said to have been baptized, if not born, in the reign of Henry II, the king responsible for the death of that same "hooly blisful martir" (A 17), Saint Thomas à Becket, to whose shrine the pilgrims are traveling. Becket was martyred in 1170, murdered by royal assassins for defending the church against the jurisdictional encroachments of Henry II (1154–89), who crafted new laws governing the relationship between church and state, as well as systematizing the Curia Regis, royal courts that heard both criminal cases and land disputes. In these royal courts, citizens could bring suit that would then be heard by appointed officers of the court rather than local officers. Beginning with Henry II we see the gradual centralizing and enlarging of the power and scope of the common law, a system of juridical government that necessarily reflected and reinforced the gender asymmetry of the state, even if it still offered a potential venue for those traditionally excluded from the courts—the secular, the non-aristocratic, women.

In the "General Prologue" to the *Canterbury Tales*, the sergeant is described, as Carolyn Dinshaw has argued, not merely as a man of the law but as a man "made up of law"; he has in his Year Books all the cases and decisions made since the Conquest, and he knows every statute entirely by heart ("And every statut koude he pleyn by rote" [A 327]). Because the common law of England "legislated land tenure, commercial relations and transactions, and the structure of the family" and reinforced royal prerogatives, the Man of Law might be said to embody "patriarchal ideology and its expressed system of law."[12] The Man of Law offers, as his version of the best "sentence and solaas," a four-part providential narrative of Christian imperial patriarchy that "romances" the suffering of the faithful.

Custance, the beautiful Christian daughter of the emperor of Rome, is given in marriage to the Muslim sultan of Syria after he, so captivated by merchants' reports of Custance's beauty, has promised to convert his entire kingdom to Christianity rather than lose her. The sultan's mother, angered by her son's apostasy and her forced conversion, kills him and casts Custance adrift in a boat, bidding her sail back to her father. Aimlessly drifting for years, Custance finally lands in Northumbria, where she is once again the instrument of conversion to Christianity, this time of the pagan king of Northumbria, Alla, whom she marries. For a second time, however, Constance is the victim of a wicked mother-in-law, who tricks her son into casting Custance and their child, Maurice, out of the kingdom and adrift on the ocean. After more wandering, and threatened with rape and death by a renegade Christian, Custance and

Maurice finally return by chance to Rome, where she is united with her father and where Alla, coincidentally, has arrived on a pilgrimage to atone for his treatment of his wife and son. Custance is restored to her husband (the transfer of daughter from father to husband is enacted yet again), and after the death of her father, Custance's son, Maurice, becomes the emperor of Rome and its Christian kingdoms.[13]

This tale of Custance, the Man of Law claims, was told to him by a merchant "goon . . . many a yeere" (B 132). The supposedly antique tale, with its repeated tropes of exile, false accusation, punishment, and conversion, has the formulaic quality of an oral narrative, reminding us of the importance of memory in constructing the social in this world, before the invention of the printing press. The tale also has the predictability of a familiar story, one passed from one narrator to another, recalling a genre of storytelling that appears to be nothing like that employed by the law or the church: the "once upon a time" of chivalric romance and fairytale. Romance and fairytale are, however, like the ideological narratives of church and state, driven by a desire for predictability, for a sure future built out of the repeated stories of the past. And so, as befits the narrative protocols of his profession and its reliance on precedent, the Man of Law turns back to what has gone before and, putting his trust in history to sanction the "truth" of his tale, fashions a Christian romance, a tale of constancy that asserts the immutability of Christian faith (in God, in law). Like the creation of legal doctrine through precedent, however, this desire for predictability is constantly undermined by the inevitability of change: every effort to assure the stability of the story by retelling it inexorably confirms its impermanence and thus generates yet more longing for the immutable, which can only be satisfied by yet another story.

Thus the repeated act of conversion in the tale models the repetitious structure of desire itself: man's longing for an ever-elusive constancy (Custance) sets the plot in motion. Just as the desire for permanence is sabotaged by the instability of narrative, however, so the desire for Custance (felt by the sultan and Alla and necessary to generate the conversion from Muslim or pagan to Christian) constantly threatens to subvert the hagiographic romance of Custance's missionary zeal and to convert it into another kind of romance in which erotic desire triumphs over divine love. As Geraldine Heng has convincingly argued, romance is a genre that is defined not by "any intrinsic subject matter, plot, style, or other content" but by the "repetition" of structures of desire through "innumerable transformations." In hagiographic romance, she contends, "the sexual formula and alchemy of an erotic trajectory that has served medieval romance for centuries since the genre's inception must give way to a different order of love."[14] The "Man of Law's Tale" embodies the conflict between these two different kinds of romance, two different kinds of love, a conflict exacerbated by the location of both *eros* and *caritas,* erotic and divine love, in the body of a woman.

In his narrative, the Man of Law suggests that a "different order of love" might be achieved through/despite the body of a woman, but only with an atypical woman such as Custance, whose constancy and self-sacrifice belie the stereotypical infidelity and insatiability of women and who therefore conjures up the only woman who embodies that ideal of Christian womanhood, the Virgin Mary. Custance must be a woman who generates desire in others and, as a daughter of Eve, will be held responsible for the consequences of the desire others feel but will not herself feel desire.[15] Subject to constant suspicion yet constantly guiltless, she is doomed as a woman to suffer repeated punishment. It is through and on Custance's body, forever traveling between the Christian and the non-Christian, between father and husband, that the "diversitee / Bitwene hir bothe lawes" (B 220–21) ("the difference between both their [i.e., the Christian and the Muslim] laws") is reconciled, although she herself plays no active part in that reconciliation. Indeed, it is precisely because she can function as the (fantasy) object of desire for both Christian and Muslim that she has value. Her body is a cipher, a blank text upon which the imperial law of the father is written, and she is thereby the bearer of the letter and spirit of that law. Although Custance, the faithful and law-embodying daughter and wife is without desire—that being the sign of her Christianity and fidelity—her mothers-in-law manifest their "otherness" in acting upon their desire, that being the sign of their infidel(ity). Doubly damned, as non-Christian and as women, these cunning ones "naturally" plot to undermine Christian patriarchal governance.

In its repetitious structure and its focus on the necessity for the subjection of the female, the "Man of Law's Tale" enacts in its narrative form those cultural transformations and exchanges essential to systems of trade, law, and ideology. The story articulates a crucial ideology: women are goods to be trafficked between men in the interests of commerce, faith, and empire; indeed, even before Custance herself travels to Syria, merchants trade reports of her beauty. Women bear the burden of reproducing both the material and spiritual conditions of the empire: its religion, its law, and its political structures. Thus Custance's religious devotion is evidence of a saintliness that is specifically rendered in terms of her willingness to travel far from home, like the merchant trader, to convert the heathen and to spread the Law/laws of the Father; in other words, her saintliness is the mark of her passivity in terms of her own desires and her activity in terms of her (Christian and secular) father's desires. Custance is an "object obliged to follow orders" rather than an active, desiring subject, just as "at the level of narrative form her exemplary role is a function of the generic authority of hagiography."[16] It is this objectification of the suffering woman of the hagiographic romance that the Wife of Bath challenges in her revision of the Arthurian romance narrative in her tale.

"The Man of Law's Tale," then, is a Christian parable that teaches, as Custance says, that "Wommen are born to thraldom and penance, / And to been under mannes governance" ("women are born to servitude and penance, and to be under man's governance") (B 286–87). Moreover, it teaches by analogy—a pedagogical procedure shared by law—that the "Other," the Muslim, is also destined to be under Christian governance. As the mother of Maurice, who becomes the Christian emperor of Rome, Custance is also the mother of the community of the faithful, who are subject to the governance of church and state. In particular, because she brings Christianity and its system of laws to England, her story retroactively "legitimize[s] a certain form of authority. . . . She is . . . the origin, the spiritual mother who gave birth to the authority of the Christian monarchs of medieval England," an authority that is inseparably both religious and legal, both spiritual and secular:

> If the people of England are historically united by the common possession of laws—common law, the 'Laws of the English'—medieval romance in the form of the Constance story ensures that we remember that the English are also united by religious faith—"lawe"—canon law, sacred literature, catechism, exhortations and creed, "credence," that bind each community.

Indeed, the Man of Law, "true to the vocabulary of his profession, evinces a preference for describing both Christianity and Islam as systems of law . . . rather than of 'creance.'"[17]

The Man of Law employs literary genres—romance, parable, and allegory—to reiterate the workings of a providence that is masculinist in its theological, political, and social intent. His is also a didactic tale that functions in the social world of the pilgrimage with the same kind of authority that the statutes, cases, and judgments that he has memorized possess in the world of the common law, a world very much present in this romance. The story is saturated with legal concepts, which are drawn from customary and common law; it invokes treason, perjury, debt, contract, laws of evidence and of accusation, as well as degrees of punishment—all manner of strategies by which the law invests a community with a sense of its identity and its difference from those who follow other rules. The Man of Law has a professional interest in hagiographic narrative, in promoting a metonymic discourse where the figure of Custance "stands in for" Christian missionary zeal and its suffering in a world of heathens.[18] As Kathleen Kelly, paraphrasing Clifford Geertz, puts it: "the saint's life is a story that Christians of late antiquity and the Middle Ages told themselves about themselves. And they told it over and over again. . . . One of the effects of this repetitive performance is to elide 'real' experience, real suffering, real death in order to privilege an Imaginary and imaginary past."[19]

Like legal historiography, hagiography depends on repetition—of like facts producing like results; in the case of the saint's life, this means that all suffering is an imitation of Christ's suffering and leads to salvation. At the same time, both narrative genres distrust the empirical reality in which the original event and its repetitions are grounded as subject to human limitations (of truthfulness, of faith). This tension between the representation of a transcendent secular or spiritual belief and its quotidian basis pervades the "Man of Law's Tale" and is most trenchantly personified in Custance's body. Reflecting the Man of Law's larger purpose, Constance's desire is "stringently regulated, disciplined, and . . . effaced—as indeed both medieval law and literature recommend."[20] The need to control Custance's excess (as sign, as woman) so that she can represent desire and its submission (to law) for both the Christian and the Muslim, for both the selfsame and the other, reduces her to an enigmatic text; rather than restraining interpretation, however, such a text incites interpretation and a promiscuity of meaning that threatens to escape the control of those in authority (and thus is conventionally linked to literature, to women, to others).

The Host pronounces the Man of Law's story a "thrifty" tale, and indeed, if one thinks of telling a story as the exchange of one thing for another,[21] an allegorical equivalency, then this lawyer has tried to be economical in his representation, endeavoring to produce an instrumental text, a parable in which signs refer, in a seemingly unambiguous and unmediated way, to their "authorized" meanings, a narrative in which a woman's body "stands in for" Christian piety. The allegory of conversion, represented by Custance's repeated exiles and returns, "privileges meaning over event and the general and exemplary over the specific" and, like law, functions as both precedent and prediction.[22] He has tried to craft his story as he would draft a legal document—so as to restrain the inevitable excess of representation, the ambiguity of language—but he is, of course, doomed to failure. Despite his obsession "with retention . . . [his] anxiety about circulation, [his fear] of the flow of things, of media, be they money or women or words," the ambiguity of language constantly threatens to defeat him, as when the name of the pagan king of Northumbria, Alla, not only recalls that of the Muslim divinity, Allah, but is a palindrome and as such captures the cunning of language, its essentially figurative (and therefore imaginary) nature.[23]

To the Man of Law, literature supplements and illustrates his political, religious, and legal ideology and the tale of Custance represents the highest values of that ideology—"constancy and fidelity," the two principles that are fundamental to the legal doctrine of precedent and religious authority.[24] Through repetition and the drive toward similitude, with its consequent restraint upon female desire and the erasure of difference, the Man of Law aims not merely to tell a story about constancy but to structure his narrative as the embodiment of that value. Despite his best efforts, however, Custance's hagiography constantly threatens to become something else: a secular romance structured by material rather than spiritual desire, a story of how men desire women and their bodies, and how that desire so constantly disrupts families and communities that it must, finally, be subjected to a higher "lawe," one that will appear to be the consequence of women's nature, not men's. Such is the inevitable implication of the Man of Law's "sentence," of his "dom"; for women, it is a judgment without much "solaas."

The Wife of Bath's "Queinte Fantasye"

When the Host calls for another professional storyteller to speak—a doctor or priest—the red-stockinged, large-hipped, loud-mouthed, five-times widowed Wife of Bath protests that she can't tolerate another tale with "termes queinte of lawe" ("quaint terms of law") (B 1189). Instead, she proposes that "her joly body . . . shal a tale telle" (B 1185). The Wife is no dreamer; she understands the authority vested in the legal and theological discourses that control women's lives. She can, however, offer a hypothetical alternative to that authority, a supplement to those "termes queinte of lawe," and in what appears to be a frontal attack on the patriarchy, she inscribes that alternative discourse in the very site that conventionally has signified her inferiority: she offers her "queinte," her "bel chose," (her "beautiful thing"), that which has been designated by the patriarchy as mere commodity and sign of sin but which the Wife of Bath claims as the source both of her "sentence" and her "solaas," of her significance and her pleasure. Challenging the lawyer's "termes queinte" with her own "queinte" (her cunt), the Wife insists that her body is not merely an object of exchange that facilitates male commerce and ideology but that it has meaning beyond that assigned by law and theology, a meaning created by the Wife's own desire and thus boundless. She offers her experience as an alternative to masculine authority, arguing that such knowledge is sufficient evidence to authorize her narrative ("Experience, though noon auctoritee / Were in this world, is right ynogh for me / To speke" [D 1–2]). Moreover, she fashions her "termes queinte" not from texts but out of her own body, its desire, and the suffering that desire has produced, signs that are, ironically, precisely the same—the body, desire, and suffering—as those that shape Christian salvation ideology and that have governed the Man of Law's story of Custance.[25]

Although the official relationship of women to law mimicked their relationship to the greatest source of authority in medieval society, the church, and thus "excluded [them] from a wide variety of legal functions, including acting as witness, making contracts and administering property,"[26] the Wife's status as a widow and wealthy merchant provided her with social independence and authority in matters of trade and law. The growth of common law during the medieval period did little to alter the law's limited representation of women: in the twelfth and early thirteenth centuries, a woman "could only bring charges against an offender for rape, miscarriage, or death of her husband. She could not bring charges for theft, burglary, or death of any other relative."[27] In other words, as property she could make claims only when that property was diminished in value—through assault on her body or her spouse. Since legally she owned nothing, she could not claim to have been robbed of anything. Unofficially, however, women of noble rank participated actively in the management of domestic affairs, especially in matters of family property: many sales contracts, leases, and donations, for example, were signed by women, or by men who identified themselves through their mother's name.

Such participation was not restricted to noblewomen. In particular, widows were named as executrices in their husband's wills and frequently undertook to manage their husband's affairs, running businesses, protecting their children's interests, and representing themselves in court. Some women could achieve a degree of independence in business and might even control, as the Wife does, the distribution of their property. During the 1300s, "women as plaintiffs in both criminal and land law gained greater access to the courts," and the development of the jury trial provided some women with an audience more closely aligned to them in class to which they might tell their stories. Balanced against these increased legal rights, however, must be the awareness that women disappeared from the court room in one major capacity: "in the early thirteenth century, we see women acting as attorneys, even for their husbands. By the end of the thirteenth century, lawyers have become an almost entirely male professional class. The common law courts have become increasingly the arena of men."[28]

It is into this increasingly professionalized, masculine world that the Wife of Bath brashly rides. Claiming her body and its experience as a site of meaning and pleasure—a somatic authority—the Wife of Bath turns upside down those theological and legal authorities that have marked the woman's body as the source of evil and sin.[29] As indicative of the continuing power of those authorities, the editor, in all but the most recent edition of the *Norton Anthology of English Literature* in which "The Wife of Bath's Prologue and Tale" are printed, has glossed the vulgar Anglo-Saxon term *queinte* by a Latin term, *pudendum,* which means "that which should be hidden, that of which one is ashamed"! We should not only mark the specific term that has been chosen to translate *queinte* but also its language. Apparently, even as late as the year 2000, the Latin language, so long the mark of privileged masculine power, still veiled a certain kind of knowledge (legal, sexual) from the laity.

In a prologue to her tale that is as self-indulgent as the Man of Law's is restrained, the Wife proposes to offer her experience of one woman's woe as counterstatement to the authority of the early Church Fathers and their commentators. Like a skilled lawyer, the Wife preemptively acknowledges that classical and theological complaints against women are well founded but insists that such behavior is warranted by male misogyny: she presents courtship as business wrangling and marriage as a property battle waged between and over her body and her husband's wealth. It is a dangerous strategy and seems to confirm precisely that which she would deny. In the almost entirely male court of public opinion that the pilgrims represent, the Wife argues like a lawyer and a priest, "glosing" (interpreting) biblical texts and the commentaries of the early Church Fathers in which she finds her own oppression authorized. Like the contemporaneous heretical practitioners of Lollardy, the Wife of Bath asserts her right to interpret those sacred texts previously reserved for the expert. "In this sermon the Wife . . . presents herself as a woman preacher— a highly troubling figure in a society in which women were prevented from officiating in any religious service, much less preaching."[30] Just as women had been excluded from the priesthood by the early Church Fathers, so now they were gradually being barred from that secular priesthood, the law. In her sermon, or opening statement, to the pilgrims, the Wife demonstrates that these two professional discourses—one spiritual, one secular—are intimately entwined in their structural and ideological affects on the female body.

The Wife's actual body is not the sealed and therefore enticingly vulnerable body of the virgin or the maternal body of the mother—both versions of female sexuality figured in Custance—nor the chaste body of the widow who has renounced remarriage, but rather the sexually active, economically independent, and constantly garrulous body of the widowed merchant Wife. She thus provokes the pervasive male fear of women's carnality, the "fear of woman's shamelessness" and of their "verbal licentiousness," characteristics that are "at once frightening and exciting." Moreover, this "double bind of antipathy and allure precipitated by feminine speech is wound more tightly when the woman happens to be old," and especially when she is a widow.[31] As one who knows about sex and can now use that knowledge freely, she is untrammeled by the social and legal restraints practiced on other women; circulating in society ("wandrynge by the weye," [A 467]), the Wife possesses her own self in a way denied to virgins and wives.

The Wife "flaunts not only her preaching" but also her prosecutorial skills: her manner of conducting what might be called a trial of gender relations is adversarial, her rhetoric, oppositional, as befits the genre.[32] Employing traditional legal tactics and rhetoric, the Wife takes the evidence of women's deceit and duplicity and shapes that evidence, circumstantially, to produce a narrative of man's sexual and economic greed, a narrative that explodes the imperial romance of women's commodification represented by the Man of Law. Her reading is a "cunning" one, a faux naive literalizing of figurative language—as, for example, when she asks how more virgins could be engendered if everyone, following Saint Paul's advice, remained chaste? In literalizing the figurative content of authoritative patriarchal texts, she reveals *their cunning,* their ideology, as a function of male misogyny. Her perversely literal reading (gloss) of scriptural and exegetical texts reminds her audience both of the essentially figurative (and therefore interpretable) nature of language and the power that resides with those who "tell the story"—a power she possesses for as long as she keeps talking.[33]

The Wife's argument, moreover, reveals that the law, whether secular or spiritual, is not "some abstract eternal principle but rather the embodied subject";[34] the law manifests itself only in its effects upon the body—penance, punishment, imprisonment, and the self-imposed habits of subjection. In particular, the Wife locates the force and affect of "lawe" (religious belief and secular law) upon the sexualized body of the woman. The "ingenious" nature of her "queinte"—it is both deceitful and marvelous—apparently demands the discipline of those "termes queinte of lawe." What for men "must be hidden," the pudendum (in order that it be found and possessed), the Wife proudly owns and names as her "cunt." Where those misogynistic sacred texts speak of the sewer that is a woman's body, of its temptations as the "gateway to Hell," the Wife celebrates her "bel chose" as that which should be enjoyed, not enjoined. By employing the texts and rhetorical strategies that had been used to denigrate women but "glosing" them in a different voice, the Wife of Bath prepares her predominantly male audience for the quaint "fantasye" (D 190) of her tale (tail), in which she revises the traditional narrative of knightly courtesy and female seduction.

Like the Man of Law, the Wife recalls a tale passed from one narrator to the next: she begins her story in "th'olde dayes of the Kyng Arthour . . . I speke of manye hundred yeres ago," a time "of which that Britons speken greet honour" (D 857–63, 858). Arthurian romance functions here to recall and cement a national identity, as did the Man of Law's tale of Custance, by invoking a mythical past that is markedly English. Moreover, the choice of an Arthurian romance, a genre that occurs only here in the *Canterbury Tales,* as the occasion for the Wife's narrative of violence, marital trials, and reconciliation is significant, given her concern with relationships of power and desire. As Geraldine Heng argues, "romance must be identified by the structure of desire which powers its narrative" and by the "innumerable transformations" of that structure. It is desire in its specifically erotic and gendered form that provokes the Wife's answer to the Man of Law's parable of Custance; indeed, her tale glosses the tale of Custance with a reading that suggests that the Man of Law's narrative of female martyrdom is really yet another of those "innumerable transformations" wrought by romance whereby women's desire is converted into the root of their suffering and the cause for their sentence.[35]

Employing the generic conventions of the medieval *pastourelle* or *chanson d'aventure,* in which a knight rapes or seduces a maiden to signify his entrance into manhood,[36] the Wife scripts the corruption of the world, a corruption located by the Judeo-Christian tradition in the nature of woman, in an alternative site: she substitutes a fantasy for a fantasy. It is, she argues, the violence done to women by men that spoils the uncorrupt, Edenic space: in the old days, it was an Arthurian knight, now it is lewd men of the church ("lymytours and othere hooly freres" [D 866]). Unlike Eve, who is traditionally represented as complicit in her downfall, the young woman of the Wife's tale who walks alone by the river is entirely innocent in her rape by the young knight of Arthur's court. Sentenced to die by the king, the knight is temporarily reprieved and given over by Arthur at Guinevere's request to her judgment and that of her all-female jury, "to chese wheither she wolde him save or spille" ("to choose whether she will save or kill him")(D 898). The young man agrees to what is, in effect, a suspended sentence: he assents to a contract in which he puts up his body as surety to return within a year and a day with the answer to the question "What thyng is it that wommen most desiren?" (D 905). In the tradition of the *chanson d'aventure,* the knight searches without success until he meets one who can save him, an old woman with whom he makes another contract: he will grant whatever she requests of him if she gives him the answer. Provided with the hag's response—that women desire "sovereignitee" (ownership/respect) over their own bodies and over their love—the knight returns to the court to fulfill his first contract. He gives the right answer, and his surety, his body, is now returned to him as whole and honorable as it was before he committed the rape—which is more than can be said for the young woman he raped, who, as befits a woman too damaged for marriage, has disappeared from the narrative.

The old woman now demands that he fulfill his second contract: he must grant her wish that she become his wife. Horrified and assuming that she only desires material goods, he begs her to take all his goods but "lat [his] body go" (D 1061). However, as the Man of Law would say, "biheste is dette" ("a promise is a debt"), and the queen's court forces the knight to keep his bargain: the old woman thus "forces" the knight to yield his body as he once forced the maiden to yield hers. That crime has its ironic fulfillment not in a publicly celebrated marriage of the hero and his chosen wife but in the secret and embarrassing ceremony between the knight and the woman he has been compelled to accept, a parodic reversal of the classical seduction of the heroine by the hero.[37] On their wedding night, the hag taunts the knight by asking him why he finds her so revolting and asks if there is nothing she can do to "amend" his discomfort; her mockery of his thwarted desire recalls the amendment, the transformation, that he has fashioned in the young woman he has raped. The knight accuses his wife of ugliness, agedness, poverty, and low class, to which she responds by suggesting that her ugliness and age will prevent him from having to worry about her infidelity, and as to her poverty and class, well, as Christ himself argued, "gentility" ("gentilesse") comes from God; gentility is not an inherent quality of the aristocracy but is made manifest in one's actions, as his own villainous behavior has proved.

She concludes her bedtime sermon by offering her husband yet another contract: to have her foul and old until she dies and thus true and constant, or else to have her young and fair and take his chances that in a world full of sexual predators, she might be unfaithful. He responds by putting himself in her "wise governance; / Cheseth yourself which may be moost plesance / And moost honour to yow and me also" (D 1231–33). Without benefit of the "spectacle" of the court (of law and crown) and its exercise of patriarchal power, the knight submits to his wife's "glossing" of her own body in the private and intimate space of their bedroom. The silence of the raped maiden has been redeemed by the garrulous discourse of the knight's wife; her insistence on choice and autonomy now redresses the knight's erasure of the maiden's selfhood. Free to realize her own "termes queinte of lawe," the old woman "amends" herself, transforming the impurity of age, ugliness, and peasantry into the purity of youth, beauty, and aristocracy; moreover, she contracts to be always so, always constant.

In her sermon, the old woman has suggested to her husband (and to the men on the pilgrimage) that rather than focusing on the unconstrained (unpropertied) body of the woman—the conventional Judeo-Christian justification for law's necessity—perhaps it is man's desires that need to be constrained. In demanding that he be forced to lie with her, his "foule" wife recalls the force with which he has raped the young woman. Moreover, the forced marriage parodies the law's response to the crime of rape, which directs the victim to marry her rapist and thus retroactively legalize the assault as marital intercourse. When his aged wife reveals her vile body to the knight, she confronts him with a symbolic representation of the effects of his sexual violence against the young woman. Thus when the knight freely acknowledges that his wife's body is her own property to dispose of as she pleases, he makes some kind of restitution for his theft of the maiden's virginity.

In the Wife's "Prologue," canon and secular law are the discursive systems that articulate and enforce inequitable gender relationships; such is the "sentence" of the "lawe." It is that same legal model that necessitates that King Arthur sentence the rapist to death—not because he cares about the damage done the young woman but because she is someone's property (her father's, her brother's), and the rapist has not only "trespassed" on that property but has deprived it of any value to its owners in the marketplace of marriage. In her story, the Wife responds to those social and legal systems that have made rape a crime of property rather than a crime of sexual violence, and as such, the tale is a direct rejoinder to the story of Custance, unpropertied by both the king's law and the law of the church. The "lusty bacheler" (D 883) of the Wife's tale is subject to the queen's law, one administered only by women. In the Wife's romance, law is transformative and offers a matriarchal model of negotiated justice and equity—the rapist can learn to see women's desires as equal in value to his own—and this is the "solaas" of the Wife's "sentence."

It is a solace, however, that remains a fantasy, as the Wife knows. Although she may appropriate "clerical misogyny . . . in order to articulate feminist truths, . . . she remains confined within the prison house of masculine language; she brilliantly rearranges and deforms her authorities to enable them to disclose new areas of experience, but she remains dependent on them for her voice."[38] Although she may be "confined by language," the choice of romance as the genre through which to examine the structures of desire and power liberates the Wife to explore the fantastic: "romance bypasses the paradigm of true and false to shift attention onto representation as magical performance."[39] In focusing on magical performance in a story about men's violence against women, the Wife does more than divert us from questions of truth and falsity; rather, her tale implies that truth and falsity are not, finally, the determinants of what is just, that truth and falsity are, perhaps, irrelevant to justice. Her narrative proposes that, like gender relationships, power relationships such as those invoked in courts of law have nothing to do with truth and falsity but everything to do with enchantment. Justice, the Wife insists, is a "magical performance," and the hag is its improbable embodiment.[40]

Unlike the "Man of Law's Tale," in which justice/power is represented as the conversion of the unlike into the like—of Muslim into Christian, of Eastern into Western, of female desire into male fantasy, of alien religious and social customs into the familiar and reliable customs of the common law—the Wife's tale is driven by difference, the difference between the past and the present, between men and women, between the king's law and the queen's law, the young and the old, male desire and female desire, the court and the country, rape and seduction, dishonor and chivalry, the "real" and the "fantastic." Justice occurs only when the knight acknowledges these differences and their individuated embodiments in himself and his wife and their irreconcilability by any set of rules or imposition of power. Only "magical performance" can reconcile these differences, and then, as with justice, only temporarily and only through narrative: "for a decision to be just and responsible it must be in its proper moment, if there is one, be both regulated and without regulation: it must conserve the law and also destroy it or suspend it enough to have to reinvent it in each case, remystify it."[41]

The "Wife of Bath's Tale" is both a fictional trial narrative and a fictional trial of narrative in which the old woman personifies the "magic" of narrative, of mythos itself; she is the *charm of literature*. The "loathly lady" holds the power to force us, like her knight-husband, to submit to a narrative not of our own making, to be made to yield to "an external force" and yet, simultaneously and paradoxically, to long for that surrender. The hag embodies that "desire to be transformed," to be "otherwise-than-ourselves," which, as Desmond Manderson insists, "is desire" and lies at the heart of narrative's power. Such transformative power must be, by definition, temporary, although it may be situated within a narrative that has the appearance of permanence and transcendence. The knight thus has to learn that meaning (like honor and "gentilesse") is contingent, a "reality" produced by choice. He also has to learn that there is a difference between obedience provoked by the threat of punishment (from Arthur or the queen) and obedience (to his wife's wishes) as a contract: "the promise of obedience in exchange for love establishes something like a social contract and certainly establishes a relationship that is most assuredly no longer unilateral in its structure." Like a child, he has to be taught how to "read" the mystery of narratives, just as he has had to learn how to read the mystery of gender relationships. Understanding both—narrative and relationship—is necessary to read the mystery of justice. Romance, it turns out, is a jurisprudential text.[42]

The narrative that is provoked by Queen Guinevere's command, with its improbabilities, discontinuities, and magical resolutions, might seem a far call from the apparent objectivity and ordered nature of legal narrative, but it serves retroactively to emphasize one crucial aspect of the Man of Law's performance—that his tale also relied on improbabilities and magical resolutions but that, couched as it is in the language of Christian faith and patriarchal law, its fantastic quality stays largely veiled. The magic of Christianity is embodied in Custance, who represents the "bride of Christ" in her journey through foreign lands. In contrast, the Wife offers a different kind of magic—the kind that is embodied in the sexualized and desiring body of the woman, who restores to Arthurian society the innocence that was lost through the unrestrained practice of man's sexual desire. This "conversion" of what was foul to what is fair thus reproduces in the material register what the tale of Custance has brought about in the spiritual register: the conversion of the dark Muslim by the fair Christian.

Although the "Wife of Bath's Tale" suggests an alternative model of justice that recognizes women's bodies as the site of difference rather than merely as provocation for the exercise of law's power, the Wife's fantasy nevertheless relies on precisely those traditional legal models and terms that she is resisting, models and terms that articulate the ideology of a system that relies on "the Latinate maxim of precedent, *procedere ad similia*," to proceed toward/on the basis of the similar.[43] Her romance represents, ironically, precisely those disruptive forces that, according to the patriarchal narrative, require policing in the first place: the old crone is a type of the sexually devious, cunning, and magically powerful women, the witch, and as such is the spectacular version of what all women have the potential to become. Her aberrant (and errant) sexuality (noted as one of the Wife's characteristics) and her ontological instability—she is a shape-shifter—aligns her both with the changeableness of the natural world and also with the world of language. The hag's deceitful body, metaphor of the unreliability of women, is linked implicitly and explicitly by Chaucer to the aging body of the Wife, whose voicing of her own fantasy confirms the paranoia of her all-male audience. Although the Wife's fiction suggests the possibility of reconstituting the marriage relationship, the tale also operates to confirm the status quo: in turning herself into a beautiful and faithful young woman, the hag bows to the knight's "worldly appetit" (D 1218). In so doing, the tale not only plays into the Wife of Bath's fantasies for youth and beauty; it also privileges the male form of desire, a desire that commodifies women's bodies. The miraculous transformation of the ugly, old, peasant woman, who represents the value of the raped maiden to the world of men— dirty, corrupt, untouchable—into the beautiful young woman confirms the sexual double standard that sanctions men's desires while it criminalizes women's. And, of course, the Wife's tale of conversion is, like the tale of Custance, infused with Christian concepts of value: it is the old woman's sermon about the "gentilesse" that comes from God, after all, that "converts" the knight and provokes his wife's "translation" from crone to aristocratic heroine.

Thus the Wife's fable simultaneously undermines and reinforces a patriarchal legal model and those narratives that promote its power, precisely as the "Man of Law's Tale" can be said both to conceal and to articulate its ideology in its formal repetitions. The hag, that familiar figure of the uncanny woman from romance narratives who both literally and figuratively enthralls the knight errant, embodies the "dom" (judgment) handed down by the queen— she is the law and, like the law, she takes on different shapes and demands different responses from those who would win her approval. Indeed, the elusiveness of law and justice is precisely captured in the tension between the "reality" of the Wife of Bath and the character she "creates" to justify her life and articulate her hidden desires. The Wife's very being is an assault on all aristocratic and patriarchal pieties—she is independent, wealthy, upwardly mobile, sexually errant, and verbally and physically unbridled—whereas the character she creates is a figure of magic and moral ambiguity (is the old woman benign or is she from the devil?) whose traditional function in romance narratives is to test the hero and demonstrate his worthiness as a member of an elite, patriarchal nobility.

LAW AND FANTASY, KNOWLEDGE AND CUNNING

One might argue that the relationship between the Man of Law and the Wife of Bath is another rehearsal of that classic, gendered antagonism between philosophy and literature, between law and poetics, between authority and experience, between history and subjectivity.[44] Yet, as I have suggested, the storytellers cannot purify their discourses of the presence of its other—whether they will or not, their stories are hybrids of learned judgments and individual fantasies, of legal fictions and imaginary bodies. At one level, the Man of Law might be seen as a mere casuist, resistant to the complexity and uncertainty that literary discourse intends. The lawyer-narrator assumes a paternalistic stance toward his subject, Custance, "standing in for" her temporal and eternal fathers and thus implying a certainty and permanence in his narrative design. Through the iteration of Custance's trials, the Man of Law seems to construct a model of divine authority, a bastion against the changeable fortunes of the world. His allegory of the soul's journey to God inevitably invokes, however, both the impermanence of human life and the hope for eternity, just as it invokes both the material reality of humankind and the miraculous presence of the divine in the Christian fantasy of the soul's salvation. Given that the king's law, which the Man of Law administers, is itself produced by and informs the Christian model of justice and mercy, it would be impossible for him to speak of human proceedings without simultaneously calling up those divine models, regardless of whether those proceedings were the allegorical trials of the faithful Christian, represented in the pale body of Custance, or the actual trials of his clients, which turn out to be no less allegorical in their implications.[45]

In a similar manner, the Wife of Bath must employ in her "Prologue" the forms and rhetorics of secular and theological antifeminists in her extended critique of the patriarchy, thus reinforcing its authority even as she argues against its power. Although illiterate legally, scripturally, and most likely, actually, the Wife nevertheless speaks eloquently and affectively as an advocate of the suffering of women. Although she has no "philosophical friends," she does have women friends and a lifetime of hearing about and experiencing men's versions of women's characters; moreover she has the skill to turn that experience, her history, into argument and fantasy. The Wife thus "subjects the discipline or doctrinal discourse [of law and scripture] to the reassertion of the form of life, the fantasmatic structure or imagination, that rhetoric ideally implies."[46] While speaking of the fantasmatic, however, the Wife inevitably remains in the real, even in her tale of Arthurian romance—indeed, especially in the romance, a "body of texts whose practices require an expressional medium that is able to perform the real as fantastical, and the fantastical as the real, without the requisite necessity of explanation or apology."[47] Despite her insistence on locating her romance in the days of the fairies and King Arthur, its "reality" exists only by virtue of its relationship to the modern world that the Wife herself occupies. Even that most "unreal" of literary forms, the romance, grounds itself in some version of the real. As Toni Morrison suggests, romance is not "an evasion of history" but rather a "head-on encounter with the very real, pressing historical forces and the contradiction inherent in them. . . . Romance [makes] possible the sometimes safe and other times risky embrace of quite specific, understandably human fears."[48]

The lawyer's and the widow's narratives, then, simultaneously rely on and yet dismiss the formal and rhetorical privileges of the genre they appear to be contesting. The Wife invents a romance that reimagines how the law might operate in order to contest a parable that conceals the workings of secular and religious law. Thus fantasy informs the real, even as the real produces fantasy. The consequence of these seemingly paradoxical moves is (a) that apparently dominant narratives of power—be they legal, theological, or literary—are revealed to be no more plausible as narratives than their alternatives are; and (b) that their power endures only so long as someone is talking and someone else is listening and interpreting. These characteristics—self-contradiction, contingency, and temporality—are not to be lamented, however, because those qualities are precisely what compel us to tell the same stories again and again, or rather to tell different versions of the same story, and thus to make judgment possible. And reiteration is what makes the re-vision of judgment possible—what we might otherwise call forgiveness and compassion. It appears then that the very qualities that inhere in narrative are qualities that make ethical response not only possible but also inevitable.

It is, moreover, those same contradictions, contingency, and temporality that inhere in the relationship between liberal arts and the law and that provoke its constant reexaminations. Just as the "Man of Law's Tale" is disturbed by the presence of those ambiguities and inevitable "translations" and "transformations" (the magic of metaphor) that accompany his parable and the Wife's story embodies the very law that she would, cunningly, dissolve before our eyes, so we must acknowledge the presence of other rhetorics and formal configurations as we struggle to define (and escape from) our own disciplinary protocols. Just as the lawyer and the widow ostensibly reject that which seems "outside" their domain of representation, so the expert in literature scorns the lawyer for being too pragmatic and the lawyer scorns the scholar of literature for being too fanciful, too imaginative. And yet, just like the Man of Law and the Wife of Bath, we cannot tell our stories without bringing into play that which we believe we can do without.

LAW AS CUNNING; FANTASY AS AUTHORITY

In this final section, I return to an issue I addressed briefly in the introduction: the gendered nature of the relationship between law and the humanities. In the tales of both the Man of Law and the Wife of Bath, gender inflects the rhetorical and formal aspects of the narrative. In both tales, law is metaphorically represented as immutable and male: the queen's court in the Wife's tale is seen as a momentary aberration from the fixity of King Arthur's judgment; he grants disposition of the case to the queen out of "grace" (D 895). Represented as an absolute institution, law is therefore to be distinguished from other social constructs, such as romance, a form that depicts an illusory and unstable reality and has therefore been symbolically associated with the feminine. Yet, as I have suggested, the apparently illusory relies on the seemingly immutable for its articulation, and vice versa. In the "Man of Law's Tale," the site of both instability and immutability is Custance's body, the place where the contest between divine and human desire is engaged, as it is also the site of the contest between the laws of the Christian and the Muslim. But Custance's body does more than simply offer a text upon which these struggles can be articulated; her body, represented as the object of desire and knowledge, actually *produces* that contest. And the body of woman, I would argue, still both makes and marks the difference between forms of knowledge; her body is a kind of proof text and, as such, both produces disciplinarity and is also the sign of the estrangement of one discipline from another—in this case, of law from literature.

My prefatory definition of the word *quaint* articulates this gendered and provisional nature of disciplinarity. When the knower is male, the term *canny* applies to both the knower (an expert) and the knowledge; when, however, the knower is female, that same knowledge becomes not canny, that is, uncanny. And that uncanniness is linked etymologically to the woman's body, to the site of her difference, her genitalia. The same concept, it appears, yields two divergent meanings, one term bringing its other into being, once again figured in the body of the woman. This conceptual contradiction and its apparently "essential" connection to the woman's body have an ancient history and find their modern "translation" in Freud's essay "The Uncanny" ("Das Unheimlich"), where he remarks that the term *canny* (*heimlich*) signifies that which is known but also that which is strange. Freud argues that *heimlich* becomes *unheimlich*, the canny becomes uncanny, when that which "ought to have remained . . . hidden . . . has become visible."[49] (Freud's etymology recalls the Norton editors' parsing of *quaint* as *pudendum*, i.e., that which should be hidden.)

Freud cites as evidence of this connection the narratives of some of his male patients, who "often . . . declare they feel there is something uncanny about the female genital organs. This unheimlich place, however, is the entrance to the former heim [home] of all human beings, to the place where everyone dwelt once upon a time and in the beginning. . . . the unheimlich is what was once heimisch, home-like, familiar; the prefix 'un' is the token of repression."[50] Freud situates the source of this double meaning, the uncanny that is canny, in the female body generally, but then he specifically locates it in that "unheimlich place," the female genitalia, and "universalizes" the repression of this knowledge in the prefix *un*. Although Freud would claim authority over both the instability and cunning of language—words say what we do not mean, mean what we cannot say—and the body of woman, his language conspires against him and reveals that he is also implicated in the pathology he diagnoses. The uncanniness he describes as reported only by his male patients escapes the representational boundaries of the psychoanalytical narrative because everyone, says Freud, suffers from homesickness, from a longing for that place where he "dwelt once upon a time and in the beginning." This nostalgia is produced by and articulated in the female body but by Freud's own account is felt as a "sickness," as an uncanny effect, only by men. Uncanniness, then, is not a universal and natural attribute of women but a desire represented to men, by women's genitalia, *as those organs are given meaning by men*.

It is precisely this "translation" of male desire into an apparently female-induced, universal, male pathology that feminism deconstructs, and not just in Freudian psychoanalytical theory and practice. Such a critique is constantly necessary within and across all disciplines because, by definition, disciplinarity generates the structural equivalent of an expert and a "patient," the latter always already assuming the role of the woman, the one upon and through whose body/text the expert will make his case. Occupying the place of the expert in one discipline does not preclude one from the possibility of becoming the "patient" in another, as, for example, the legal scholar does when she speaks of literature, or as the literary critic does when he speaks of the law. The plausibility and authority of any specific disciplinary narrative are contingent on its difference from other kinds of knowledge, certain of which may call into question the privileges the specific discipline claims. Thus, for example, to return to the question of rape in the "Wife of Bath's Tale": to define rape as a "trespass" against a property owned by another is to limit issues of sexuality and violence to a model that privileges a patriarchal social structure. Within that disciplinary narrative, rape can never be articulated from the victim's perspective because to do so would require one to imagine the unimaginable—that property might be sentient. It takes a critique that stands outside of disciplinarity itself to translate that familiar legal concept (woman as object of property) into a strange and new claim (woman as owner of self), to convert the canny into the uncanny.

Latour addresses this resistance to interdisciplinarity: "Offer the established disciplines . . . some lovely translations," says Latour, and each discipline resorts to defending its own privileged knowledge. "That a delicate shuttle should have woven together . . . [bodies], texts, souls, and moral law—this remains uncanny, unthinkable, unseemly." What is uncanny is precisely the magic of language, its "lovely translations," its facility to bring into play many different understandings of the sign and its referent and thus invoke the paradoxical. And it is exactly this capacity for "translation" (or perhaps one might call it "conversion") and for ambiguity that has been traditionally attached to the sign of the woman. Despite the post-Enlightenment belief in a "luminous dawn that cleanly separated material causality from human fantasy," argues Latour, "meaning and mechanism, signs and things" are inextricably bound, and the disciplines have only a provisional and contingent existence.[51] The consequence of this representational paradox is an inevitable restraint upon both the authority and plausibility of any disciplinary narrative.

Feminism's interdisciplinarity, which celebrates contingency, allows it to address these issues of disciplinary privilege from a position that is both within and outside the traditional epistemological model. Feminism has been able to interrupt the conversation "from a source relating 'otherwise' (allegorein = speaking otherwise) to the continuing unfolding of the main system of meaning."[52] This allegorical speaking—a kind of which I have proposed in this essay—is neither a call for help from other disciplines outside law and literature nor the supplement of one discipline by another, as argued by Harold Berman in 1954, who suggested that law is "taught interstitially in most political science courses . . . and *perhaps elsewhere*." Moreover, Berman insisted that the law "needs other disciplines. . . . It needs constantly recurring guidance *from the outside*."[53] In both cases Berman speaks of an "elsewhere" and an "outside" that are still represented as part of a traditionally gendered and hierarchical system of knowledge. Just as Custance enacts the fantasies of the Christian in the world of the Oriental (and vice versa), just as the hag enacts the fantasies of the knight in a world of masculine desire and spiritual courtliness, and the knight figuratively enacts the aristocratic fantasies of the worldly and sexually charged Wife of Bath, so too does literature try the fantasies of law and law ratify the possibilities of literature, each cultural production representing an elsewhere to the other. This essay proposes a reading of the relationship between the law and liberal arts, an interruption from elsewhere, that unsettles the privileges of both systems of knowledge and affirms that there is no place, Edenic or otherwise, that is law-less, and no law that comes unattended by fantasy. Such a claim brings with it, I would suggest, the promise of both "sentence and solaas," both meaning and pleasure.

NOTES

1. My thanks to those who helped me formulate my ideas, especially Marianne Constable, Dirk Hartog, Bill MacNeil, Austin Sarat, Susan Silbey, Martha Umphrey, and James Boyd White. Further refinements were enabled by the helpful comments of colleagues Phil Barrish and Elizabeth Cullingford and the scholarship of Geraldine Heng and Jorie Woods. Special thanks to Peggy Bradley, who clarified the difference between a "true" story and a "real" story.

2. Harold Berman, *On the Teaching of Law in the Liberal Arts Curriculum* (Brooklyn: Foundation Press, 1956).

3. Berman's historical perspective on the relationship between law and the liberal arts is hardly surprising, given his own contribution to the history of the law; see, e.g., Harold Berman, *Law and Revolution: The Formation of the Western Legal Tradition* (Cambridge: Harvard University Press, 1983).

4. Peter Goodrich, "Rhetoric and Somatics: Training the Body to Do the Work of Law," *Law/Text/Culture* 5 (special North American issue) (2002): 241, 253. Peter Fitzpatrick, *Modernism and the Grounds of Law* (Cambridge: Cambridge University Press, 2001), 17.

5. W. B. Yeats, "The Second Coming," in *The Collected Poems* (New York: Macmillan, 1965), 134.

6. Bruno Latour, *We Have Never Been Modern* (Cambridge: Harvard University Press, 1993), 35.

7. Maria Aristodemou, *Law and Literature: Journeys from Her to Eternity* (New York: Oxford University Press, 2000), 28, 15, 8 (quoting Goodrich).

8. For a detailed discussion of these issues, see *The Riverside Chaucer,* 3rd ed., ed. Larry Benson (Boston: Houghton Mifflin, 1987), 854–58, 864–65, 872–73 (all quotations in the text from *Canterbury Tales* are taken from this edition); and *The Wife of Bath,* ed. Peter Beidler (Boston: Bedford Books, 1996).

9. Clifford Geertz, *The Interpretation of Cultures: Selected Essays* (New York: Basic Books, 1973), 17, as quoted in Hendrik Hartog, "Romancing the Quotation," in this collection. Other contributors to this collection note the growing juridification of society, with its consequences for our ability to undertake certain intimate relationships in society (see the chapters by Bybee, and Goodman and Silbey). Such observations would not have seemed inappropriate in the late fourteenth century. See Paul Brand, *The Origins of the English Legal Profession* (Cambridge, Mass.: Blackwell, 1992), esp. chaps. 2 and 3.

10. Carolyn Dinshaw, *Chaucer's Sexual Poetics* (Madison: University of Wisconsin Press, 1989), 91.

11. *Riverside Chaucer,* 811. F. N. Robinson, *The Canterbury Tales,* 2nd ed. (Cambridge, Mass.: Riverside Press, 1957), 658.

12. Dinshaw, *Chaucer's Sexual Poetics,* 89, 90.

13. "The Man of Law's 'Tale' is based on a story in the Anglo-Norman Chronicle of Nicolas Trivet [ca. 1334] and on Gower's version of Trivet's tale in his *Confessio amantis* [begun ca. 1386]. The most significant difference between Chaucer's version and those of Trivet and Gower is the highly elaborated style in which the tale is told. Such a style is well suited to the Man of Law, who uses all the devices recommended by medieval rhetoricians to move our pity for the heroine, almost as if he were pleading her case in a court of law" (*Riverside Chaucer,* 9).

14. Geraldine Heng, *The Magic of Empire: Medieval Romance and the Politics of Cultural Fantasy* (New York: Columbia University Press, 2003), 3–4, 183.

15. Unlike many subjects of hagiographies, Custance is never violated sexually (unless one counts the forced marriage to the sultan as a kind of marital rape), and her body never becomes the physical site of her martyrdom, as is so frequently the case in saints' lives. Her sexuality is erased, despite the fact that it is *precisely* that sexuality which provokes both the sultan and Alla to convert to Christianity.

16. Desmond Manderson, "From Hunger to Love: Myths of the Source, Interpretation and Constitution of Law in Children's Literature," *Law and Literature* 15, 1 (Spring 2003): 87, 117. Lee Patterson, "Feminine Rhetoric and the Politics of Subjectivity: La Vieille and the Wife of Bath," in *Rethinking the Romance of the Rose: Text, Image, Reception,* ed. Kevin Brownlee and Sylvia Huot (Philadelphia: University of Pennsylvania Press, 1992), 344.

17. Heng, *Magic of Empire,* 395 (quoting María Bullón-Fernández, "Engendering Authority: Father, Daughter, State, and Church in Gower's 'Tale of Constance' and Chaucer's 'Man of Law's Tale,' " in *Re-visioning Gower,* ed. R. F. Yaeger [Asheville, N.C.: Pegasus, 1998]), 409.

18. See Marianne Constable's essay in this volume, in which she inquires into the rhetorical effect of something "standing for" something else. In particular, she quotes Pierre Schlag: "the metaphor of stance can quickly become a kind of closure device that works to exclude from view any intellectual activity that does not consist in stance-taking."

19. Kathleen Coyne Kelly, "Useful Virgins in Medieval Hagiography," in *Constructions of Widowhood and Virginity in the Middle Ages,* ed. Cindy L. Carlson and Angela Jane Weisl (New York: St. Martin's Press, 1999), 157.

20. Heng, *Magic of Empire,* 200.

21. Dinshaw, *Chaucer's Sexual Poetics,* 91.

22. Kelly, "Useful Virgins," 136.

23. Heng, *Magic of Empire,* 395. She argues persuasively that the Alla/Allah confusion is one that the medieval world did not share, given that the God of the Muslims would be referred to as Mahomet. But she speaks only of the written confusion of the two words. One can assume that Chaucer's audience would recognize the homophonic analogy. If they were thinking Muslim and Mahomet, they might very well associate the name of the Northumbrian king, Alla, with Allah, when they *heard* it, even if they would not have written "Allah" (403n40).

24. Peter Goodrich, "Laws of Friendship," *Law and Literature* 15, 1 (Spring 2003): 30. In his essay, Goodrich argues that "friendship . . . is at its root a theory of precedent, a theory of similars proceeding according to the logic of similarity. My friend—in law French, mon semblable—is my other self" (27).

25. For a discussion of the "intellectual intersection between the facts of knowledge gained through the body and the role of the body in Christian Salvation ideology," see Louise M. Bishop, " 'Of Goddes Pryvetee nor of His Wyf': Confusion of Orifices in Chaucer's Miller's Tale," *Texas Studies in Literature and Language* 44, 3 (Fall 2002): 231–46.

26. Ian Maclean, *The Renaissance Notion of Woman* (Cambridge: Cambridge University Press, 1980), 77.

27. Ruth Kittel, "Women under the Law in Medieval England, 1066–1485," in *The Women of England: From Anglo-Saxon Times to the Present: Interpretive Bibliographical Essays,* ed. Barbara Kanner (Hamden, Conn.: Archon Books, 1979), 131.

28. Ibid.

29. Somatic authority: Goodrich, "Rhetoric and Somatics," 241. Woman's body as the source of sin: "Though Mary's purity was said to provide a way for women to avoid the corruption brought about by Eve, the rhetoric of women's responsibility for original sin worked too much in the ecclesiastical establishment's favor for it to be put to rest. Not only did it help to maintain general systems of patriarchal authority, but it also provided invaluable in quelling heretical movements (like that of the Lollards in fourteenth-century England) in which women claimed equal access to the divine." Kathleen M. Hobbs, "Blood and Rosaries: Virginity, Violence, and Desire in Chaucer's 'Prioress's Tale,' " in Carlson and Weisl, *Constructions of Widowhood and Virginity,* 183. Despite her exaggerated and self-serving argument, the Wife speaks to issues that were traditionally the provenance of the clergy (scriptural interpretation), and it is for this that she is suspected of being a Lollard.

30. Lee Patterson, " 'Experience woot well it is noght so': Marriage and the Pursuit of Happiness in the Wife of Bath's Prologue and Tale," in *Wife of Bath,* 140.

31. Patterson, "Feminine Rhetoric," 328.

32. Patterson, " 'Experience woot well,' " 141.

33. The Wife of Bath "offers a mode of reading that is at once literal and moral; and she insists that interpretation must be deferred, that meaning (whether literary or personal [or, we might add, legal] is available only at the end (whether of a narrative or a life [or a trial]" (Patterson, "Feminine Rhetoric," 346).

34. Goodrich, "Rhetoric and Somatics," 242.

35. Heng, *Magic of Empire,* 3–4. For the relationship between the "Man of Law's Tale" and Arthurian romance narrative, consider the following hypothesis: "At the inaugural moments of Arthurian romance, we ... find in operation violence of related kinds: the rape and sacrificial death of women; domination of racial and religious others; and aggressive empire formation" (ibid., 49).

36. See Marjorie Curry Woods, "Rape and the Pedagogical Rhetoric of Sexual Violence," in *Criticism and Dissent in the Middle Ages,* ed. Rita Copeland (Cambridge: Cambridge University Press, 1996), 56–85. Woods argues that in medieval pedagogical texts, boys and young men "learned about sexual violence as a method of defining their manhood and controlling their own lives. . . . Rape scenes function . . . as the paradigmatic site for working out issues of power and powerlessness" (73).

37. The conventional medieval romance narrates the chivalric rescue of the aristocratic maiden by the knightly hero and frequently includes the socially inferior scapegoat victim whose fate foreshadows, in a lower register, that of the heroine. I am suggesting that in the Wife's tale, the scapegoat (the raped maiden) returns in the form of the old woman who "rescues" the knight from shame by teaching him how to be knightly. This revision of the romance narrative thus constitutes a model of how justice is achieved—by the retelling of a familiar story in a way that demands a rethinking of conventional moral and legal certainties: what is known (canny) is shown to be unknown (uncanny).

38. Patterson, "Feminine Rhetoric," 337.

39. Heng, *Magic of Empire,* 53.

40. See Peter Brown, "Sorcery, Demons, and the Rise of Christianity: From Late Antiquity to the Middle Ages," in *Religion and Society in the Age of Saint Augustine,* ed. P. Brown (New York: Harper and Row, 1972), quoted in Edward Peters, *The Magician, the Witch, and the Law,* 3rd ed. (Philadelphia: University of Pennsylvania Press, 1992), 9. Brown argues that magic appears when there is a "clash within the one society" between "two sources of power: On the one hand, there is articulate power, power defined and agreed upon by everyone (and especially by its holders): authority vested in precise persons; admiration and success gained by recognized channels. Running counter to this may be other forms of influence less easy to pin down . . . inarticulate power: the disturbing intangibles of social life; the imponderable advantages of certain groups; personal skills that succeed in a way that is unacceptable or difficult to understand. Where these two systems overlap, we may expect to find the sorcerer."

41. Manderson, "From Hunger to Love," 123 (paraphrasing Derrida).

42. Ibid., 92, 121. See Manderson's argument about the Middle Ages and the chansons de geste: "Notions of fealty and revenge were the pillars of feudal law. They created personal and emotional obligations—not generalized normative ones—through and between every level of government. Such a legal order requires a way of binding subjects to it through affect. It is to be sustained not by legal science but by legal romance. Peter Goodrich has perhaps been almost alone in taking this argument seriously. The chansons de geste, therefore, were the major jurisprudential texts of the period" (114). I would add that romance functions in the same way to bind subjects to the legal order through affective relations.

43. Goodrich, "Laws of Friendship," 27.

44. Lee Patterson argues that in "the Man of Law and his Tale, Chaucer has dramatized the aspect of authorship that he seems to have found most problematic. This is the tyranny of orthodox authority, a force that, whether it be embodied in the patron, in the source, or in the poet himself, is at once inhibiting and enabling, oppressive and supportive. Moreover, in . . . the Man of Law's Tale that authority is conceived in terms of gender, as male dominion over women, an ascendancy that is sanctimoniously assumed in the name of feminine virtue" ("Feminine Rhetoric," 343).

45. "The gnomic utterance is hardly more foreign to statute law than to literature; in the common law tradition, at least, a case is perhaps best understood as a parable; the Code Napoleon is full of its aphorisms and pensées" (Manderson, "From Hunger to Love," 131).

46. Goodrich, "Rhetoric and Somatics," 243.

47. Heng, *Magic of Empire,* 43.

48. Heng, 16 (quoting) Toni Morrison, *Playing in the Dark: Whiteness and the Literary Imagination* (Cambridge: Harvard University Press, 1992).

49. Sigmund Freud, "The Uncanny," in *On Creativity and the Unconscious,* ed. Benjamin Nelson (New York: Harper, 1958), 129.

50. Ibid., 152–53.

51. Latour, *We Have Never Been Modern,* 5, 35.

52. Mark Sanders, "Ambiguities of Mourning: Law, Custom, Literature, and Women before South Africa's Truth and Reconciliation Commission," *Law/Text/Culture* 4, 2 (1998): 236.

53. Berman, *Teaching of Law,* 13, 12 (italics in both quotations are mine).

Contributors

Jeffrey Abramson is the Louis Stulberg Professor of Law and Politics at Brandeis University, where he teaches political theory and constitutional law. He is the author, most recently, of *We, the Jury: The Jury System and the Ideal of Democracy* (Harvard University Press, 2000) and has served as law clerk to the chief justice of the California Supreme Court and as an assistant district attorney and special assistant attorney general in Massachusetts.

Keith J. Bybee is Associate Professor and Michael O. Sawyer Chair of Constitutional Law and Politics at Syracuse University. He is also Senior Research Associate, Campbell Public Affairs Institute, The Maxwell School, and Associate Professor of Law (by courtesy appointment), Syracuse University College of Law. His publications include *Mistaken Identity: The Supreme Court and the Politics of Minority Representation* (Princeton: Princeton University Press, 1998), "The Jurisprudence of Uncertainty," Law and Society Review 35 (2001): 501–14, and "The Political Significance of Legal Ambiguity: The Case of Affirmative Action," *Law and Society Review* 34 (2000): 263–90.

Marianne Constable is associate professor of rhetoric at the University of California at Berkeley. She is author of *The Law of the Other: The Mixed Jury and Changing Conceptions of Citizenship, Law, and Knowledge* (University of Chicago Press, 1994; winner of the Hurst Prize in Legal History) and *Just Silences: The Limits and Possibilities of Modern Law* (unpublished manuscript).

Douglas J. Goodman is an assistant professor in the Department of Comparative Sociology at the University of Puget Sound. His books include *Consumer Culture* (ABC-Clio, 2003) and, with George Ritzer, *Sociological Theory, Classical Sociological Theory,* and *Modern Sociological Theory* (all published by McGraw-Hill, 2003).

Hendrik Hartog is Class of 1921 Bicentennial Professor of the History of American Law and Liberty at Princeton University. His books include *Public Property and Private Power: The Corporation of the City of New York in American Law, 1730–1870* (University of North Carolina Press, 1983) and

Man and Wife in America: A History (Harvard University Press, 2000). He has been awarded a variety of national fellowships and lectureships, and for a decade he co-edited Studies in Legal History, the book series of the American Society for Legal History.

Susan Sage Heinzelman is an associate professor of English at the University of Texas at Austin. She is co-editor, with Zipporah Batshaw Wiseman, of *Representing Women: Law, Literature, and Feminism* (Duke University Press, 1994) and author of several articles on the representation of women in law and literature, including " 'Going Somewhere': Maternal Infanticide and the Ethics of Judgment," in *Literature and Legal Problem Solving: Law and Literature as Ethical Discourse* (Carolina Academic Press, 1998), and "Black Letters and Black Rams: Fictionalizing Law and Legalizing Literature in Enlightenment England," *Law/Text/Culture* 5 (2001): 377–407.

Austin Sarat is William Nelson Cromwell Professor of Jurisprudence and Political Science at Amherst College and co-founder of Amherst's Department of Law, Jurisprudence, and Social Thought. Among his books are *When the State Kills: Capital Punishment and the American Condition* (Princeton University Press, 2001), *Dissent in Dangerous Times* (University of Michigan Press, 2004), and *Something to Believe In: Politics, Professionalism, and Cause Lawyers,* with Stuart Scheingold (Stanford University Press, 2005). He is a past president of the Law and Society Association and of the Association for the Study of Law, Culture, and the Humanities.

Susan S. Silbey is professor of sociology and anthropology at the Massachusetts Institute of Technology. Her work *The Common Place of Law* explores the role of law in everyday life (University of Chicago Press, 1998). She is currently at work on a study of legal regulation, risk control, and surveillance in contemporary science.

James Boyd White is Hart Wright Professor of Law, professor of English, adjunct professor of classical studies, and chair of the Michigan Society of Fellows at the University of Michigan. From his volumes *The Legal Imagination* (University of Chicago Press, 1973) to *The Edge of Meaning* (University of Chicago Press, 2001), his work has been concerned with the difficulties and possibilities of making meaning with language, in law, in literature, and in the rest of life.

Acknowledgments

The essays in this book were first presented at the Conference on Legal Scholarship in the Liberal Arts, Amherst College, April 26–27, 2002. I am grateful to all those who participated in that event, in particular to Ronald Kahn, Elizabeth Spelman, David Mednicoff, Valerie Hans, Martha Umphrey, Timothy Kaufman-Osborn, and Lawrence Douglas. I am grateful for the indispensable intellectual companionship of my colleagues and students in Amherst College's Department of Law, Jurisprudence, and Social Thought. I am also grateful for support, financial and otherwise, provided by Lisa Raskin, former dean of the faculty, Amherst College; the Department of Law, Jurisprudence, and Social Though, Amherst College; the Department of Sociology and Criminal Justice, University of Delaware; the Office of the President, Oberlin College; and the Office of the President, Whitman College.

A. S.

Index

Abortion, 148–49
Abraham (biblical figure), 125–27
Abramson, Jeffrey, 10–11, 62, 140–54
Ackerman, Bruce, 142
Aesthetic, repression of the, 168
Affirmative duty, 30–31, 39n20
Alienation, 32, 115
Allah, 174
Al Qaeda, 149. *See also* Terrorism
Ambiguity, significance of, 57–62
American Bar Association, 63n2
American Bar Foundation, 71–72, 81n6
American Kinship (Schneider), 157–64
American Legal Studies Association, 5
American Political Science Association, 5
American Psychological Association, 5
American Society for Legal History, 5
Amherst College, 86, 119–22
Anthropology, 11, 102, 155, 156–64
Antigone, 91
Antipositivism, 11
Antistructuralism, 11. *See also* Structuralism
Antivocationalism, 7, 42, 48–50
Appleby, Joyce, 142
Argentina, 3
Argumentation, judicial, 58, 62
Aristocracy, 12, 48, 51, 180, 189
Aristodemou, Maria, 167, 168
Aristotle, 4
Arkes, Hadley, 86
Association for the Study of Law, Culture, and the Humanities, 5
Athens, 48, 50–51
Auerbach, Jerold, 141
Austin, J. L., 76
Authenticity, 113, 123
Authority, concept of, 4, 125, 174

Babb, Lawrence, 13n12
Baird, Theodore, 119
Bakhtin, M. M., 155
Baldwin, Roger, 98
Bennett, William, 19
Berman, Harold, 8, 69, 74, 79, 81, 166, 188
Bible, 3, 125–27. *See also* Religion

Blackmun, Harry A., 129–30, 132–33, 135–36, 138n8
Blackstone, William, 11, 166
Bloom, Alan, 19
Bonsignore, John, 80
Bradshaw v. Rawlings, 31
Brandeis University, 141
Brazil, 3
Breneman, David, 19
Briand, Aristide, 79
Brown, Peter, 192n40
Buckley v. Valeo, 143, 151
Bureaucracy, 32
Burke, Edmund, 11
Burton, Harold, 101
Bush, George W., 150
Bybee, Keith J., 7–8, 10, 11, 41–68, 70, 140–41

California Supreme Court, 95
Canada, 28, 45, 80, 145
Canterbury Cathedral, 169
Canterbury Tales (Chaucer), 12, 168–84
Capitalism, 32, 37. *See also* Economy, market
Capital punishment, 100–101, 105n54
Cardozo, Benjamin, 84–85, 93
Carrington, Paul, 90, 104n21
Carter, Lief, 56
Cases, legal: *Bradshaw v. Rawlings,* 31; *Buckley v. Valeo,* 143, 151; *Coghlan v. Beta Theta Pi Fraternity,* 31; *Dixon v. Alabama,* 22; *Francis v. Resweber,* 100–101, 103, 105n54; *Palsgraf v. Long Island Railroad,* 84–85, 88, 92–93, 97, 101, 103; *Roe v. Wade,* 148; *Thomas v. Collins,* 133–37; *United States V. Holmes,* 99; *Virginia Pharmacy Board v. Consumer Council,* 127–37; *West Virginia State Board of Education v. Barnette,* 135; *Yania v. Bigan,* 92–94, 103
Catholic Church, 141, 150
Cavell, Stanley, 78
Center for Advanced Study in Behavioral Sciences (Stanford University), 158
Chanson d'aventure, tradition of, 179